Langenscheidt

C000156903

Deutsch in 30 Tagen

by Christoph Obergfell

Langenscheidt

München · Wien

Deutsch in 3o Tagen
Herausgegeben von der Langenscheidt-Redaktion

Fachlektorat: Magdalena Obergfell
Gestaltungskonzept: Farnschläder & Mahlstedt, Hamburg
Zeichnungen: Claas Janssen, Frankfurt/Main
Corporate Design Umschlag: KW43 BRANDDESIGN, Düsseldorf
Umschlaggestaltung: Guter Punkt, München

Auf **www.langenscheidt.de/Deutsch-in-30-Tagen** steht Ihnen der kostenlose
Service-Download des gesamten Audio-Materials zur Verfügung. Registrieren
Sie sich dazu mit dem Code **DE049**.

www.langenscheidt.de

© 2017 by Langenscheidt GmbH & Co. KG, München
Satz: Franzis print & media GmbH, München

ISBN 978-3-468-28049-8

17010

User Advice

Welcome to your new language course "German in 30 days". We're glad you want to learn German with us.

Once you've completed this course, you will be able to talk in German about common topics in easy, everyday and routine situations. This corresponds to level A2 of the Common European Framework of Reference for Languages.

How is this course built?

- The course consists of **30 consecutive daily portions** ordered in four sections containing six to eight days respectively.
- The modules are accompanied by an enjoyable **serial story**. Pierre, an engineering student from France, comes to Berlin for an internship. Iwona, a business woman from Poland, got sent to a new position in Germany by her firm. In Berlin they meet and become friends in a German class led by the friendly Martina. Martina and her boyfriend Jens, Pierre's colleague as it happens, make friends with the two as they encounter many everyday experiences together. We will accompany them in their language class, their everyday life, on a journey to Munich and in their business life. It's going to be interesting!
- First, a short quiz helps you find out what type of learner you are.
- This course starts with the chapter **Tips for learning German** in which we reveal helpful tips to make listening, reading, talking and writing in a foreign language easy for you. However, if you'd rather start right away, just skip the first day and start with day 2.
- As you know: practice makes perfect! Therefore we would like to encourage you to repeat what you've learned on a regular basis. For this reason you'll find a **unit for repetition** and a **short test** after 5–7 chapters. Here you'll be able to test how far you've mastered the material and where there's still need for practice. After day 30 you can find the **final test**, with exercises from the whole book.
- In order to assist you with your self-learning, we provide you with an extensive **appendix** at the end of the book. There you'll find a systematic short grammar to consult, a verb table for irregular German verbs, solutions to all the exercises and tests, scripts for all listening texts and an alphabetical vocabulary with all words from this course plus a phonetic transcription.

How is a lesson built?

At the beginning of each lesson we present the **learning goals**, so you know what awaits you.

Read the **dialogue** while listening to the recording on the CD. Try to catch the general meaning of the dialogue as a first step without lingering on each new word.

You'll find the most important new words of the lesson in the **vocabulary** afterwards, neatly alphabetically ordered or summarised in small thematic tables. You can listen to the new vocabulary from each chapter in the Audio Vocabulary Trainer.

Under the heading **Exercises** you practise what you've just learned in various ways. The symbols (see on p. 6) show you the emphasis of each exercise: listening, speaking, reading or writing.

Dialogue questions

(Mark with a cross:

	right	wrong
1. Pierre has two sisters.	☐	☐
2. Robert is Iwona's son.	☐	☐
3. Pierre's father is an architect.	☐	☐
4. Iwona's mother works in a nursery.	☐	☐

And your family?

Martina presents today's subject in her German class.

Martina Today, I would like you to talk about your families. Each of you will ask your neighbour about their family. For instance: What's your father's name? Or: Do you have any brothers or sisters? OK? Then go ahead!

Iwona and Pierre are sitting at the same table today ...

Iwona Pierre, do you have any brothers or sisters?
Pierre Yes, I have two sisters. Their names are Julie and Camille.
Iwona And how old are they?
Pierre Camille is 21. But Julie is still young. She's only 14. Do you have a sister too?
Iwona No, I don't have any sisters. I have a brother. His name is Robert and he's already has a son.
Pierre You're an auntie then! How old is Robert's son?
Iwona He's one year old. He's very sweet and so small. What does your father do for living?
Pierre My father's an architect. He works a lot. My mother works at a nursery. What do your parents do?
Iwona My father's a lawyer. My mother does not work any more. She visits her grandson often now. Robert's wife likes that. She has more time for herself. Both are happy then.
Martina So .. are you done? You're all doing really well! I'm very pleased.

fünfunddreißig 35

····● If you answer the following **dialogue questions**, you'll see, that you've already understood a lot.

Grammar and means of expression

Adjective comparison · §6.1

For most adjectives you simply add ..-er for the comparative and am ..-(e)sten for the superlative (some adjectives get an umlaut too – see the short grammar!). Ein Spaziergang ist interessant. *A walk is interesting.* Das Ägyptische Museum ist interessanter. *The Egyptian Museum is more interesting.* Das Mauermuseum ist am interessantesten. *The Wall Museum is the most interesting.*

The most important irregular adjectives and adverbs

	Positive	Comparative	Superlative
good	gut	besser	am besten
gladly	gern	lieber	am liebsten
much	viel	mehr	am meisten

Simple future · §8.4

An easy and common way to speak about the future is the use of the present tense and a temporal adverbial. Wir gehen am Abend auf den Fernsehturm. *We're going to go up the television tower in the evening.* Wir gehen morgen in ein Museum. *Tomorrow we're going to go to a museum.*

Time

There are two ways to say what time it is in German. The first is a bit more formal (e.g. as heard at a train station) and it uses the 24 hour clock. The other is less formal and uses the 12 hour clock.

What time is it?		
written	spoken (formal)	spoken (less formal)
21.00 Uhr	Es ist einundzwanzig Uhr.	Es ist neun (Uhr).
16.30 Uhr	Es ist sechzehn Uhr dreißig.	Es ist halb fünf.
22.45 Uhr	Es ist zweiundzwanzig Uhr fünfundvierzig.	Es ist Viertel vor elf.
02.15 Uhr	Es ist zwei Uhr fünfzehn.	Es ist Viertel nach zwei.

einundvierzig 41

····● Under the heading **Grammar and means of expression** new grammar is explained in a plain manner. There are also references to the **short grammar** in **the appendix**, where the topics are presented in a more comprehensive way.

Kulturtipp Germans and football

Football is one of the most popular sports in Germany – even before the World Cup in Germany in 2006. A lot of Germans spend Saturday afternoon in a football stadium or – after 6 pm – in front of the television watching the **Sportschau** with the results of the **Bundesliga** *German Football League.* The matches of the national football team draw an even greater TV audience or – since 2006 during the World or European Cup – there is **Public Viewing** (yes, that's German!), where the matches are shown on big screens open to the public.

Thanks to the great successes of the women's national football team, women's football has become very popular and is one of the fastest growing sports in Germany.

If you want to play sports actively check out the local **Sportvereine** *sports clubs* where you can participate in your favourite sport for small fees.

What can you already do?

- give advice ☐☐☐ – U1
- talk about your daily routine ☐☐☐ – U1
- present your interests, hobbies and favourite sports ☐☐☐ – U1

Learning a foreign language is like sport. You have to stay on the ball. And if you do, you'll get better and better and it's as much fun – but with a lot less sweating! And don't forget that learning a language is a team sport. Sooner or later you're out there "competing" – why not already assemble a team for training!

neunundvierzig 49

····● The last page of each lesson – under the heading **Culture tip** – offers interesting hints and information about Germany and its people.

The last part of each lesson is entitled **What can you already do** and allows you to evaluate your learning success.

What symbols are used?

◉ 1/2 This text or exercise is on the CD. The first number is the CD's number, the second the track's number. We've recorded the dialogues from day 2 to 13 in two different rates. Once in "normal" everyday life speech and once a bit slower.

exercise with emphasis on speaking

exercise with emphasis on listening

exercise with emphasis on reading

exercise with emphasis on writing

▸ *§1 reference to short grammar | exercise | lesson*

Achtung:
important grammar note

The author and the editorial staff at Langenscheidt wish you a lot of fun and success learning German.

Content

Deutsch

Basics — Let's start with German!

Everyday life – German for every day

Travel – German to go

Job – German for your job

Appendix

Pronunciation, stress and spelling

Vowels

[a]	a	similar to a in British English *cat*	gefallen
[aː]	a, aa, ah	like a in *father*	Bahn, ein paar
[ɛ]	e	like e in *bed*	am besten, essen
[eː]	e, ee, eh	formed similarly to a long [iː] but the mouth a bit more open	lesen, sehen, Tee
[ə]	-e	non-stressed -e endings, like a in *about*	bitte, danke
[ɪ]	i	like i in *list*	du bist, richtig
[iː]	i, ie, ieh	like ee in *see*	Kantine, er sieht
[ɔ]	o	similar to o in *not*	offen, Post
[oː]	o, oo, oh	formed similar to the [ɔ] but the lips more rounded and closed	Obst, wohnen
[ʊ]	u	like u in *put*	um, Lust
[uː]	u, uh, ou	like ou in *you*	Uhr, Radtour, Juni

Diphthongs and umlauts

[aɪ]	ai, ei (ay, ey)	like y in *my*	Mai, heißen (Bayer, Meyer)
[au]	au	like ou in *mouth*	Auto, einkaufen
[ɔY]	äu, eu	like oy in *boy*	Räume, neu, teuer
[ɛ]	ä	like e in *bed*	Erkältung, Hände
[ɛː]	ä, äh	like ai in *fair*	erzählen, Gespräch
[œ]	ö	something between [ɔ] and [ɛ]	plötzlich, öffnen
[øː]	ö, öh	something between [oː] and [eː]	nervös, Söhne
[Y]	ü	similar to [yː] but the mouth is a bit more open and it's short	Mütter, müssen
[yː]	ü, üh	formed like [iː] but the lips are formed for [uː]	Gemüse, früher

Consonants

[ç]	ch	no English equivalent, can occur as an allophone of [h] in front of vowels (like *huge* or *hue*)	ich, welche
[ɪç]	-ig	only as a word ending	wenig
[x]	ch	after German a, o, u, au – no English equivalent, like the Scottish ch in *loch*	Nacht, auch
[f]	f, ff, ph, v	like the English f	fünf, Vater
[j]	j	like y in *New York*	ja, Jacke
[k]	k, ck, c, -g	like ck in *jacket*	Jacke, weg
[ŋ]	ng	like ng in *wrong*	länger

Consonants			
[p]	p, pp, -b	like the English p	Pause, gib
[r]	r, rr	no English equivalent, like the Scottish r in *curd*	rot
[ɐ]	-er	similar to the English u in *but*	Lehrer
[z]	s	like z in *zero*	lesen
[s]	s, ss, ß	like s in *say*	Wasser, Straße
[ʃ]	sch	like sh in *show*	schwarz
[ʃp], [ʃt]	st-, sp-	combination of [ʃ] and [p] or [t] when sp and st are combined at the beginning of a word	Sport, studieren
[t]	t, dt, -d	like the English t	gut, Stadt, wird
[tʃ]	tsch	like ch in *chat*	deutsch
[v]	w	like v in *voice*	wirklich
[ts]	z, tz	like ts in *let's*	Zimmer, putzen

Some pronunciation rules

[:] means that the previous vowel is a long vowel.
A lot of consonants (b, d, g, h, k, l, m, n, p, t) are generally spoken the same (or very similarly) to their English counterparts.
Vowels in front of double consonants are always short: **Treppe**, **passieren**
Double vowels, ie and vowel + h are always long: **Tee**, **pass*ie*ren**, **s*eh*en**
b, d, g at the end of a word are spoken like p, t, k: **weg**, **gib**, **wird**
h after a vowel is not spoken – it only prolongs the vowels: **s*eh*en**, **g*eh*en**
The German [r] is formed in the throat and spoken like when you are clearing your throat or gurgling.

Stress

Usually the first syllable is stressed in a word. However, the stress in German is relatively free and similar looking words can be stressed differently. The primary stress is signalled with ['] , the secondary with [ˌ].

Spelling

In German the beginning of a sentence and all nouns are written with a capital letter. Additionally all pronouns for formal address (**Sie, Ihr** ...) are written with a capital letter.

Alphabet and abbreviations

Alphabet											
A	[aː]	F	[ɛf]	L	[ɛl]	Q	[kuː]	Ü	[yː]
Ä	[ɛː]	G	[geː]	M	[ɛm]	R	[ɛr]	V	[fau]
B	[beː]	H	[haː]	N	[ɛn]	S	[ɛs]	W	[veː]
C	[tseː]	I	[iː]	O	[oː]	ß	[ɛs'tsɛt]	X	[ɪks]
D	[deː]	J	[jɔt]	Ö	[øː]	T	[teː]	Y	['ʏpsilɔn]
E	[eː]	K	[kaː]	P	[peː]	U	[uː]	Z	[tsɛt]

Abbreviations

Pl   Plural
Sg   Singular
m   masculine
f   feminine
n   neuter
Nom. Nominative
Acc. Accusative
Dat. Dative

Which learner type are you?

Not all people learn the same way. Using the statements below, try to establish which type of learner you are and adjust your learning habits accordingly. Remember that you don't always have to follow your own way of doing things. You could assume the methods of another type of learner, even if it may seem less agreeable at first.

Auditive learner

☐ You follow lectures easily and memorize the contents.
☐ You like listening to audio books and having things explained.
☐ You're able to quickly get along with listening to spoken foreign languages.
☐ You have few problems understanding different English accents.

Visual and reading learner

☐ You like to read and take the contents in with your eyes.
☐ You know which page a word is listed on in a vocabulary book as well as which words precede and follow it.
☐ You memorize new words with visual mnemonics.
☐ You read grammar rules several times.

Writing learner

☐ You mark keywords and write them down.
☐ You like written exercises.
☐ You quickly want to be able to write e-mails in the new language.
☐ You like word lists and mind maps.

Action and speaking learner

☐ You want to actively use the new language.
☐ You want to meet native speakers.
☐ You like to talk and don't worry too much about correct grammar at the start.
☐ You like to give new words and sentences a try in role plays.

Read the following chapter to learn more about which method of learning is the most effective for each type of learner to reach his individual goals.

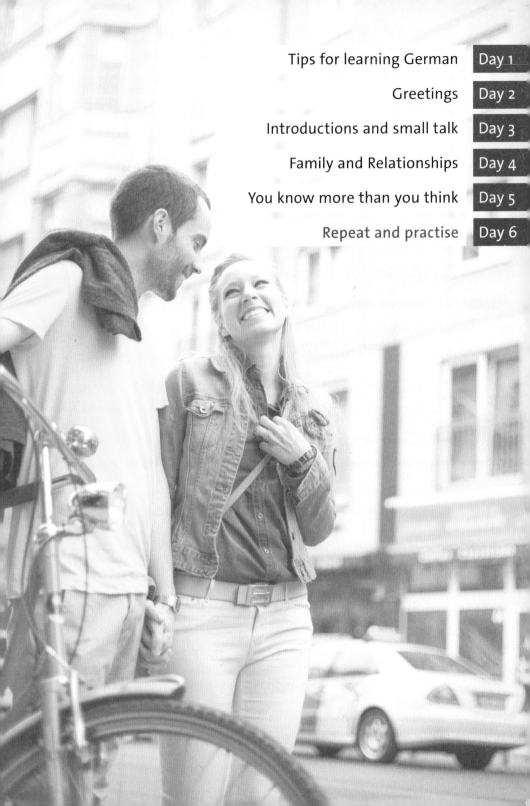

Tips for learning German

Vocabulary learning tips

Have you ever been in a house or flat with almost every object labelled in a foreign language using little stickers or post-it notes? They were trying, probably with success, to memorize things of everyday use in another language. It's an apt technique. You are constantly reminded of the new word when you look at or take the object and say the related word in your head or speak it out loud. It won't take long for you to remember that the toilet tank is *der Toilettenspülkasten*, the rolling pin *das Nudelholz* and the wrench *der Schraubenschlüssel*.

If this method is a bit too cumbersome for you, you can try learning with vocabulary notebooks, index cards, mind maps or books with thematical vocabulary or you make use of digital media like computers, tablets and smartphones.

To learn your vocabulary we recommend e.g. a file card box with four or five compartments. Words you haven't learned yet stay in the first compartment. Keep going over your cards. Words you're still unsure of go to the next compartment. The better you know a word the further to the back it goes. Once it reaches the last compartment, it means you have learned the word.

Reading tips

Reading is an important task while learning a new language. Especially at the beginning reading tasks should be carefully planned and reading should be practiced regularly. There are three methods that can be used in turn.

Imagine three cars: a fast sports car, a (big/medium-sized) family car and a small city car. At the start of your learning career you can only afford the small car: You read single words slowly and repeatedly speak them out loud. You should look up the pronunciation in the vocabulary list in the appendix or in a dictionary if you are not sure. Don't fear the phonetic transcription; you'll know those few special characters soon enough. Wherever you have internet connection, the Langenscheidt dictionary online is easily accessible. For every foreign-language entry you can find a sound version spoken by a native speaker, so you can absolutely rely on the pronunciation.

Don't wait too long before changing to the family car and start reading whole sentences, slowly at first, then a bit faster. It's good to try to bear in mind the rhythm of speech typical to the country. As soon as you feel comfortable on the foreign roads, read bigger paragraphs at a time and so dare to get into the sports car at last. Keep in mind though: there is no reason to drive as fast as the locals. Enjoy the scenery of the language with medium reading speed and take the time to pause for a moment at certain terms – you might risk missing the beauty of single words – but also read fast sometimes to get a fair step ahead.

Speaking tips

Speaking is closely connected to reading. It's the hardest part while learning a foreign language since usually there aren't any native speakers around who could sensitively correct your mistakes. But maybe there's another learner around who would be happy to have someone to communicate with. Meet at home or at a café and try some small talk in your "new" language. Be courageous! Or read the dialogues from the textbook to each other and maybe even learn them by heart.

If there's no one to learn the dialogue with in assigned roles, do it on your own. Take over one part and try to think of what could be said additionally in each situation and have a conversation with imaginary partners. If you find this method slightly embarrassing, try it where nobody can see you, for example in the morning in front of your bathroom mirror.

Why not try it with lyrics or movies? Buy a German version of your favourite film – or maybe a German film you have heard of and would like to see – and watch it, particularly with German subtitles on.If you pause from time to time to write down single phrases or small sections and learn them, you can use them later as a starting point for short role plays. Put yourself in each particular situation and "chat" with the actors. You can practice this kind of communication even with yourself while jogging or having a shower.

Listening tips

Considerably easier than speaking is listening. The new media available these days offer a wide variety of possibilities which you didn't dare to dream of a few years ago.

You only need a few clicks to tune in to a foreign radio station or to listen to a podcast. Even if you don't understand much at first because they speak too fast for you, just accept it. Keep listening and get accustomed to the sound of the language you're learning – that's all that matters at the beginning. There's a good chance of getting into a holiday mood – and there's no harm in that, is there?

Listening and comprehending is like jogging. If you're a beginner running a marathon, you're likely to be soon standing breathless on the roadside. Take your time and be patient: Constant input will train the brain. That means: the more you expose yourself to spoken language, the more you keep listening, be it concentrated or just casually, the faster your listening comprehension will progress. You'll get the feeling for words and intonation. If you like listening to audio books or watching DVDs, pause from time to time and listen carefully to single sections a few times in a row. You

will see: at the third repetition you'll already understand a lot more. And if you make use of the text too – if you have it – you'll take a large step forward in comprehension.

Writing tips

Writing is an easy but very effective exercise. Even the mere copying of words or dialogues improves your understanding of a language considerably and helps you to easily memorize those words or sections.

You can start with writing down the exercises or dialogues from this book. As your next step, you can change them or even write new ones. Writing down short scenes in different situations is a brilliant exercise – not only for prospective writers. But you should try to find someone to read your writing and point out possible mistakes.

Of course this should not prevent an electronic exchange of ideas. Try to find chat partners, for example in social networks and write each other short messages. You can write about simple everyday matters. You'll see that it's not as easy as it sounds. Even writing just a shopping list for your spouse or child in the new language will require a lot of leafing through dictionaries. Make it a rule to write short messages for your family and friends in German or change the text recognition on your mobile phone to German and surprise your friends with "foreign" text messages. Who knows, maybe one of them will also write back "foreign".

Greetings

In this lesson you will learn

- to introduce yourself
- to say hello and good-bye
- to count to 12

⊙ 1/2 **Erste Stunde im Deutschkurs**
⊙ 1/3

Die meisten Lerner sind schon da. Iwona kommt zur Tür herein.

Iwona	Guten Tag. Ist hier der Deutschkurs?
Martina	Ja, genau. Dort vorne ist noch ein Platz frei ...
Iwona	Danke.
Martina	Hallo, herzlich willkommen. Wir sagen „du" und benutzen den Vornamen. Ist das O. K.?

Die Lerner nicken zustimmend.

Ja? Super! Wir stellen uns jetzt vor – das ist nicht schwer. Ihr sagt einfach euren Vornamen, wie alt ihr seid und aus welchem Land ihr kommt. Ich beginne: Mein Name ist Martina. Ich bin neunundzwanzig Jahre alt. Ich komme aus Deutschland. Machst du bitte weiter?

Brian	Ich? O. K. Hi! Ich bin Brian und ich bin neunzehn Jahre alt. Ich bin aus Australien.
Susan	Hallo, mein Name ist Susan. Ich bin dreiundzwanzig Jahre alt und aus England.
Pierre	Salut! Ich heiße Pierre. Ich bin vierundzwanzig. Ich komme aus Frankreich.
Iwona	Hallo. Mein Name ist Iwona. Ich bin dreißig Jahre alt und ich komme aus Polen.
Yoko	Ich heiße Yoko. Ich bin einundzwanzig Jahre alt. Ich komme aus Japan.

Die restlichen Lerner stellen sich der Reihe nach vor ...

Martina Vielen Dank, das war echt gut!

Dialogue questions

Cross out the wrong answer.

1. The teacher's name is *Iwona | Martina*.
2. Iwona learns *German | English*.
3. Martina is *19 | 29* years old.
4. *Brian | Susan* is from England.
5. Pierre is from *Australia | France*.

The first lesson in German class

Most students are already there. Iwona steps in.

Iwona   Good day. Is this the German class?

Martina   Yes, exactly. There's an empty seat at the front ...

Iwona   Thank you.

Martina   Hello, welcome. Let's say "du" and use our first names. Is that OK with you?

The students nod in agreement.

Yes? Great! We will introduce ourselves now – it's not difficult.
You just say your first name, how old you are and which country you
come from. I shall start: my name's Martina. I'm twenty-nine years old.
I come from Germany. Will you continue?

Brian   Me? OK. Hi! I'm Brian and I'm nineteen years old. I'm from Australia.

Susan   Hello, my name is Susan. I'm twenty-three years old and from England.

Pierre   Salut! I'm Pierre. I'm twenty-four. I come from France.

Iwona   Hello. My name is Iwona. I'm thirty years old and I come from Poland.

Yoko   I am Yoko. I'm twenty-one years old. I come from Japan.

The remaining students introduce themselves in turn ...

Martina   Thank you, that was really good!

Vocabulary

3/2

alt	old
Auf Wiedersehen!	Good-bye!
bitte	please
danke	thanks, thank you
Deutschkurs, -e *m*	German class
Deutschland	Germany
Dialog, -e *m*	dialogue
die USA (*only Pl*)	USA
England	England
Frankreich	France
frei	free, empty
Hallo!	Hello!
Herzlich willkommen!	Welcome!
Hi!	Hi!, Hey!
ich bin	I am
ich heiße	my name is
ich komme aus	I come from
ja	yes
Jahr, -e *n*	year
Japan	Japan
Kontinent, -e *m*	continent
Land, Länder *n*	country
Lektion, -en *f*	lesson
Lerner, – *m*	student
Name, -n *m*	name
nein	no
Platz, Plätze *m*	here: seat
Polen	Poland
sagen	say
Schottland	Scotland
Stunde, -n *f*	hour, here: lesson
Tschüs!	Bye!
Vorname, -n *m*	first name
weitermachen	continue

Learning tip

To memorize the gender of a noun, we think it's best to learn the definite article (**der/die/das**) together with the noun – and not **m**, **f** or **n** (see grammar on next page). You'll also see words or endings behind a noun: that's the plural (e.g. plural of **Dialog, -e** is **Dialoge** and of **Lerner, –** it's **Lerner** without an ending). Memorize it at once with each noun!

Greetings

Guten Morgen.	Good morning.
Guten Tag.	Good day.
Guten Abend.	Good evening.
Gute Nacht.	Good night.

Continents

Afrika	Africa
Amerika	America
Asien	Asia
Australien	Australia
Europa	Europe

Numbers from 1 to 12

eins	1
zwei	2
drei	3
vier	4
fünf	5
sechs	6
sieben	7
acht	8
neun	9
zehn	10
elf	11
zwölf	12

Grammar and means of expression

Personal pronouns ▸ §3.1

ich	I	wir	we
du	you	ihr	you
er/sie/es	he/she/it	sie	they

Verb conjugation in the singular ▸ §8.1

Ich **komme** aus Frankreich. *I come from France.*
Machst du bitte weiter? *Will you continue?*
The following table shows you the endings for the singular of most verbs.

I	**ich** komme	**ich** mache	**ich** heiße
you	**du** kommst	**du** machst	**du** heißt
he/she/it	**er/sie/es** kommt	**er/sie/es** macht	**er/sie/es** heißt

Word order I ▸ §10

The "normal" word order in a declarative sentence (main clause) is similar to the English: subject – verb – object.
Mein Name ist Martina. *My name is Martina.*
However, the German word order is not so fixed. The subject doesn't always have to be in the first position. But: The conjugated verb is always in the second!

Gender ▸ §1.1

German nouns have three genders: masculine (*m*), feminine (*f*) and neuter (*n*).
But it's very often difficult to determine the gender of a noun. There are some rules – look out for them in the vocabulary sections!
Like English, German has a definite and an indefinite article. The definite article always shows the gender!

The German definite and indefinite article				
	m	f	n	Pl
the (definite)	der	die	das	die
a/an (indefinite)	ein	eine	ein	—*

* The indefinite article **ein** has no plural since it means not only *a* but also *one*.

1 These declarative sentences are a mess. Put them back in the right order.

1. ist / Pierre / Mein Name / .

....

2. aus Australien / Ich / komme / .

....

3. Yoko / 21 Jahre alt / ist / .

....

4. kommt / aus England / ist / Susan / und / 23 / .

....

5. komme / bin / aus / 30 / Ich / alt / Jahre / und / Polen / .

....

⊙ 1/4 **2** Listen to the numbers on the CD, repeat them and cross them off the list. One number remains. Which is it?

12   3   2   17   20   14   16   7   9   5   8

3 Read the sentences and fill in the missing personal pronouns or verb endings.

1. .... machst einen Deutschkurs.

2. Die Lehrerin heiß .... Martina. .... kommt aus Deutschland.

3. .... bin aus England.

4. Pierre komm........ aus Frankreich. .... ist 24 Jahre alt.

5. Ich komm........ aus Japan.

⊙ 1/5 **4** Where are your fellow students from? Listen to the CD and complete the sentences.

| Australien   den USA   Schottland   England |

1. Paul kommt aus ....

2. Mary ist aus ....

3. Lucy kommt aus ....

4. George ist aus ....

Kulturtipp Saying hello and good-bye

Guten Tag! is the standard way to say hello in Germany and **Auf Wiedersehen!** is the most common way to say good-bye. The less official forms are **Hallo!** and **Tschüs!** respectively.

However, you will encounter many other forms of saying hello and good-bye during your stay in Germany. This depends where you are in Germany and whom you are talking to.

In Northern Germany you will hear **Moin!** all day long when people say hello (this is also used to say good-bye) or **Tach!**. In Southern Germany **Grüß Gott!** is usually used to say hello and the French word **Adieu!** or the adapted form **Ade!** to say good-bye. Among friends you can often hear **Servus!** in Western and Southern Germany as a way to say hello as well as good-bye.

Young people use **Hi!** or **Hey!** to say hello. The Italian **Ciao!** (or the German **Tschau!**) is used to say good-bye.

So you see, there are no boundaries for language!

....

What can you already do?

☺ ☺ ☹

▪ say your name	☐ ☐ ☐	▸Ü1
▪ say where you come from	☐ ☐ ☐	▸Ü1
▪ say how old you are	☐ ☐ ☐	▸Ü3
▪ understand where someone is from	☐ ☐ ☐	▸Ü4
▪ count to 12	☐ ☐ ☐	▸Ü2

Welcome to the end of your first lesson! You've learned a lot already, haven't you? Don't worry, you don't have to know all by heart yet. The next lessons will allow you to deepen, extend and repeat your knowledge. Keep on and you'll see: practice makes perfect!

Introductions and small talk

In this lesson you will learn

- to start a conversation, ask others how they are and answer such questions
- to ask and answer further questions about place of origin
- to talk about your length of stay
- to exchange basic information about work

⊙ 1/6
⊙ 1/7

Vor dem Sprachkurs

Vor der Sprachschule treffen sich Pierre und Iwona vor ihrer zweiten Unterrichtsstunde.

Pierre Hallo Iwona, wie geht es dir?

Iwona Gut, danke. Du bist Pierre aus Frankreich, ja?

Pierre Ja, ich komme aus Rennes. Das liegt in der Bretagne. Entschuldigung, woher kommst du?

Iwona Ich bin aus Polen, aus Rzeszów. Das ist in der Nähe von Krakau. Bist du schon lange in Deutschland?

Pierre Nein, erst seit einem Monat. Und du? Arbeitest du hier?

Iwona Ja, ich habe einen neuen Job hier in Berlin. Ich bin aber erst seit zwei Wochen hier.

Pierre Und was machst du?

Iwona Ich arbeite in einer Consultingfirma. Und du?

Pierre Ich studiere Maschinenbau. Ich bin fast fertig und mache jetzt ein Praktikum in einer deutschen Firma.

Martina und Jens kommen dazu.

Martina Hallo Iwona, hallo Pierre. Darf ich euch meinen Freund Jens vorstellen?

Iwona Freut mich ...

Pierre Was? Jens, Martina ist deine Freundin?

Martina Woher kennt ihr euch denn?

Jens Hi, ihr beiden. Pierre und ich arbeiten in der gleichen Firma.

Martina Das ist ja toll! Oh, die anderen kommen schon. Der Unterricht beginnt gleich. Gehen wir hinein?

Jens Gut, dann viel Spaß. Bis später!

Dialogue questions

Mark with a cross:

	right	wrong
1. Iwona is from Cracow.	☐	☐
2. Pierre has been in Germany for a month.	☐	☐
3. Iwona studies in Berlin.	☐	☐
4. Martina is Jens' girlfriend.	☐	☐
5. Martina and Pierre work at the same company.	☐	☐

Before the language class

Pierre and Iwona meet in front of the language school before their second class.

Pierre	Hello Iwona, how are you?
Iwona	Well, thank you. You are Pierre from France, right?
Pierre	Yes, I come from Rennes. It's in Brittany. Sorry, where are you from?
Iwona	I am from Poland, from Rzeszów. It's not far from Cracow. Have you been in Germany long?
Pierre	No, only a month. And you? Do you work here?
Iwona	Yes, I have a new job here in Berlin. But I have only been here for two weeks.
Pierre	And what do you do?
Iwona	I work at a consulting company. And you?
Pierre	I study mechanical engineering. I'm almost finished and now I am doing a placement at a German company.

Martina and Jens join them.

Martina	Hello Iwona, hello Pierre. May I introduce you to my boyfriend Jens?
Iwona	Pleasure ...
Pierre	What? Jens, Martina is your girlfriend?
Martina	So where do you know each other from?
Jens	Hi, you two. Pierre and I work for the same company.
Martina	This is cool! Oh, the others are already coming. The class is about to start. Shall we go inside?
Jens	Ok, have fun. See you later!

Vocabulary

⊙ 3/3

arbeiten	work
beginnen	start
Bis später!	See you later!
Consultingfirma, -firmen *f*	consulting company
Darf ich Jens vorstellen?	May I introduce Jens?
Das ist toll!	This is cool!
dürfen	may
Entschuldigung! *f*	sorry
fertig	done
Firma, Firmen *f*	company
gehen	go
in der Nähe von	not far from
Job, -s *m*	job
kommen aus	come from
lang(e)	long
leben	live
Maschinenbau (*only Sg*) *m*	mechanical engineering
Monat, -e *m*	month
Praktikum, Praktika *n*	placement
sich kennen	know each other
sich treffen	meet
studieren	study
Tag, -e *m*	day
toll	cool
Unterricht (*only Sg*) *m*	class
Viel Spaß!	Have fun!
was	what
wie	how
Wie geht's?/ Wie geht es dir/ Ihnen?	How are you?
wo	where
Woche, -n *f*	week
woher	from where
wohnen	live (e.g. in a flat)
Wohnung, -en *f*	flat

Numbers from 13 to 100

13	dreizehn
14	vierzehn
15	fünfzehn
16	sechzehn
17	siebzehn
18	achtzehn
19	neunzehn
20	zwanzig
21	einundzwanzig
22	zweiundzwanzig
23	dreiundzwanzig
24	vierundzwanzig
30	dreißig
40	vierzig
50	fünfzig
60	sechzig
70	siebzig
80	achtzig
90	neunzig
100	(ein-)hundert

Information about the length of the stay

Ich bin hier seit einem Tag/ einer Woche/ einem Monat/ einem Jahr.	I've been here for a day/ a week/a month/a year.
Ich bin hier seit zwei/drei/... Tagen/Wochen/ Monaten/Jahren.	I've been here for two/ three/... days/weeks/ months/years.

Grammar and means of expression

Wh Questions ▸ §3.3, §10

These questions always start with an **interrogative pronoun** (they all start with **W**).
Wie geht es dir? *How are you?*
Woher kommst du? *Where do you come from?*
Was machst du? *What do you do?*
Like in a normal positive sentence (▸ *Day 2*), the verb takes the second position in the
sentence.

Yes/No Questions

This type does not involve an interrogative pronoun. Unlike Wh Questions,
these questions can just be answered with a **Yes** or **No**. Like in English, the **verb
takes the first position** in the sentence.
Bist du schon lange in Deutschland? *Have you been in Germany long?*
Arbeitest du hier? *Do you work here?*

Verb conjugation in the plural ▸ §8.1

In the previous lesson, you learned how the verbs conjugate in the singular.
Now take a look at some **verbs in the plural**:
Wir arbeit**en** in der gleichen Firma. *We work at the same company.*
Woher kenn**t** ihr euch denn? *So where do you know each other from?*
Die anderen komm**en** schon. *The others are already coming.*

This is how regular verbs conjugate in the plural			
we	**wir** arbeiten	**wir** kennen	**wir** kommen
you	**ihr** arbeitet	**ihr** kennt	**ihr** kommt
they	**sie** arbeiten	**sie** kennen	**sie** kommen
you*	**Sie*** arbeiten	**Sie*** kennen	**Sie*** kommen

* To address someone formally you use **Sie** (with a capital) for both singular and plural.

1 These questions are totally mixed up. Put the words in the correct order and answer the questions.

1. a) du / woher / kommst / ? _____
   b) Answer: _____
2. a) geht / wie / dir / es / ? _____
   b) Answer: _____
3. a) ist / das / wo / ? _____
   b) Answer: _____
4. a) machst / was / du / ? _____
   b) Answer: _____
5. a) aus Deutschland / kommst / du / ? _____
   b) Answer: _____
6. a) schon / lange / in Deutschland / du / bist / ? _____
   _____
   b) Answer: _____
7. a) hier / du / arbeitest / ? _____
   b) Answer: _____

2 Choose the right forms of the verbs *arbeiten* and *kommen* from the box in the grammar section and fill in the gaps.

1. Woher _____ ihr?

2. Wir _____ in Berlin.

3. Wir _____ aus England.

4. Pierre und Jens _____ in der gleichen Firma.

5. Wo _____ ihr?

6. Jens und Martina _____ aus Deutschland.

⊙ 1/8   **3** You're talking to Jens now. Listen to his answers and then ask him the appropriate question after the beep. Choose your questions in the right order from the box. Listen to the correct question and answer again after each of your questions.

Wo ist das?   Hallo Jens, wie geht's?   Und was machst du?   Woher kommst du?

Kulturtipp Wie geht's?

To start small talk with friends you can use the question:
Wie geht's?/Wie geht es dir?
How are you?
If you want to address someone formally use: **Wie geht es Ihnen?**
How are you?
Sometimes others use this phrase only to start a conversation. If you have the feeling that they don't really want to know how you are, then answer with one of the following:

(Mir geht es) prima/toll/super/sehr gut. *(I'm doing) great/OK/well/fine.*
Gut, danke. *Well, thank you.*
Es geht. *Not bad.*
So lala. *So so.*
Nicht so gut. *Not so good.*
Schlecht. *Bad.*

If you think the other person cares and you're feeling bad and you want to talk about it, then answer truthfully and tell your story. But – vice versa – be prepared to hear the full story if you ask someone how she/he is!

And of course you can counter with your own question by putting **Und (wie geht's) dir?** *And (how are) you?* after your answer.

....

What can you already do?

	☺	☺	☹	
■ conduct a short conversation	□	□	□	▸Ü1
■ ask how others are and answer if you're asked	□	□	□	▸Ü3
■ ask and answer questions about place of origin	□	□	□	▸Ü1
■ ask others about the length of their stay	□	□	□	▸Ü1
■ answer questions about the length of your stay	□	□	□	▸Ü1
■ talk about work	□	□	□	▸Ü1, Ü2, Ü3

In this lesson you will learn

- to talk about your family
- how to ask others about their family
- to name some professions

⊙ 1/9 Und deine Familie?
⊙ 1/10

Martina stellt in ihrem Deutschkurs das heutige Thema vor.

Martina Heute sprechen wir über unsere Familien. Jeder fragt seinen Nachbarn zur Familie. Zum Beispiel: Wie heißt dein Vater? Oder: Hast du Geschwister? O. K.? Dann los!

Iwona und Pierre sitzen heute am gleichen Tisch ...

Iwona Pierre, hast du Geschwister?

Pierre Ja, ich habe zwei Schwestern. Ihre Namen sind Julie und Camille.

Iwona Und wie alt sind sie?

Pierre Camille ist 21. Aber Julie ist noch jung. Sie ist erst 14. Hast du auch eine Schwester?

Iwona Nein, ich habe keine Schwester. Ich habe einen Bruder. Er heißt Robert und er hat schon einen Sohn.

Pierre Dann bist du ja Tante! Wie alt ist Roberts Sohn?

Iwona Er ist ein Jahr alt. Er ist sehr süß und so klein. Was ist dein Vater von Beruf?

Pierre Mein Vater ist Architekt. Er arbeitet sehr viel. Meine Mutter arbeitet in einem Kindergarten. Was machen deine Eltern?

Iwona Mein Vater ist Rechtsanwalt. Meine Mutter arbeitet nicht mehr. Sie besucht jetzt sehr oft ihren Enkel. Roberts Frau mag das. Sie hat mehr Zeit für sich. Dann sind beide glücklich.

Martina So ... seid ihr fertig? Ihr macht das alle wirklich gut! Ich bin sehr zufrieden.

Dialogue questions

Mark with a cross:

	right	wrong
1. Pierre has two sisters.	☐	☐
2. Robert is Iwona's son.	☐	☐
3. Pierre's father is an architect.	☐	☐
4. Iwona's mother works in a nursery.	☐	☐

And your family?

Martina presents today's subject in her German class.

Martina   Today, I would like you to talk about your families. Each of you will ask your neighbour about their family. For instance: What's your father's name? Or: Do you have any brothers or sisters? OK? Then go ahead!

Iwona and Pierre are sitting at the same table today ...

Iwona   Pierre, do you have any brothers or sisters?

Pierre   Yes, I have two sisters. Their names are Julie and Camille.

Iwona   And how old are they?

Pierre   Camille is 21. But Julie is still young. She's only 14. Do you have a sister too?

Iwona   No, I don't have any sisters. I have a brother. His name is Robert and he already has a son.

Pierre   You're an auntie then! How old is Robert's son?

Iwona   He's one year old. He's very sweet and so small. What does your father do for living?

Pierre   My father's an architect. He works a lot. My mother works at a nursery. What do your parents do?

Iwona   My father's a lawyer. My mother does not work any more. She visits her grandson often now. Robert's wife likes that. She has more time for herself. Both are happy then.

Martina   So ... are you done? You're all doing really well! I'm very pleased.

Vocabulary

⊙ 3/4

beide	both
Beruf, -e *m*	profession
besuchen	visit
erst	only
Familie, -n *f*	family
fragen	ask
glücklich	happy
jung	young
Kindergarten, -gärten *m*	nursery
klein	small
mehr	more
Nachbar, -n *m*	neighbour
nicht mehr	not anymore
Seid ihr fertig?	Are you done?
sprechen	speak, talk
süß	sweet
verheiratet	married
Verwandte, -n *m+f*	relative
wirklich	really
Zeit, -en *f* (mostly only *Sg*)	time

Family	
Eltern	parents
Mutter, Mütter *f*	mother
Vater, Väter *m*	father
Kind, -er *n*	child
Tochter, Töchter *f*	daughter
Sohn, Söhne *m*	son
Geschwister *Pl*	brothers and sisters
Bruder, Brüder *m*	brother
Schwester, -n *f*	sister
Großeltern *Pl*	grandparents
Großmutter *f*	grandmother
Großvater *m*	grandfather
Tante, -n *f*	aunt
Onkel, – *m*	uncle

Possessive pronouns (used like an article)	
mein	my
dein	your
sein/ihr/sein	his/her/its
unser	our
euer	your
ihr/Ihr formal, *Sg+Pl*	their/your

Professions	
Architekt, -en *m*	architect
Kindergärtner, – *m*	nursery teacher
Lehrer, – *m*	teacher
Rechtsanwalt, -anwälte *m*	male lawyer
Rechtsanwältin, -nen *f*	female lawyer
Kellner, – *m*	waiter
Professor, -en *m*	professor
Ich bin Lehrer.	I'm a teacher.

German professions don't take the indefinite article as in English!
Each profession also has a female form!
Normally you just add -**in** to the male form:
e.g. **Kellner** *m* and **Kellnerin** *f*.

Grammar and means of expression

haben and *sein* ▸ *§8.5*

haben have		sein be	
ich habe	wir haben	ich bin	wir sind
du hast	ihr habt	du bist	ihr seid
er/sie/es hat	sie haben	er/sie/es ist	sie sind

Negation ▸ *§4*

As you've already seen in the previous dialogues you can use **nicht** (*not*) to negate words or sentences:

Das ist **nicht** schwer. *That's not difficult.*

Kein only negates nouns and stands right in front of them, just like the indefinite article (see table below):

Ich habe **keine** Schwester. *I don't have a sister.*

Cases: Nominativ and Akkusativ I ▸ *§1.3*

The German equivalent of the direct object is the accusative. It's used for things or people you have, see or in general do something with.

Ich habe **einen Bruder**. *I have a brother.*

The good news is: The noun usually does not change – only the little word in front of it. Here you can see the accusative forms of the indefinite article, **kein** or a possessive pronoun that are all very similar.

	m	f	n	Pl
Nom.	ein	eine	ein	—
	kein	keine	kein	keine
	mein, dein ...	meine ...	mein ...	meine ...
Acc.	einen	eine	ein	—
	keinen	keine	kein	keine
	meinen ...	meine ...	mein ...	meine ...

Achtung: ....
Remember that there's no indefinite article for plurals!

Exercises

1 *Haben* or *sein*? Fill in the gaps with the correct forms of *haben* or *sein*.

1. Mein Vater _____ Architekt.

2. _____ ihr aus Polen?

3. Ich _____ 24 Jahre alt.

4. Jens und Martina _____ noch keine Kinder.

5. _____ du eine Schwester?

⊙ 1/11 **2** Listen to the questions on the CD and write the answers down.

1. Mein Name ist _____

2. Ich komme _____

3. Ich _____

4. _____

5. _____

3 Connect the questions with the right answers.

1. Wo arbeitest du?

2. Arbeitet deine Mutter viel?

3. Was macht dein Bruder?

4. Wer arbeitet in einem Kindergarten?

5. Bist du Rechtsanwältin?

6. Was machen deine Eltern?

a) Meine Schwester arbeitet in einem Kindergarten.

b) Er ist Kellner.

c) Sie arbeiten nicht mehr.

d) Ja, sie arbeitet sehr viel.

e) Ich arbeite in einer Firma.

f) Ja, ich bin Rechtsanwältin.

4 Fill in the missing words in their appropriate form (gender, accusative). The numbers in brackets show what to use:

0 = *kein*, 1 = *ein*, all other numbers = this number as a German word.

1. Ich habe _____ Schwestern. (2)

2. Du hast _____ Bruder. (0)

3. Wir haben _____ Kinder. (0)

4. Sie hat _____ Freund. (1)

5. Er hat _____ Freundin. (1)

6. Ihr habt _____ Brüder. (3)

Kulturtipp *Du* or better *Sie*?

Use **Du** and the first name with people you're familiar with and who you like. For all others, you're on the safe side with **Sie** and the last name.

If you're not sure, look around to see what others say and follow their lead. It's never a mistake to use **Sie** but it might be embarrassing to say **Du** (if someone hasn't proposed it yet).

Students often use **Du** and the first name with each other, regardless of age. But don't use **Du** with your professors and teachers (unless they propose it).

You can often read that a tie (and a suit) is accompanied by **Sie** (even if the wearer is a 12-year younger bank clerk). If you are new in a company, use **Sie**, especially with your managers. They'll tell you if they prefer it otherwise.

However, in some companies the hybrid form of **Sie** plus first name exists. It suggests more familiarity than **Sie** and the last name but not as much as the use of **Du** would. On the contrary, **Du** and the last name can be heard (especially with children) but is normally not used!

....

What can you already do?

	☺	☺	☹	
■ introduce your family	☐	☐	☐	▸ *Ü3, Ü4*
■ ask questions about family	☐	☐	☐	▸ *Ü1, Ü2, Ü3*
■ answer questions about family	☐	☐	☐	▸ *Ü1, Ü2, Ü3*
■ ask and answer questions about professions	☐	☐	☐	▸ *Ü2, Ü3*

You know more than you think

In this lesson you will learn

- to say that you don't understand
- to ask for help
- to deal with false friends

 1/12
1/13

Deutsch ist einfach! Oder?

Im Deutschkurs

Martina Brian, kannst du bitte den Beamer holen? Er steht dort hinten.

Brian Entschuldigung, das verstehe ich nicht. Kannst du das bitte wiederholen?

Martina Der Beamer. Für Filme und Präsentationen am Laptop.

Brian Oh, meinst du einen „video projector"?

Martina Ja, genau! Das Wort Beamer kennst du nicht? Es ist doch englisch ...

Brian Nicht wirklich, ich kenne nur „beam".

Iwona Das ist aber seltsam. Passiert so etwas oft?

Martina Ich weiß es nicht. Ich muss das nachschlagen. Aber es gibt sehr viele echte englische Wörter im Deutschen. So wie der Laptop hier zum Beispiel.

Pierre Heißt es übrigens der Laptop oder das? Ein Kollege sagt immer „das Laptop".

Martina Ja, das kommt vor. Bei Laptop ist beides möglich.

Brian Es gibt auch deutsche Wörter im Englischen: „Sauerkraut" zum Beispiel.

Martina Stimmt. Und ziemlich viele Wörter haben gemeinsame Wurzeln. Diese Wörter sind heute oft sehr ähnlich: „garden" und „der Garten" oder „fish" und „der Fisch".

Iwona Aber „Chips" sind hier etwas ganz anderes als „chips" in London.

Martina Ja, leider gibt es auch einige falsche Freunde! Wer kennt denn noch andere falsche Freunde aus seiner Muttersprache?

Dialogue questions

Cross out the wrong answer.

1. A Beamer is a *laptop | video projector.*
2. There are *some | no* English words in the German language.
3. Garden and fish have *similar | other* words in German.
4. Chips in London are *the same as | something completely different* than "Chips" in Berlin.

German is easy! Isn't it?

In the German class

Martina	Brian, can you get the "Beamer", please? It's over there at the back.
Brian	Sorry, I didn't understand that. Can you repeat, please?
Martina	The "Beamer". For videos or presentations on a laptop.
Brian	Oh, you mean the video projector?
Martina	Yes, exactly. You don't know the word "Beamer"? But it's English ...
Brian	No, not really, I only know "beam".
Iwona	That's strange. Does this happen a lot?
Martina	I don't know. I have to look it up. But there are a lot of real English words in German. Like "der Laptop" here for instance.
Pierre	Is it "der Laptop" or "das" by the way? One colleague always says "das Laptop".
Martina	Yes, it is used. With Laptop both are possible.
Brian	There are German words in English too: "Sauerkraut" for instance.
Martina	Right. And quite a few words have common roots. These words are very similar today: "garden" and "der Garten" or "fish" und "der Fisch".
Iwona	But "Chips" here are something completely different than "chips" in London.
Martina	Yes, unfortunately there are also some false friends. Who knows any other false friends in his native language?

Vocabulary

3/5

ähnlich	similar, alike
Beamer, – m	video projector
dieser, diese, dieses	this/that
diese Pl	these
dort	there
echt	real
etwas ganz anderes	something completely different
Film, -e m	film, movie
Fisch, -e m	fish
Garten, Gärten m	garden
gemeinsam	common
Haus, Häuser n	house
hinten	(at the) back
holen	get, fetch
können	can
langsam	slow
Laptop, -s m/n	laptop
möglich	possible
müssen	have to, must
nachschlagen	look up
oft	often, a lot
passieren	happen
planen	plan, arrange, design
Präsentation, -en f	presentation
Restaurant, -s n	restaurant
sehr viel	a lot of
sehr	very
stehen	stand (here: be)
Stimmt.	Right.
verstehen	understand
wiederholen	repeat
wissen	know
Wort, Wörter n	word
Wurzel, -n f	root

Some false friends

Chip, -s m (mostly only Pl)	crisps
Mord, -e m	murder
Mörder, – m	murderer
Pommes (frites) (Pl)	chips, fries
fast	almost
schnell	fast
Geschenk, -e n	gift
Gift, -e n	poison
Chef, -s m	boss, manager
Koch, Köche m	chef
bekommen	get
werden	become

Learning tip I

Most internationalisms or English words used in German have -s as a plural ending. E.g.: Chips, Chefs, Laptops, Singles, Restaurants.

Learning tip II

German nouns with -ion as suffix are always feminine! E.g.: die Präsentation.

Grammar and means of expression

The modal verbs *können* and *müssen* ► *§8.6*

können		müssen	
ich kann	wir können	ich muss	wir müssen
du kannst	ihr könnt	du musst	ihr müsst
er/sie/es kann	sie (Sie) können	er/sie/es muss	sie (Sie) müssen

Modal verbs and sentence frame ► *§10*

Remember: In declarative sentences and Wh Questions, the conjugated verb
(here the modal verb) is in the second place (the first in Yes/No Questions):
Ich **muss** das **nachschauen**. *I have to look it up.*
Kannst du das bitte **wiederholen**? *Can you repeat, please?*
The second (uninflected) verb goes – as you see – to the last place and together they
build this frame-like structure: the **Satzklammer** *sentence frame.*

Definite vs. indefinite article ► *§2.1*

The use of the appropriate article should in most cases be the same as in English.
Use the definite article with nouns when you refer to a singular distinct and known
thing (or things).
Kannst du bitte **den** Beamer holen? *Can you get the video projector please?*
If you refer to a noun in general or something yet unknown, use the indefinite article.
Meinst du **einen** „video projector"? *You mean a video projector?*

Cases: Nominativ and Akkusativ II ► *§2.1*

Let's develop the table of accusative forms from the previous lesson. Here you can
see the accusative forms of the definite article.

	m	f	n	Pl
Nom.	der	die	das	die
Acc.	den	die	das	die

Exercises

 1 False friends. Connect the German words with the correct translation.

1. die Chips	a) fast	4. fast	d) gift
2. das Geschenk	b) almost	5. das Gift	e) crisps
3. die Pommes	c) chips	6. schnell	f) poison

⊙ 1/14   **2** Read the phrases below. Now listen to the CD, repeat each sentence and strike it off the list. One phrase remains. Which one?

> Heißt es der Laptop oder das Laptop?   Dieses Wort kenne ich nicht.
> Entschuldigung, ich verstehe das nicht. Leider gibt es einige falsche Freunde.
> Das ist etwas ganz anderes.   Kannst du das wiederholen?
> Garten und *garden* sind sehr ähnlich.

3 Put the mixed up sentences in the right order. Remember the position of the modal verb and the infinitive. Translate them afterwards.

1. a) den Satz / wiederholen / muss / er / . ...

   b) Translation: ....

2. a) kannst / den Beamer / holen / bitte / du / ? ....

   b) Translation: ....

3. a) viel / arbeiten / musst / du / ? ....

   b) Translation: ....

4. a) diese Wörter / Iwona / muss / nachschauen / . ...

   b) Translation: ....

5. a) oft / unseren Sohn / besuchen / können / wir / . ...

   b) Translation: ....

6. a) ich / das / nicht / verstehe / . ...

   b) Translation: ....

7. a) wiederholen / Sie *(formal!)* / das / können / bitte / ? ....

   b) Translation: ....

Kulturtipp
German and English

You might have thought that English and German are not very similar. But as they both have Germanic origins, it's easy to spot similarities (either in writing or pronunciation): **das Haus** *house*, **der Mann** *man*, **gut** *good*, **singen** *sing*, **das Wasser** *water*.

But be careful! There are also some false friends as you've learned in this lesson. And it wouldn't be good to confuse *a gift* and **das Gift**!

You'll notice that the Germans use a lot of English words today – especially around computers and the internet. Those are either real English words: **Software aus dem Internet auf den Computer downloaden** *to download software from the internet on the computer* is actually a German sentence! Or (as in the dialogue) pseudo-anglicisms: **das Handy** *mobile/cell phone*, **der Beamer** *video projector* for presentations and **Bodybags** *shoulder/cross-body bag* for carrying your stuff.

....

What can you already do?

☺ ☺ ☹

■ say that you don't understand	▪ ▪ ▪	▸*Ü2, Ü3*
■ ask for help	▪ ▪ ▪	▸*Ü2, Ü3*
■ detect some common false friends	▪ ▪ ▪	▸*Ü1*

Congratulations, you've now mastered the first part of this book! Wasn't as difficult, was it? Now you can delve into the next lesson with a lot of opportunities to practise what you've learned ... Have fun!

Repeat and practise

Here you repeat

- asking and answering questions about yourself and others
- talking about your family
- talking about professions
- conducting short conversations

1 Write the sentences again. This time use personal pronouns given in brackets instead of the names and don't forget to adapt the verbs.

1. Iwona arbeitet in einer Consultingfirma. (du) ....

2. Pierre studiert noch. (er) ....

3. Jeff ist aus den USA. (wir) ....

4. Monika ist Rechtsanwältin. (sie *Sg*) ....

2 The possessive pronouns are missing. Fill the gaps with the right pronoun in the nominative case.

1. Wir haben zwei Kinder. .... Kinder sind 7 und 8 Jahre alt.

2. Ich habe einen Bruder. .... Bruder heißt Michael.

3. Iwona und Pierre lernen Deutsch. .... Lehrerin heißt Martina.

4. Sie kommt aus Deutschland. .... Freund kommt aus England.

5. Ihr habt eine Schwester. .... Schwester ist verheiratet.

6. Haben Sie ein Kind? Wie alt ist .... Kind? *(Caution: formal Sie!)*

3 Two people are having a little chat but the phrases got mixed up. Can you put them back in their original order?

1. Ja, Rzeszów liegt in der Nähe von Krakau. Bist du aus Deutschland? ☐
2. Ich kenne Berlin. Ich arbeite dort. Arbeitest du auch? ☐
3. Hallo! Mein Name ist Iwona. Wie heißt du? ☐
4. Nein, ich studiere noch. ☐
5. Ich komme aus Rzeszów. ☐
6. Ich heiße Claudia. Woher kommst du? ☐
7. Ist das in Polen? ☐
8. Ja, ich bin aus Potsdam. Das ist in der Nähe von Berlin. ☐

4 Write the correct numbers in German in the puzzle. The coloured boxes will reveal another number when you've finished.

a) = 4   c) = 11   e) = 10   g) = 8
b) = 2   d) = 3   f) = 7   h) = 9

5 Listen to the CD. Then read the sentences below and listen to the CD again.   ⊙ 1/15
Mark the correct information with a cross.

1. Martin ist   a) ☐ Deutschlehrer.   b) ☐ Architekt.
2. Martin ist seit   a) ☐ einem Jahr   b) ☐ fünf Jahren in Berlin.
3. Lynn kommt aus   a) ☐ Deutschland.   b) ☐ England.
4. Lynn ist Martins   a) ☐ Schwester.   b) ☐ Freundin.

6 Read the short word lists. Then choose the words from the box that go with each list and write them down. One does not fit!

> Deutschland   Guten Abend   Geschäftsmann
> Eltern   Onkel   Auf Wiedersehen   Monat

1. Tante, Vater, Sohn, ...

2. Kellner, Lehrer, Architekt, ...

3. Stunde, Woche, Tag, ...

4. Frankreich, England, Polen, ...

5. Guten Tag, Hallo, Hi, ...

6. Großeltern, Kinder, Geschwister, ...

7 *Sie* or *du*? Which one would you normally use when talking to the people in the table below? Mark:

	Sie	du
1. dein Chef	☐	☐
2. deine Familie	☐	☐
3. ein Freund aus dem Deutschkurs	☐	☐
4. ein neuer Kollege	☐	☐
5. eine Kellnerin	☐	☐
6. dein Professor	☐	☐

8 *Kein* or *nicht*? Write the sentences in the negative.

1. Das ist schwer. _____

2. Martina hat eine Schwester. _____

3. Ich verstehe das. _____

4. Das ist ein englisches Wort. _____

5. Du weißt es. _____

6. Ich habe einen Laptop. _____

9 Read the short text. Then read the phrases below and decide whether they are right or wrong.

Martina ist Deutschlehrerin in Berlin. Sie lebt dort mit ihrem Freund Jens. Martinas Eltern wohnen nicht in Berlin. Sie wohnen in München. Martina hat eine Schwester, aber keinen Bruder. Ihre Schwester heißt Kathrin. Kathrin wohnt in Potsdam. Potsdam liegt in der Nähe von Berlin. Sie studiert und arbeitet als Kellnerin. Martina besucht sehr oft ihre Schwester in Potsdam. Jens hat keine Geschwister. Jens kommt aus Jena. Aber er lebt seit sechs Jahren in Berlin. Er arbeitet dort in einer großen Firma. Er ist Informatiker.

	right	wrong
1. Martinas Eltern wohnen in Hamburg.	☐	☐
2. Jens' Schwester heißt Kathrin.	☐	☐
3. Kathrin wohnt in der Nähe von Berlin.	☐	☐
4. Kathrin besucht sehr oft ihre Schwester.	☐	☐
5. Jens hat keine Schwester.	☐	☐
6. Jens arbeitet in Jena.	☐	☐

10 What do you say? Choose your replies from the box.

> Hallo!   Es geht.   Bis später!   Viel Spaß!   Freut mich!

1. Wie geht es dir? – ....
2. Das ist mein Freund Jens. – ....
3. Der Unterricht beginnt. – ....
4. Tschüs! – ....
5. Hi! – ....

11 Build sentences. Use the information in their right forms.

ich / haben / 2 / Bruder *Ich habe zwei Brüder.*
1. sie *Pl* / sehen / 2 / Mann ....
2. wir / haben / – / Schwester ....
3. du / haben / 1 / Sohn ....
4. sie *Sg* / haben / 4 / Geschwister ....

12 Connect the short descriptions with the correct profession.

1. Er macht den Deutschkurs.	a) der Professor
2. Er plant Häuser.	b) die Kindergärtnerin
3. Sie arbeitet in einem Restaurant.	c) der Architekt
4. Sie arbeitet mit Kindern.	d) die Kellnerin
5. Er arbeitet an der Universität.	e) der Deutschlehrer

13 Pierre introduces himself and his family. Read the text and then introduce yourself following Pierre's example.

> Hallo, mein Name ist Pierre. Ich komme aus Rennes. Das liegt in der Bretagne. Ich bin 24 Jahre alt. Ich studiere Maschinenbau. Ich mache ein Praktikum in einer deutschen Firma in Berlin. Ich habe zwei Schwestern. Sie heißen Camille und Julie. Camille ist 21 und Julie ist 14. Mein Vater ist Rechtsanwalt von Beruf. Meine Mutter arbeitet in einem Kindergarten.

....
....
....
....
....

☑ **14** The following sentences and questions are in a mess. Please sort them out. But be careful: all the verbs are in the infinitive and you have to put them in the right form!

1. sehen / können / den Mann / du / ? ....
2. ich / Deutsch / müssen / lernen / . ...
3. arbeiten / wo / du / ? ....
4. du / in einer Consultingfirma / arbeiten / ? ....
5. sehr viel / wir / müssen / lernen / . ...
6. sie (*Pl.*) / können / verstehen / diese Wörter / nicht / . ...

....

15 Read the short e-mail. Then write back answering the questions.

Neue E-Mail

Hallo,

wie geht es dir? Danke für deine E-Mail. Du schreibst gut deutsch.
Das ist toll! Wie lange bist du schon in Deutschland? Machst du einen
Deutschkurs? Ist Deutsch schwer?
Und arbeitest du? Kennst du schon viele Deutsche?
Tschüs!

....
....
....
....
....
....

☑ **16** Definite article, indefinite article, or nothing? Complete the sentences with the words from the box.

— der der die ein eine einen einen einen

1. Hast du .... Laptop? – Nein, ich habe keinen Laptop.

2. a) .... Beamer ist kaputt. Ich hole b) .... neuen Beamer.

3. Kennst du .... Restaurant hier?   4. Seine Schwester ist .... Architektin.

5. Ich sehe a) .... Mann. b) .... Mann hat c) .... Frau. d) .... Frau ist jung.

17 Read the answers below. Then listen to the first question on the CD, pause ⊚ 1/16
after the beep and answer. You can hear the correct answer afterwards.
Then continue.

> Nein, ich bin Single.   Ja, kein Problem.   Mir geht es prima.
> Mein Vater ist Rechtsanwalt. Meine Mutter ist Architektin.
> Ja, ich habe einen Bruder.   Ich bin seit 6 Monaten hier.

18 Pierre wrote an e-mail but the verbs are still missing. Read the e-mail and
help Pierre fill in the missing verbs in the right form.

> machen   sein   haben   sein   arbeiten   machen   gehen
> heißen   sein   kommen   kennen

Neue E-Mail

Lieber Michael,

wie _____ (1.) es dir? Ich _____ (2.) jetzt in Berlin und _____ (3.)
einen Deutschkurs. Deutsch _____ (4.) nicht sehr schwer! Ich _____
(5.) viel Spaß!

Eine Freundin aus dem Kurs _____ (6.) Iwona. Sie _____ (7.) aus
Polen.

Mein Praktikum _____ (8.) auch toll. Ich _____ (9.) schon viele
Menschen hier.

Was _____ (10.) du? _____ (11.) du noch in der Firma?

Viele Grüße

Pierre

19 Listen to the five short dialogues on the CD. Listen to how they say hello ⊚ 1/17
or good-bye. Do you know what time these people are meeting? Write the
dialogue numbers.

1. 8 am _____   2. 2 pm _____   3. 10 pm _____

20 Read the phrases. Now say them aloud using the formal *Sie* this time.

1. Du fragst deinen Nachbarn.   4. Kannst du das bitte wiederholen?
2. Woher kommst du?   5. Du bist aus Deutschland.
3. Arbeitest du viel?

Intermediate test 1

1 Which article is right? Strike out the wrong ones.

1. *der | die | das* Architektin
2. *der | die | das* Präsentation
3. *der | die | das* Garten
_/8 4. *der | die | das* Zeit

5. *der | die | das* Monat
6. *der | die | das* Restaurant
7. *der | die | das* Woche
8. *der | die | das* Dialog

2 Write the following sentences again but this time use the modal verb given in brackets.

1. Sie holt den Laptop. *(müssen)* ....

2. Ich spreche über meine Familie. *(können)* ....

3. Ihr wiederholt den Satz. *(müssen)* ....

_/4 4. Arbeiten Sie sehr viel? *(müssen)* ....

◉ 1/18 **3** Read the following phrases. Then listen to the CD and decide ...

	right	wrong
1. Frau Schneider versteht alles.	☐	☐
2. Martina muss einen falschen Freund wiederholen.	☐	☐
3. Martina ist nicht zufrieden.	☐	☐
4. Yoko hat einen Bruder.	☐	☐
_/5 5. Jens ist nicht glücklich.	☐	☐

4 Either the plural or the singular is missing. Write down the form.

Singular	Plural
1. Land	
2.	Stunden
3.	Firmen
4. Familie	
5. Lehrer	
6.	Söhne
7. Schwester	
8. Mutter	
9.	Häuser
_/10 10. Restaurant	

5 Read the following answers. Then write down appropriate questions using either the formal *Sie* or the informal *Du* as stated.

1. _____ (Sie)

Herr Schneider: „Ich komme aus Deutschland."

2. _____ (Du)

Claudia: „Ja, ich kann das wiederholen."

3. _____ (Du)

Brian: „Ja, ich hole den Beamer."

4. _____ (Sie)

Frau Maier: „Ich arbeite in einer Consultingfirma."   __/4

6 Here is a short e-mail from a German friend. After you have read it, mark the right numbers with a cross in the questions below.

Neue E-Mail
An:
Kopie:
Betreff:
Von: Michael

Hallo,

das ist meine Familie: Mein Vater heißt Robert. Er ist Lehrer. Meine Mutter heißt Johanna und arbeitet in einem Kindergarten. Ich habe auch eine Schwester. Ihr Name ist Julia und sie ist zwölf. Ich habe keinen Bruder. Mein Vater hat viele Geschwister: Drei Schwestern und einen Bruder. Aber meine Mutter hat mehr Geschwister: vier Brüder und zwei Schwestern. Meine Eltern kennen sich seit vierzehn Jahren. Und deine Familie?

Tschüs!

Michael

1. Julia ist
   a) ☐ 2 Jahre alt.
   b) ☐ 12 Jahre alt.
   c) ☐ 20 Jahre alt.

2. Michaels Vater hat
   a) ☐ 1 Schwester.
   b) ☐ 2 Schwestern.
   c) ☐ 3 Schwestern.

3. Johanna hat
   a) ☐ 6 Geschwister.
   b) ☐ 7 Geschwister.
   c) ☐ 8 Geschwister.

4. Robert und Johanna haben
   a) ☐ kein Kind.
   b) ☐ 1 Kind.
   c) ☐ 2 Kinder.

5. Roberts Eltern haben
   a) ☐ 5 Kinder.
   b) ☐ 6 Kinder.
   c) ☐ 7 Kinder.

__/5

7 Complete the questions with the correct interrogative pronoun: *Wie, wo, woher.*

1. .... kommst du?

2. .... liegt das?

3. .... lange bist du schon in Berlin?

4. .... heißt du?

5. .... arbeitest du?

__/6 6. .... alt ist deine Mutter?

⊙ 1/19 **8** Read the three business cards. You can see some information is missing. Now listen to the three short introductions on the CD and fill in the missing information.

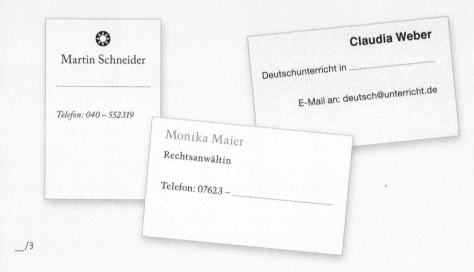

__/3

9 Translate the following sentences.

1. Can you help me? ....

2. I have to get the laptop. ....

3. He has to work a lot. ....

4. Jens can visit his mother often. ....

__/5 5. Can you repeat these words, please? ....

__/50

Day 7 Shopping

In this lesson you will learn

- to buy food
- to ask about prices
- to get to know common quantities and packaging

⊙ 1/20 **Auf dem Markt**
⊙ 1/21

Verkäuferin	Na, junger Mann? Was darf's denn sein?
Pierre	Ich möchte Obst kaufen. Was kosten die Pfirsiche?
Verkäuferin	Die Pfirsiche? Ein Kilo kostet 2,60 Euro.
Pierre	O. K., dann bitte vier Pfirsiche. Und noch Weintrauben, bitte. Ein halbes Kilo.
Verkäuferin	Aber gern. Noch etwas?
Pierre	Ja, noch Gemüse. Ich brauche rote Paprika und Zucchini.
Verkäuferin	Wie viel möchten Sie denn?
Pierre	Ich möchte zwei Paprikas und eine Zucchini, bitte.
Verkäuferin	Johannes, gib dem Mann bitte das Gemüse. Ist das dann alles?
Pierre	Ja, vielen Dank.
Verkäuferin	Möchten Sie auch eine Tüte?
Pierre	Oh ja, bitte.
Verkäuferin	Das macht dann zusammen 11,50 Euro. Was gibt es denn zum Essen?
Pierre	Ich möchte Ratatouille kochen.
Verkäuferin	Ah, schön! So, Sie bekommen noch 3 Euro und 50 Cent zurück. Bitte.
Pierre	Danke. Auf Wiedersehen.
Verkäuferin	Auf Wiedersehen.
Pierre	Mal sehen … Ich brauche noch Schinken, eine Flasche Wein, einen Karton Milch und zwei Dosen Tomaten. Aber jetzt treffe ich mich erst mit Iwona. Sie wartet sicher schon auf mich …

Dialog questions

Mark with a cross:

	right	wrong
1. Pierre ist im Supermarkt.	☐	☐
2. Er kauft ein Kilo Pfirsiche.	☐	☐
3. Pierre kauft vier Paprikas.	☐	☐
4. Pierre kauft Zutaten für Ratatouille.	☐	☐
5. Die Waren kosten 3,50 Euro.	☐	☐
6. Pierre braucht noch Zucchinis.	☐	☐

At the market

Saleslady	Hello, young man. What would you like to buy?
Pierre	I'd like to buy some fruit. How much are the peaches?
Saleslady	The peaches? One kilo costs 2,60 Euro.
Pierre	OK, then four peaches, please. And grapes, please. Half a kilo.
Saleslady	Certainly. Anything else?
Pierre	Yes, some vegetables. I need red peppers and courgettes.
Saleslady	How much do you want?
Pierre	I would like two peppers and one courgette, please.
Saleslady	Johannes, give the man the vegetables, please. Is that all then?
Pierre	Yes, thank you very much.
Saleslady	Would you like a bag?
Pierre	Oh yes, please.
Saleslady	That's 11,50 Euro altogether. What are you going to cook?
Pierre	I'd like to cook Ratatouille.
Saleslady	Oh, nice. So, 3 Euro and 50 Cents for you. Here you are.
Pierre	Thanks. Good bye.
Saleslady	Good bye.
Pierre	Let's have a look ... I still need ham, a bottle of wine, a carton of milk and two cans of tomatoes. But now, I'm going to meet Iwona first. She's probably waiting for me already ...

Vocabulary

bekommen	get
brauchen	need
Einkaufsliste, -n *f*	shopping list
geben	give
Geld *(only Sg) n*	money
Gemüse *(only Sg) n*	vegetable(-s)
gern, gewiss	certainly
Ich möchte ...	I would like ...
kaufen	buy
kosten	cost
Lebensmittel, – *n (mostly Pl)*	food
Markt, Märkte *m*	market
Milchprodukt, -e *n*	dairy product
Obst *(only Sg) n*	fruit
Preis, -e *m*	price
pro (Kilo)	per (kilo)
Sonderangebot, -e *n*	special offer
Supermarkt, -märkte *m*	supermarket
Verpackung, -en *f*	packaging
warten	wait
Wechselgeld *(only Sg) n*	change
wie viel/viele	how much/many

Weight & packaging

Kilo, – *n*	kilo (kilogramme)
Gramm, – *n*	gramme/gram
Liter, – *m*	litre
Dose, -n *f*	can
Flasche, -n *f*	bottle
Karton, -s *m*	carton
Packung, -en *f*	package, pack
Stück, -e *n*	piece
Tüte, -n *f*	bag

Food

Apfel, Äpfel *m*	apple
Birne, -n *f*	pear
Brot, -e *n*	bread
Brötchen, – *n*	bun
Butter *(only Sg) f*	butter
Ei, -er *n*	egg
Fisch, -e *m*	fish
Fleisch *(only Sg) n*	meat
Gurke, -n *f*	cucumber
Hähnchen, – *n*	chicken
Kartoffel, -n *f*	potato
Käse *(only Sg) m*	cheese
Marmelade, -n *f*	jam
Milch *(only Sg) f*	milk
Möhre, -n *f (also* Karotte, -n *f)*	carrot
Müsli, -s *n*	muesli
Paprika, -s *m/f*	peppers
Pfirsich, -e *m*	peach
Sahne *(only Sg) f*	cream
Schinken *(only Sg) m*	ham
Tomate, -n *f*	tomato
Wein, -e *m*	wine
Weintraube, -n *f*	grape
Wurst, Würste *f*	sausage
Zucchini, -s *f*	courgette
Zwiebel, -n *f*	onion

Grammar and means of expression

Imperative ▸ §8.9

The imperative is the form for commands and requests. The verb goes always to the front of the sentence. Depending on who you address you need one of the following imperative sentences.

Declarative sentence	Rule	Imperative
Du gibst dem Mann das Gemüse.	no pronoun omit ending -st	**Gib** dem Mann das Gemüse.
Ihr gebt dem Mann das Gemüse.	no pronoun	**Gebt** dem Mann das Gemüse.
Sie geben dem Mann das Gemüse. *(formal)*	keep the pronoun	**Geben** Sie dem Mann das Gemüse.

Cases: *Dativ* ▸ §2.1

The English indirect object is the **Dativ** in German. Certain verbs (like **geben** – see the example for the imperative) and prepositions need an object in the dative. With verbs the dative usually is an object that receives something. A noun in the dative gets an **-n** ending – but only in the plural and when not already there.

Dative of the definite article				
	m	f	n	Pl
Nom.	der	die	das	die
Dat.	dem	der	dem	den (noun+n)

Dative of the indefinite article				
	m	f	n	Pl
Nom.	ein	eine	ein	—
Dat.	einem	einer	einem	— (noun+n)

Remember that the forms of the possessive pronouns and **kein** are similar to the indefinite article. Their plural form is **keinen, meinen, deinen** …

Nullartikel ▸ §2.2

Nullartikel means you need no article in front of the noun. Like in English, you use nouns of unspecified quantity without any article:
Ich brauche noch Schinken. *I still need ham.*

1 Take the food table from the vocabulary section and sort the items into the following table.

Obst

Gemüse

Milchprodukte

Anderes (others)

2 Connect the questions with the right answers.

1. Was kosten die Orangen?	a) Geben Sie mir bitte zwei Stück.
2. Ist das dann alles?	b) Ein Kilo kostet 3 Euro.
3. Was darf's denn sein?	c) Nein, ich brauche noch Gemüse.
4. Wie viele Gurken möchten Sie?	d) Ich möchte Wurst kaufen.

1/22 **3 Listen to the special offers on the CD. Now write the right prices of the food items.**

1. Kartoffeln: .... pro Kilo

3. Schinken: .... pro Packung

2. Birnen: .... pro Kilo

4. Wein: .... pro Flasche

Kulturtipp Shopping in Germany

If you want to go shopping in Germany keep in mind that, at least in some states (like Bavaria), the opening hours of shops on working days are limited. Bigger supermarkets are at least open till 8 pm. But smaller shops like butchers or bakers normally still close around 6 or 7 pm.

On Saturday some shops close still earlier, some even as early as 1 or 2 pm and on Sunday all shops are closed. All shops? No, there are some exceptions: petrol stations often sell food too and they are mostly open on Sundays and shops at the station (at least in bigger cities) can open on Sundays too.

If you prefer fresh food directly from the farmer go to the **Wochenmärkte** *weekly farmers' markets* like Pierre. They offer a wide variety of food and now a lot of organic products as well. They take place at least once a week, often on two days and usually in central (market) places.

What can you already do?

	☺	☺	☹	
■ know common food	■	■		▸*Ü1*
■ ask about prices	■	■		▸*Ü2*
■ buy food	■	■		▸*Ü2*
■ understand prices and packaging	■	■		▸*Ü3*

So, this was your first lesson in the second part. If you don't understand everything at the beginning, don't let that discourage you. That's normal for everyone!
Just listen to the texts on the CD several times and don't forget the appendix – the short grammar section, the complete vocabulary section and the solutions are there to help you!

In a restaurant

In this lesson you will learn

- to order something to eat or drink
- to ask for the bill in a restaurant or café
- to speak about food

⊚ 1/23 **Für mich einen Kuchen**
⊚ 1/24

Iwona and Pierre sitzen in einem Café.

Kellner Guten Tag. Was hätten Sie denn gerne?

Iwona Guten Tag. Für mich eine Tasse Kaffee und ein Stück Apfelkuchen, bitte.

Kellner Und für Sie?

Pierre Ich hätte gerne einen Milchkaffee und ein Stück Schokoladen-torte.
Könnte ich bitte auch etwas Schlagsahne bekommen?

Kellner Ja, natürlich.

Iwona Kommst du jetzt vom Markt?

Pierre Ja! Und der Markt ist toll – viel besser als ein Supermarkt. Es gibt
sogar einen Stand mit französischen Spezialitäten. Das muss ich meiner
Mutter erzählen!

Iwona *(etwas später)* Und? Wie ist deine Torte?

Pierre Sehr lecker! Möchtest du sie probieren?

Iwona Gern! Oh ja, sehr lecker! Hier, probier auch von meinem Kuchen.

Pierre Danke. Mmm, schmeckt mir sehr!

Kellner *(noch etwas später)* Darf ich Ihnen noch etwas bringen?

Iwona Nein danke, aber könnten wir bitte die Rechnung bekommen?

Kellner Ja, sehr gern.

Pierre Wie ist das in Deutschland? Geben wir dem Kellner auch Trinkgeld?

Iwona Ja, etwas Trinkgeld ist üblich. Und dann müssen wir gehen.
Jens und Martina warten sicher schon.

Pierre Jens und Martina? Treffen wir uns nicht morgen?

Iwona Nein Pierre, wir treffen uns heute!

Dialog questions

Cross out the wrong answer.

1. Iwona isst ein Stück *Apfelkuchen | Schokoladentorte*.
2. Pierre möchte *etwas | keine* Schlagsahne.
3. Iwona findet Pierres Torte *nicht | sehr* lecker.
4. Pierre und Iwona treffen sich *heute | morgen* mit Jens und Martina.

A pie for me ...

Iwona and Pierre are in a café.

Waiter	Good afternoon. What would you like?
Iwona	Good afternoon. A cup of coffee and a slice of apple pie for me, please.
Waiter	And for you?
Pierre	I'd like a café au lait and a slice of chocolate gateau. Could I have some whipped cream too, please?
Waiter	Yes, of course.
Iwona	Have you just come from the market?
Pierre	Yes! And the market is great – much better than a supermarket. There was even a market stand with French specialties. I have to tell my mother about it!
Iwona	*(a bit later)* And? How is your gateau?
Pierre	Delicious! Would you like to taste it?
Iwona	Yes, please! Oh yes, very tasty! Here, try my pie as well.
Pierre	Thanks. Mmm, I like it very much!
Waiter	*(later yet)* May I get you anything else?
Iwona	No thanks, but could we have the bill please?
Waiter	Yes, of course.
Pierre	How is it in Germany? Do we tip the waiter?
Iwona	Yes, you normally tip. And then we have to go. Jens and Martina for sure are waiting already.
Pierre	Jens and Martina? Aren't we meeting them tomorrow?
Iwona	No Pierre, today!

3/7

Beilage, -n *f*	side dish
bestellen	order
bringen	get, bring
Café, -s *n*	café
erzählen	tell
essen	eat
Essen, – *n*	meal
Gabel, -n *f*	fork
Glas, Gläser *n*	glass
Hauptgericht, -e *n*	main dish
Ich hätte gern...	I'd like (to have)...
ja, natürlich	yes, of course
Könnte ich ...?	Could I...?
Kuchen, – *m*	cake, pie
Löffel, – *m*	spoon
Messer, – *n*	knife
Nachtisch, -e *m*	dessert
probieren	taste, try
Rechnung, -en *f*	bill
schlecht	bad
schmecken	taste
lecker	delicious
Serviette, -n *f*	napkin
sicher	for sure
Tasse, -n *f*	cup
Teller, – *m*	plate, dish
Torte, -n *f*	gateau
trinken	drink
Trinkgeld (only Sg) *n*	tip
üblich	normal, common
warten	wait

Something to drink

Getränk, -e *n*	beverage, drink
Kaffee, -s *m*	coffee
Tee, -s *m*	tea
(stilles) Wasser, – *n*	(non sparkling) water
Sprudel, – *m*	sparkling water
Bier, -e *n*	beer
Cola, -s *n/f*	coke
Saft, Säfte *m*	juice
Schorle, -n *f*	juice or wine mixed with sparkling water

Popular dishes

Schnitzel, – *n*	schnitzel
Kartoffeln *(here mostly Pl)*	potatoes
Nudeln *(mostly Pl)*	noodles
Reis *(only Sg) m*	rice
Pommes (frites) *(only Pl)*	chips
Suppe, -n *f*	soup
Salat, -e *m*	salad

Some temporal adverbials

heute	today
morgen	tomorrow
übermorgen	the day after tomorrow
gestern	yesterday
vorgestern	the day before yesterday
jetzt	now
später	later
früher	earlier

Grammar and means of expression

Polite forms ▸ §8.6

You've seen in the dialogues from this and the previous lessons what Pierre and Iwona say to get what they want:

Ich möchte zwei Paprikas, bitte. *I would like two peppers, please.*
Ich hätte gerne einen Milchkaffee. *I'd like (to have) a café au lait.*
Könnte ich etwas Schlagsahne bekommen? *Could I have some whipped cream?*
These are the polite forms you can use when you want something.

Personal pronouns ▸ §3.1

A pronoun usually replaces a noun, like with the nominative (e.g. **er** instead of **Pierre**):
Er kauft Obst. *He buys fruit.*
It's the same with the accusative and the dative.
You've already seen it in the dialogue:
Möchtest du **sie** probieren? *Would you like to taste it?* (accusative)
Darf ich **Ihnen** noch etwas bringen? *May I get you anything else?* (dative)

The personal pronouns in the nominative, accusative and dative						
Nom.	ich	du	er/sie/es	wir	ihr	sie/Sie
Acc.	mich	dich	ihn/sie/es	uns	euch	sie/Sie
Dat.	mir	dir	ihm/ihr/ihm	uns	euch	ihnen/Ihnen

More examples are:
Was hätten **Sie** denn gerne? *What would you like?* (nominative)
Das schmeckt **mir** sehr. *I like it very much.* (dative)
Und für **Sie**? *And for you?* (accusative)
Könnten **wir** die Rechnung bekommen? *Could we have the bill?* (nominative)

Three- and four-digit numbers

200	zweihundert	1000	(ein-)tausend
300	dreihundert	2000	zweitausend
768	siebenhundertachtundsechzig	4179	viertausendeinhundertneun-undsiebzig

1 Order your lunch. Read the menu and underline what you would like.

Suppen
Tomatensuppe	
Gemüsesuppe	2€
Nudelsuppe	2€
Zwiebelsuppe	1,80€
	1,80€

Beilagen
Pommes	
Reis	
Nudeln	2€
Kartoffeln	1,80€
Gemüse	2€
kleiner Salat	1,50€
großer Salat	1,80€
	1,50€
	3€

Hauptgerichte
	5€
Schnitzel	5€
Fisch	4,50€
Hähnchen	3,50€
Ratatouille	

Getränke
	2€
Cola	1,50€
Wasser	2€
Apfelsaft	2,50€
Bier	1€
Tee	1,80€
Kaffee	

⊙ 1/25 **2** Martina and Jens are in a restaurant. Listen to the short dialogue on the CD and mark who orders what.

	Martina	Jens
Wasser	☐	☐
Bier	☐	☐
Salat	☐	☐
Suppe	☐	☐
Schnitzel mit Pommes	☐	☐
Fisch mit Kartoffeln	☐	☐
Rechnung	☐	☐

3 Imagine you're in a restaurant. What would you say to get the following dishes?

eine Tasse Tee   ein Schnitzel mit Kartoffeln   ein Glas Cola
ein Stück Apfelkuchen   eine Suppe   ein Salat

Kulturtipp Eat and drink

Apart from the common meals through-out the day, **das Frühstück** *breakfast*, **das Mittagessen** *lunch* and **das Abend-essen** *supper,* the Germans like to have **Kaffee und Kuchen** *coffee and cake* in the afternoon. Often there's only time for this in the afternoon at weekends. Like Iwona and Pierre, people enjoy meeting in the city to have their coffee and cake in a café.

By the way, coffee is one of the most popular beverages in Germany besides **Bier** *beer* and **Sprudel** *sparkling mineral water.*

When you're in a restaurant or café with other people and you ask for the bill, the waiter may ask if you want to pay **getrennt oder zusammen**. This means he wants to know if each person is paying for her-/himself individually or if the whole sum is going to be paid in one go. Usually it's no problem to divide the sum in other ways: e.g. you pay for the drinks and your friend for the food.

....

What can you already do?

	☺	☺	☹	
■ order something to eat or drink	■	■	■	▸ *Ü2, Ü3*
■ ask for the bill	■	■	■	▸ *Ü2*
■ understand a basic menu	■	■	■	▸ *Ü1*

Leisure time in a city

In this lesson you will learn

- to talk about your leisure time
- to express your wishes and preferences
- to buy tickets for a museum

⊙ 1/26 **Berliner Sehenswürdigkeiten**
⊙ 1/27

Iwona, Martina, Pierre und Jens treffen sich am Brandenburger Tor.

Jens	Hallo Iwona! Hi Pierre. Wie geht's euch?
Iwona	Gut, danke.
Pierre	Hi. Was unternehmen wir denn heute?
Jens	Wart ihr schon auf dem Fernsehturm am Alexanderplatz?
Iwona	Nein, aber können wir nicht lieber einen Spaziergang durch die Stadt machen?
Martina	Das Wetter ist heute nicht so gut. Am besten finde ich ein Museum!
Pierre	Ja, und das ist sicher interessanter als ein Spaziergang.
Iwona	O. K, aber welches Museum?
Martina	Auf der Museumsinsel sind einige Museen.
Jens	Martina, die Museen dort machen alle schon um 18 Uhr zu. Es ist halb vier – das ist zu wenig Zeit. Aber kennt ihr schon das Mauermuseum? Das ist länger offen.
Pierre	Nein, was gibt es da zu sehen?
Jens	Alles rund um die Berliner Mauer. Wir gehen dann am Abend noch auf den Fernsehturm und sehen Berlin bei Nacht!
Iwona	Ja, das hört sich toll an. Das machen wir.

Die vier kommen am Mauermuseum an.

Pierre	Bitte vier Eintrittskarten. Gibt es eine Ermäßigung für Studenten?
Verkäuferin	Ja. Wie viele Studentenkarten möchten Sie?
Pierre	Eine Karte für einen Studenten und drei normale, bitte.
Verkäuferin	Darf ich bitte Ihren Studentenausweis sehen? Danke. Das macht dann zusammen 47 Euro ...

Dialogue questions

Mark the right answer.

1. War Iwona schon auf dem Fernsehturm?   a) ☐ Ja.   b) ☐ Nein.
2. Wer möchte einen Spaziergang machen?   a) ☐ Martina.   b) ☐ Iwona.
3. Wohin gehen die vier?   a) ☐ Museum.   b) ☐ Berliner Mauer.
4. Wer bekommt eine Ermäßigung?   a) ☐ Pierre.   b) ☐ Iwona.

Berlin's sights

Iwona, Martina, Pierre and Jens meet at the Brandenburg Gate.

Jens   Hello Iwona! Hi Pierre. How are you?
Iwona   Well, thanks.
Pierre   Hi. What are we going to do today?
Jens   Have you been to the television tower on Alexanderplatz yet?
Iwona   No, but can't we go for a walk through the city instead?
Martina   The weather's not so good today. I think a museum would be best!
Pierre   Yes, and it's certainly more interesting than a walk.
Iwona   OK, but which museum?
Martina   There are some museums on the museum island.
Jens   Martina, the museums there close at 6 pm.
               It's half past 3 now – that's too little time. But
               do you know the Wall museum? It closes later.
Pierre   No, what's there to see?
Jens   Everything about the Berlin Wall. Then we can
               go up the television tower in the evening and see
               Berlin by night!
Iwona   Yes, that sounds great. Let's do it.

The four arrive at the Wall museum.

Pierre   Four tickets please. Is there a discount for students?
Ticket seller Yes. How many tickets for students do you want?
Pierre   One ticket for a student and three normal, please.
Ticket seller May I see your student ID? Thanks. That's 47 Euro altogether ...

Vocabulary

3/8

Abend, -e *m*	evening
alles rund um	all about
ankommen	arrive
bezahlen, zahlen	pay
Das hört sich toll an.	Sounds great.
einige	some
Eintrittskarte, -n *f*	ticket
Ermäßigung, -en *f*	discount
Freizeit *(only Sg) f*	leisure time
geschlossen	closed
groß	big
interessant	interesting
Museum, Museen *n*	museum
Nacht, Nächte *f*	night
normal	normal
offen	open
Öffnungszeit, -en *f*	opening hours
sehen	see
Sehenswürdig-keit, -en *f*	sight
Spaziergang, -gänge *m*	walk
Student, -en *m*	student
Studenten-ausweis, -e *m*	student ID
Um wie viel Uhr ...?	What time ...?

unternehmen	do, undertake
wann	when
Wetter *(only Sg) n*	weather
zumachen	close

Learning tip

Nouns with the suffixes **-ung** and **-keit** are always feminine – like **die Ermäßigung** and **die Sehenswürdigkeit**.

What to do in your leisure time?

auf ein Konzert gehen	go to a concert
ein Museum besichtigen	visit a museum
eine Stadtrund-fahrt machen	go on a sightseeing tour
einkaufen, shoppen	go shopping, shop
faulenzen	do nothing
in eine Ausstellung gehen	go to an exhibition
ins Kino/Theater gehen	go to the cinema/theatre
spazieren (gehen)	stroll, walk

Grammar and means of expression

Adjective comparison ▸ §6.3

For most adjectives you simply add ...**-er** for the comparative and **am** ...**-(e)sten** for
the superlative (some adjectives get an umlaut too – see the short grammar!).
Ein Spaziergang ist interessant. *A walk is interesting.*
Das Ägyptische Museum ist interessant**er**. *The Egyptian Museum is more interesting.*
Das Mauermuseum ist **am** interessant**esten**. *The Wall Museum is the most interesting.*

The most important irregular adjectives and adverbs			
	Positive	Comparative	Superlative
good	gut	besser	am besten
gladly	gern	lieber	am liebsten
much	viel	mehr	am meisten

Simple future ▸ §8.4

An easy and common way to speak about the future is the use of the present tense
and a temporal adverbial.
Wir gehen **am Abend** auf den Fernsehturm.
We're going to go up the television tower in the evening.
Wir gehen **morgen** in ein Museum.
Tomorrow we're going to go to a museum.

Time

There are two ways to say what time it is in German. The first is a bit more formal
(e.g. as heard at a train station) and it uses the 24 hour clock. The other is less formal
and uses the 12 hour clock:

What time is it?		
written	spoken *(formal)*	spoken *(less formal)*
21.00 Uhr	Es ist einundzwanzig Uhr.	Es ist neun (Uhr).
16.30 Uhr	Es ist sechzehn Uhr dreißig.	Es ist halb fünf.
22.45 Uhr	Es ist zweiundzwanzig Uhr fünfundvierzig.	Es ist Viertel vor elf.
02.15 Uhr	Es ist zwei Uhr fünfzehn.	Es ist Viertel nach zwei.

Exercises

1 Complete the sentences. Put the adjective/adverb in the comparative. Use any additional information in brackets for your sentence.

1. Hamburg ist groß. Berlin _____ .
2. Iwona geht gern in die Stadt. Martina _____
   (in ein Museum gehen).
3. Ein Spaziergang ist gut. Eine Stadtrundfahrt _____ .
4. Jens geht gern ins Kino. Martina _____
   (ins Theater).
5. Das Ägyptische Museum ist interessant. Das Mauermuseum

   _____ .

6. Berlin bei Tag ist toll. Berlin bei Nacht _____ .

2 How would you react in the following situations? Choose the right reply from the box and say it loud.

> Ich möchte lieber eine Stadtrundfahrt machen.   Ich faulenze lieber.
> Gibt es eine Studentenermäßigung?   Was kostet eine normale Eintrittskarte?
> Ich hätte gerne eine normale Eintrittskarte und zwei für Studenten.
> Ich gehe lieber einkaufen als ins Theater.   Um wie viel Uhr macht das Museum zu?

1. You want to buy tickets. You need two tickets for students.
2. You'd rather go shopping than to the theatre.
3. You want to know when the museum closes.
4. You need to know if there's a discount for students.
5. You tell your friend that you want to go on a sightseeing tour.
6. You prefer doing nothing.
7. You want to know how much a normal ticket costs.

⊙ 1/28   **3 Listen to the CD. In each sentence you'll hear a time. Write the number of this sentence next to the correct time below. One time has no matching sentence.**

1. 11.15 Uhr: _____   5. 19.15 Uhr: _____
2. 14.00 Uhr: _____   6. 15.30 Uhr: _____
3. 9.45 Uhr: _____   7. 18.30 Uhr: _____
4. 8.45 Uhr: _____   8. 15.00 Uhr _____

Kulturtipp
A weekend in Berlin

You want to spend a weekend in Berlin? Berlin has a lot to offer but you'd have to stay a long time there to see everything that's worth seeing.

If you're a fan of museums then you could start with one of the five museums on the **Museumsinsel** *museum island* in the center of the city. You're more interested in recent history? The **Haus am Checkpoint Charlie**, the **Mauermuseum**, tells you all about the history of the Berlin Wall.

But maybe it's a nice day and you don't want to stay inside. You could go to one of the two zoos or take a stroll along the great boulevard **Unter den Linden** and walk through the **Brandenburger Tor** *Brandenburg Gate*. Once there, head over to the **Reichstagsgebäude** *Reichstag building* and enjoy the view from the newly built dome on the roof.

You like shopping too? Then don't miss the **Kaufhaus des Westens** *Department Store of the West*, the **KaDeWe**.

....

What can you already do?

	☺	☺	☹	
■ talk about your leisure time				▸Ü1, Ü2
■ express your wishes and preferences				▸Ü1, Ü2
■ buy tickets for a museum				▸Ü2
■ understand time				▸Ü3

In this lesson you will learn

- to give advice
- to talk about your daily routine
- to present your interests, hobbies and favourite sports

⊙ 1/29   **Sport in Berlin**
⊙ 1/30

Iwona und Martina gehen nach dem Deutschkurs ein Stück zusammen.

Iwona   Martina, ich will wieder mehr Sport machen. Kannst du mir ein paar Tipps geben?

Martina   Ja, klar. Was machst du denn gerne?

Iwona   Am liebsten spiele ich Volleyball. Aber ich gehe auch gern joggen. Wo kann ich das gut machen? Ich laufe nicht gern an der Straße.

Martina   Ja, das kann ich verstehen. Du könntest zum Beispiel im Tiergarten laufen. Es gibt auch tolle Laufstrecken außerhalb des Stadtzentrums ... Da musst du aber erst hinfahren.

Iwona   Ich stehe gerne früh auf und gehe joggen. Danach will ich in Ruhe duschen und frühstücken. Ich habe keine Zeit, noch weit zu fahren. Aber wie ist das mit Volleyball?

Martina   Das weiß ich nicht. Aber du solltest mal im Internet suchen – am besten such nach einem Sportverein, vielleicht auch bei der Volkshochschule oder an der Uni.

Iwona   Ja, das mache ich. Danke! Welchen Sport machst du denn gerne?

Martina   Ich fahre viel Rad in der Stadt. Sonst mache ich keinen Sport. Am Wochenende machen wir manchmal eine Radtour. Wir nehmen dich auch gerne einmal mit!

Iwona   Super! Aber ich habe kein Fahrrad ...

Martina   Das ist kein Problem. Du leihst einfach ein Fahrrad aus!

Dialogue questions

Mark with a cross:

	right	wrong
1. Martina gibt Iwona Tipps.	☐	☐
2. Iwona will nicht in der Stadt joggen.	☐	☐
3. Sie joggt am liebsten nach dem Frühstück.	☐	☐
4. Martina ist in einem Sportverein.	☐	☐
5. Iwona hat ein Fahrrad.	☐	☐

Sport in Berlin

Iwona and Martina walk a short way together after German class.

Iwona   Martina, I want to work out more again. Can you give me a few tips?

Martina   Yes, of course. What do you like to do?

Iwona   I like volleyball the most. But I like to jog too. Where's a good place for this? I don't like running near a street.

Martina   Yes, I understand that. You could jog in the Tiergarten park for instance. There are some great running routes out of town too ... But you have to get there first.

Iwona   I like to get up early and jog. Afterwards I want to take a shower in peace and eat breakfast. I don't have time for long drives. But what about volleyball?

Martina   I don't know. But you should search the internet – the best idea would be to look for a sports club, maybe even at the Volkshochschule or at the university.

Iwona   Yes, I will do that. Thanks! What sport do you like?

Martina   I cycle a lot in town. Otherwise I don't work out. At weekends we go on a bicycle tour sometimes. We'll gladly take you along some time!

Iwona   Super! But I don't have a bike ...

Martina   That's no problem. Just borrow one!

Vocabulary

3/9

ausleihen	borrow
außerhalb	out of
Beispiel, -e *n*	example
danach	afterwards
einmal	once
Fahrrad, -räder *n*	bicycle, bike
früh	early
geben	give
hinfahren	get/drive there
Hobby, -s *n*	hobby
Interessen (*only Pl*)	interests, hobbies
Internet (*only Sg*) *n*	internet
ja, klar	yes, of course
manchmal	sometimes
mitnehmen	take along
oft	often
Park, -s *m*	park
Problem, -e *n*	problem
Radtour, -en *f*	bicycle tour
Ruhe (*only Sg*) *f*	peace
Sport* (*only Sg*) *m*	sport
Sportart**, -en *f*	sport
Sportverein, -e *m*	sports club
Stadt, Städte *f*	town, city
Stadtzentrum, -zentren *n*	city centre
Straße, -n *f*	street
suchen	search
Tipp, -s *m*	tip
vielleicht	maybe
weit	far, long
Wochenende, -n *n*	weekend

* sport in general
** different kinds of sport

Daily routine

aufstehen	get up
frühstücken	eat breakfast
etw. zum Frühstück essen	eat sth. for breakfast
duschen	take a shower
Zähne putzen	brush one's teeth
in die Arbeit gehen/fahren	go/drive to work
arbeiten	work
zu Mittag/ Abend essen	have lunch/dinner
nach Hause kommen	return home
fernsehen	watch TV
ins Bett gehen	go to bed
schlafen	sleep

Times of the day

Morgen *m*	morning
Vormittag *m*	morning
Mittag *m*	noon
Nachmittag *m*	afternoon
Abend *m*	evening
Nacht *f*	night

Sport & hobbies

joggen, laufen	jog, run
Judo/Karate/ Aikido/... machen	do judo/karate/aikido/...
klettern	climb
Rad fahren	cycle
schwimmen	swim
Volleyball/Fuß- ball/Tennis/ ... spielen	play volleyball/football/ tennis/...

Grammar and means of expression

Trennbare Verben ▸ §8.7

Some German verbs have a prefix (usually a preposition) that is **trennbar** *separable*.
Let's have a look at the examples from the dialogue:
Wir **nehmen** dich **mit**. *We'll take you along.*
Du **leihst** ein Fahrrad **aus**. *You borrow a bike.*
Their infinitives are **mitnehmen** and **ausleihen**. But when you use them in the
present tense the prefix goes to the last position in the sentence.
With a modal verb you use the normal infinitive:
Du musst mich **mitnehmen**. *You have to take me along.*
Sie kann ein Fahrrad **ausleihen**. *She can borrow a bike.*

The modal verbs *wollen* and *sollen* ▸ §8.6

sollen shall/are to		wollen want	
ich soll	wir sollen	ich will	wir wollen
du sollst	ihr sollt	du willst	ihr wollt
er/sie/es soll	sie/Sie sollen	er/sie/es will	sie/Sie wollen

Advice ▸ §8.6

To give someone advice you can use the imperative (▸ *Day 7*) or the forms **sollt-**
and **könnt-**:
Such im Internet! *Search the internet.*
Lauf im Tiergarten! *Jog in the Tiergarten park.*
... or ...
Du **solltest** im Internet suchen. *You should search the internet.*
Du **könntest** im Tiergarten laufen. *You could jog in the Tiergarten park.*
These forms are more polite than the imperative. And **könnt-** is more like a proposition.
For advice you mainly need the forms of the second person *(Sg/Pl)* and the formal **Sie**:
du sollt**est** ..., ihr sollt**et** ..., Sie sollt**en** ...
du könnt**est** ..., ihr könnt**et** ..., Sie könnt**en** ...

1 Connect the phrases with the right advice.

1. Ich will nicht an der Straße joggen.
2. Ich jogge nicht gerne morgens.
3. Ich habe leider kein Fahrrad.
4. Wo finde ich einen Sportverein?
5. Ich spiele gern Fußball.
6. Ich fahre sehr gern Rad.

a) Du könntest eine Radtour mit uns machen.
b) Du solltest im Park laufen.
c) Du solltest mal im Internet suchen.
d) Du könntest ein Rad ausleihen.
e) Du könntest abends joggen.
f) Du solltest einen Sportverein suchen.

⊙ 1/31 **2 Read the sentences below. Then listen to the three short descriptions of daily routines on the CD. Mark them:**

	right	wrong
1. Pierre isst nichts zum Frühstück.	☐	☐
2. Nach der Arbeit geht er einkaufen.	☐	☐
3. Martina steht gern früh auf.	☐	☐
4. Sie trinkt nur einen Kaffee zum Frühstück.	☐	☐
5. Iwona kommt oft erst am Abend nach Hause.	☐	☐
6. Am Abend liest sie gern.	☐	☐

3 Iwona posted on an internet forum about sport. Read what she wrote and write a similar text about yourself and your favourite sport.

Hallo,
ich mache gern Sport. Am Morgen gehe ich oft joggen. Am liebsten jogge ich in einem Park. Ich fahre auch gerne Rad, aber ich habe kein Fahrrad in Deutschland. Am liebsten spiele ich Volleyball. Ich bin auch gut. Wo kann ich hier in Berlin Volleyball spielen? Kann mir jemand helfen? Vielen Dank!
Iwona

Kulturtipp Germans and football

Football is one of the most popular sports in Germany – even before the World Cup in Germany in 2006. A lot of Germans spend Saturday afternoon in a football stadium or – after 6 pm – in front of the television watching the **Sportschau** with the results of the **Bundesliga** *German Football League*. The matches of the national football team draw an even greater TV audience or – since 2006 during the World or European Cup – there is **Public Viewing** (yes, that's German!), where the matches are shown on big screens open to the public.

Thanks to the great successes of the women's national football team, women's football has become very popular and is one of the fastest growing sports in Germany.

If you want to play sports actively check out the local **Sportvereine** *sports clubs* where you can participate in your favourite sport for small fees.

What can you already do?

☺ ☺ ☹

- give advice   ▪ ▪ ▪   ‣ *Ü1*
- talk about your daily routine   ▪ ▪ ▪   ‣ *Ü2*
- present your interests, hobbies and favourite sports   ▪ ▪ ▪   ‣ *Ü3*

Learning a foreign language is like sport. You have to stay on the ball. And if you do, you'll get better and better and it's as much fun – but with a lot less sweating! And don't forget that learning a language is a team sport. Sooner or later you're out there "competing" – why not already assemble a team for training?

Forming new friendships

In this lesson you will learn

- to introduce others and become introduced
- to welcome guests
- to congratulate someone

(•) 1/32
(•) 1/33

Jens' Geburtstagsparty

Iwona und Pierre stehen vor der Wohnung von Martina und Jens und klingeln an der Tür ...

Jens Hallo Iwona! Hi Pierre! Kommt herein. Hier könnt ihr eure Jacken aufhängen.

Iwona Hallo Jens. Herzlichen Glückwunsch zum Geburtstag.

Pierre Ja, alles Gute zum Geburtstag. Und vielen Dank für die Einladung.

Iwona Wir haben ein kleines Geschenk für dich. Hier, bitte.

Jens Mensch, vielen Dank! Und willkommen in unserer Wohnung.
Martina ist noch in der Küche. Die anderen Gäste sind im Wohnzimmer.
Es sind erst zwei da. Ich stelle euch kurz vor: Das ist Kathrin, Martinas
Schwester, und ihr Freund Andreas. Und das hier sind Iwona und Pierre.
Sie sind aus Martinas Kurs und Pierre ist auch ein Kollege von mir.

Kathrin Hallo! Schön, euch kennenzulernen.

Iwona Hallo.

Pierre Hi, freut mich!

Andreas Hallo, sehr angenehm.

Jens Da hinten auf dem Tisch sind Getränke. Bedient euch einfach.

Einige Zeit später

Kathrin Du kannst echt gut Deutsch. Sprichst du in der Arbeit auch Deutsch?

Iwona Nicht viel. Wir sprechen dort fast nur Englisch. Wir haben viele
internationale Kollegen und Kunden.

Kathrin Das ist alles echt interessant! Komm uns doch mal in Potsdam besuchen.
Dann reden wir und besichtigen die Stadt.

Dialogue questions

Answer the questions briefly.

1. Wer hat Geburtstag? ....
2. Wer ist Andreas? ....
3. Wo stehen die Getränke? ....
4. Wo wohnt Kathrin? ....

Jens' birthday party

Iwona and Pierre stand in front of Martina's and Jens' flat and ring the doorbell ...

Jens	Hello Iwona! Hi Pierre! Come on in. You can put your jackets there.
Iwona	Hello Jens. Happy birthday.
Pierre	Yes, all the best for your birthday. And thanks a lot for the invitation.
Iwona	We have a small present for you. Here you go.
Jens	Gosh, thanks a lot! And welcome to our flat. Martina is still in the kitchen. The other guests are in the living room. There are only two at the moment. I'll introduce you briefly: That's Kathrin, Martina's sister, and her boyfriend Andreas. And this is Iwona and Pierre. They are from Martina's class and Pierre is a colleague of mine too.
Kathrin	Hello! Nice to meet you.
Iwona	Hello.
Pierre	Hi, pleased to meet you!
Andreas	Hello, pleased to meet you too.
Jens	Back there are drinks on the table. Just help yourself.

Some time later

Kathrin	You speak German very well. Do you speak German at work too?
Iwona	Not much. We speak almost only English. We have a lot of international colleagues and clients.
Kathrin	That's really interesting! Come and visit us in Potsdam. We'll be able to talk a lot and visit the city.

⊙ 3/10

aufhängen	put
Einladung, -en *f*	invitation
empfangen	welcome
Freund, -e *m*	(boy-) friend
Freundin, -nen *f*	(girl-) friend
Gast, Gäste *m*	guest
Geburtstag, -e *m*	birthday
Geschenk, -e *n*	present
hereinkommen	come in
international	international
Jacke, -n *f*	jacket
kennenlernen	meet, get to know
Kollege, -n *m*	(male) colleague
Kollegin, -nen *f*	(female) colleague
Kunde, -n *m*	client
Mensch!	Gosh!
noch	still
Raum, Räume *m*	room
sich bedienen	help oneself
Tisch, -e *m*	table
vorstellen	introduce, present
willkommen	welcome
wünschen	wish
Zimmer, – *n*	room

Rooms

Bad, Bäder *n* (also Badezimmer, – *n*)	bathroom
Flur, -e *m*	corridor
Gästezimmer, – *n*	guest room
Kinderzimmer, – *n*	nursery (children's room)
Küche, -n *f*	kitchen
Schlafzimmer, – *n*	bedroom
Toilette, -n *f*	bathroom, lavatory
Wohnzimmer, – *n*	living room

Learning tip

You'll often see composite nouns in German like **Wohnzimmer** or **Schlafzimmer**. The gender (and the plural) of those nouns is always that of the last noun in the composition (**Zimmer, – *n*** in our example). So **das Wohnzimmer** is also neuter and the plural is **die Wohnzimmer**.

Some adverbs of place

hier	here
da	here/there
dort	there
oben	above
unten	below
hinten	back
vorne	in front
rechts	right
links	left

Languages

Chinesisch	Chinese
Deutsch	German
Englisch	English
Französisch	French
Polnisch	Polish
Russisch	Russian
Spanisch	Spanish

Grammar and means of expression

Prepositions of place with the dative ▸ §5.1

There are a few prepositions of place that need an object either in the dative or in the accusative.

The prepositions that can have either dative or accusative					
in	in	über	over	zwischen	between
an	at	unter	beneath	vor	in front of
auf	on	neben	by/next to	hinter	behind

There's an easy rule to determine if you need dative or accusative:

If you ask	**where?**	the preposition is followed by a noun in the	**dative.**
	where to?		accusative.

Achtung: ....
So the dative is used when the preposition specifies a position
(and not a direction).
....

In this lesson's dialogue there were some of those prepositions with the dative.
Do you remember?
Da hinten **auf** dem Tisch sind Getränke. *Back there are drinks on the table.*
Sprichst du **in** der Arbeit auch deutsch? *Do you speak German at work?*
Komm uns **in** Potsdam besuchen. *Come and visit us in Potsdam.*

Attention: in + dem ▸ **im**, an + dem ▸ **am**
Die anderen Gäste sind **im** Wohnzimmer. *The other guests are in the living room.*

Temporal and local statements ▸ §7.1

If you use a temporal and a local statement in your sentence, you normally put the temporal first.
Ich bin **morgen hier**. *I'm here tomorrow.*
Wir sitzen **später im Wohnzimmer**. *We'll sit in the living room later.*
Additionally you can often see the temporal adverb in the first place of the sentence.
In this case the personal pronoun comes directly after the verb.
Morgen bin ich **hier**. *Tomorrow I'm here.*
Später sitzen wir **im Wohnzimmer**. *Later we'll sit in the living room.*

⊙ 1/34 🎧 **1** Listen to the short dialogues on the CD. Which dialogue belongs to which situation?

1. Gäste vorstellen ☐
2. Small Talk ☐
3. etwas zu trinken holen ☐
4. zum Geburtstag gratulieren ☐
5. Gäste empfangen ☐

2 Who is in which room? Read the text and mark.

Auf der Party von Jens sind viele Gäste. Jens ist gerade im Flur und spricht mit Martinas Schwester Kathrin. Kathrin wartet auf ihren Freund Andreas.
Andreas ist auf der Toilette. Iwona sucht Martina. Martina ist nicht in der Küche. Iwona findet sie im Wohnzimmer. Die anderen Gäste sind auch im Wohnzimmer und reden. Aber wo ist Pierre? Er ist nicht im Wohnzimmer.
Er ist im Bad.

	Bad	Flur	Küche	Toilette	Wohnzimmer
Andreas	☐	☐	☐	☐	☐
Jens	☐	☐	☐	☐	☐
Kathrin	☐	☐	☐	☐	☐
Martina	☐	☐	☐	☐	☐
Pierre	☐	☐	☐	☐	☐

3 Can you put the mixed up sentences back in their right order?

1. kennenzulernen / Sie / freut / sehr / mich.

2. alles Gute / dir / ich / zum Geburtstag / wünsche /.

3. vorstellen / möchte / euch / kurz / ich /.

4. in / willkommen / unserer / herzlich / Wohnung /.

5. mein / Paul / Kollege / das / ist /.

Kulturtipp Happy birthday!

The most important personal holiday is one's **Geburtstag** *birthday*. Formerly, **der Namenstag** *the name day* was a popular holiday in Catholic regions, but is now rarely celebrated. On a birthday the person celebrating her/his birthday is **das Geburtstagkind** *the birthday child* and usually gets **Geburtstagsgeschenke** *birthday presents* and **einen Geburtstagskuchen** *a birthday cake* with one candle for each year.

Herzlichen Glückwunsch (zum Geburtstag) *best wishes / happy birthday* and **Alles Gute (zum Geburtstag)** *all the best* are the standard congratulations – but beware: congratulating before the actual birthday is said to bring bad luck in Germany! There's often **eine Geburtstagsparty** *a birthday party* for family and/or friends too on that day or one of the following weekends.

Attaining full age (with 18) or a so called **runder Geburtstag** *literally a round birthday* (30, 40, 50 ...) are often specially celebrated. But no matter how old you've become, your friends might consider it necessary to sing you a birthday song. The most popular in Germany is probably **Happy Birthday to You**. It's often sung in English, but there's a German translation too and that often causes funny moments when the singers sing different versions.

....

What can you already do?

	☺ ☺ ☹	
■ introduce others and become introduced	▪ ▪ ▪	▸ Ü1, Ü3
■ welcome guests	▪ ▪ ▪	▸ Ü1, Ü3
■ congratulate someone on her/his birthday	▪ ▪ ▪	▸ Ü1, Ü3
■ give a present	▪ ▪ ▪	▸ Ü1, Ü3
■ name basic rooms in a flat/house	▪ ▪ ▪	▸ Ü2

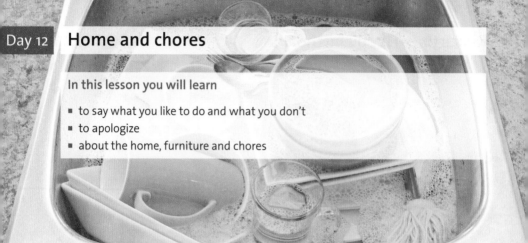

Home and chores

In this lesson you will learn

- to say what you like to do and what you don't
- to apologize
- about the home, furniture and chores

⊙ 1/35 ## Aufräumen nach der Party
⊙ 1/36

Die Party ist zu Ende und die meisten Gäste sind weg. Nur Iwona und Pierre sind noch da.

Iwona Die Party war toll! Wir hatten wirklich viel Spaß!

Martina Und ihr wollt uns jetzt sicher beim Aufräumen helfen?

Pierre Klar! Das ist ja nicht viel Arbeit! Was sollen wir denn machen?

Martina Pierre, auf der Kommode im Wohnzimmer stehen noch saubere Gläser. Kannst du diese Gläser bitte ins Regal stellen?

Pierre Ja, mache ich.

Martina Und trägst du bitte das dreckige Geschirr in die Küche, Iwona? Stell die Sachen dort einfach auf den Tisch.

Jens Und was darf ich machen?

Martina Das darfst du dir aussuchen: abspülen oder kehren.

Jens Kehren mag ich nicht! Ich spüle lieber ab. Wir brauchen dringend einen Geschirrspüler ...

Martina Das ist gut. Kehren ist in Ordnung. Aber ich spüle nicht gern ab. Bringst du dann später Iwona und Pierre zur Tür? ... Und nimmst den Müll mit?

Jens Na ja ...

Pierre Oh nein!

Martina Was ist los?

Pierre Entschuldigung, zwei Weingläser sind kaputt. Das tut mir leid!

Martina Das macht nichts. Die Gläser waren nicht teuer. Ich mache gleich die Scherben weg.

Dialogue questions

Cross out the wrong answer.

1. Pierre räumt *im Wohnzimmer | in der Küche* auf.
2. Jens *kehrt gerne | spült gerne ab.*
3. *Iwona | Pierre* macht die Weingläser kaputt.
4. Die Weingläser waren *sehr | nicht* teuer.

Cleaning up after the party ...

The party is over and most of the guests are gone. Only Iwona and Pierre are still there.

Iwona	The party was great! We really had a lot of fun!
Martina	And you really want to help us clean up now?
Pierre	Sure! There's not much to do! What should we do?
Martina	Pierre, there are still some clean glasses on the chest of drawers in the living room. Can you put those glasses on the shelf please?
Pierre	OK, I can do that.
Martina	And would you please carry the dirty dishes into the kitchen, Iwona? Just put them on the table.
Jens	And what may I do?
Martina	You may choose: washing-up or sweeping.
Jens	I don't like sweeping! I'd rather do the washing-up. We badly need a dishwasher ...
Martina	That's good. Sweeping is fine. But I don't like doing the washing-up. Will you show Iwona and Pierre to the door later? ... And take the rubbish with you?
Jens	Oh well ...
Pierre	Oh no!
Martina	What's the matter?
Pierre	Sorry, two wine glasses are in pieces. I'm really sorry!
Martina	Never mind. The glasses weren't expensive. I'll clear the shards away.

Vocabulary

aussuchen	choose
brauchen	need
bringen	bring
Das ist in Ordnung.	That's fine/OK.
Das macht nichts.	Never mind.
Das tut mir leid!	I'm (really) sorry!/My apologies!
dreckig	dirty
Entschuldigung, -en *f*	apology
Geschirr *(only Sg) n*	dishes
Glas, Gläser *n*	glass
Hausarbeit, -en *f*	chore
Ich mag ...	I like ...
Klar!	Sure!
legen	lay
liegen	lie
Möbel, – *(mostly Pl) n*	furniture
Müll *(only Sg) m*	rubbish
Ordnung *f*	order
Party, -s *f*	party
Sache, -n *f*	thing
sauber	clean
setzen	put
sitzen	sit
Spaß *m*	fun

stehen	stand
stellen	put
teuer	expensive
tragen	carry
Was ist los?	What's the matter?
Weinglas, -gläser *n*	wine glass

Chores	
abspülen	wash up
aufräumen	clean up
bügeln	iron
fegen, kehren	sweep
Müll wegbringen	take the rubbish out
staubsaugen	hoover
Wäsche waschen	do one's laundry

Furniture	
Kommode, -n *f*	chest of drawers
Lampe, -n *f*	lamp
Regal, -e *n*	shelf
Schrank, Schränke *m*	cupboard
Sofa, -s *n*	couch
Stuhl, Stühle *m*	chair
Tisch, -e *m*	table

Grammar and means of expression

Local prepositions with the accusative ▸ *§5.1*

Look at the examples from the dialogue first:
Kannst du die Gläser **in** den Schrank stellen? *Can you put the glasses in the cupboard?*
Stell die Sachen **auf** den Tisch. *Put the things on the table.*

These are the very same prepositions you learned about in the previous lesson's grammar. However, now they don't specify a point but a direction!

Let's repeat the rule. Now the second line is highlighted:

If you ask	where?	the preposition is followed by a noun in the	dative.
	where to?		**accusative.**

Attention: in + das ▸ **ins**, an + das ▸ **ans**
Kannst du diese Gläser **ins** Regal stellen? *Can you put these glasses on the shelf?*

Certain verbs indicate **where** an object is. These are for example **sein, stehen, sitzen, liegen**.
Other verbs indicate **where** an object moves/is moved **to**, like **stellen, setzen, legen, bringen, tragen**.

haben and *sein* in the simple past ▸ *§8.5*

Die Party **war** toll! Wir **hatten** wirklich viel Spaß!
The simple past is called **Präteritum** in German. It's mainly used in written German like in novels or reports. But **haben, sein** and the modal verbs are used in the **Präteritum** in spoken German as well.
Let's have a look now at the **Präteritum** forms of **haben** and **sein** – we'll show you the forms of the modal verbs in the next lesson.

haben		sein	
ich hatte	wir hatten	ich war	wir waren
du hattest	ihr hattet	du warst	ihr wart
er/sie/es hatte	sie/Sie hatten	er/sie/es war	sie/Sie waren

⊙ 1/37   **1** Listen to the dialogue on the CD. Iwona and Pierre are talking about chores. If you hear a chore, decide who does it and if she/he likes (☺) it or not (☹) and fill it in the table.

	☺	☹
Iwona		
Pierre		

2 How would you react in the following situations? Choose the right reply from the box and say it out loud.

> Das macht nichts.   Abspülen ist in Ordnung.   Das tut mir leid!
> Was ist los?   Was soll ich machen?   Kehren mag ich nicht.
> Stell das dreckige Geschirr in den Geschirrspüler.

1. Say that washing the dishes is OK.
2. The sound of breaking glass can be heard. You want to know what happened.
3. Ask your friend to put the dirty dishes in the dishwasher.
4. Someone stepped on your toe and apologizes – but it didn't hurt.
5. You want to help clean up but you don't know what to do.
6. You broke a plate while cleaning up.
7. You don't like sweeping.

3 Fill the gaps with the furniture given in brackets and it's article. Be careful to use the appropriate form (accusative or dative).

1. Die Gläser stehen im .... (shelf)

2. Pierre legt seine Jacke auf .... (couch)

3. Iwona sitzt auf .... (chair)

4. Der Stuhl steht unter .... (table)

5. Jens stellt die Teller in .... (cupboard)

6. Martina steht vor .... (chest of drawers)

7. Die Flasche ist neben .... (lamp)

8. Das Messer und die Gabel liegen neben .... (plate)

Kulturtipp Living and waste separation

For some Germans, having a house of their own is their life's goal. But nevertheless renting a flat (or house) is popular. Among young people and students **Wohngemeinschaften** *flat share*, so called **WGs**, are quite common. If you need to find an accommodation for a longer stay check the internet but don't forget the local newspaper. There's often a special day during the week for **Wohnungsanzeigen** *flat advertisements*.

"Could you please take out the rubbish?" Maybe not one of the most loved chores but it sounds quite easy, doesn't it? You might want to change your mind after being asked that question during your stay in Germany. The Germans segregate their rubbish. Most households have at least two rubbish bins and maybe up to five! The city councils issue leaflets with long lists of all kinds of waste and the appropriate way to dispose of it. You'll have to separate glass and paper, organic waste, different kinds of plastic, metal and other recyclable materials...

What can you already do?

☺ ☺ ☹

▪ say what you like doing and what you don't	☐	☐	☐	►*Ü1, Ü2*
▪ apologize	☐	☐	☐	►*Ü1*
▪ name basic furniture and chores	☐	☐	☐	►*Ü1, Ü2, Ü3*

In this lesson you will learn

- to talk about TV programs
- to search and present short information about mass media

◉ 1/38 **Ein Fernsehabend**
◉ 1/39

Von der Party ist noch Essen übrig. Martina und Jens laden Iwona und Pierre noch einmal ein.

Iwona Das Essen war sehr lecker! Danke.

Martina Kein Problem! Ihr wolltet gestern auf der Party ja nicht alles essen. Also war noch viel Essen übrig.

Pierre Ich wollte ja, aber ich konnte nicht noch mehr essen! Du kochst fantastisch!

Martina Danke!

Jens Sehen wir uns vielleicht noch einen Film an? Habt ihr Lust?

Pierre Ja. Was kommt denn heute Abend im Fernsehen?

Jens Moment, ich hole die Fernsehzeitschrift. Also ... es gibt eine Komödie auf einem Privatsender. Eine Quizsendung ... Oh, im Ersten kommt ein Tatort!

Iwona Was ist Tatort?

Jens Das ist eine Krimiserie. Normalerweise kommt jeden Sonntag ein Fall aus einem anderen Bundesland ...

Martina Wo spielt er denn heute?

Jens So ein Zufall! Heute ermitteln die Kommissare aus Berlin!

Pierre Das hört sich gut an. Was meinst du, Iwona?

Iwona Ja, gerne.

Jens Gut, ihr könnt euch schon auf das Sofa setzen. Trinken wir einen Wein?

Pierre Natürlich!

Jens Rot oder weiß?

Iwona Rotwein, bitte.

Pierre Ja, für mich auch.

Dialogue questions

Mark with a cross:

	right	wrong
1. Martina kann gut kochen.	☐	☐
2. Pierre hat keine Lust auf einen Film.	☐	☐
3. Iwona möchte eine Krimiserie ansehen.	☐	☐
4. Iwona und Pierre trinken beide Rotwein.	☐	☐

An evening in front of the TV

There's still food left from the party. Martina and Jens invite Iwona and Pierre once again.

Iwona The meal was delicious! Thank you.

Martina No problem! You didn't want to eat everything at the party yesterday. So there was a lot of food left over.

Pierre I wanted to, but I couldn't eat any more. You're a great cook!

Martina Thanks!

Jens What about watching a film? Are you up for it?

Pierre Yes. What's on TV tonight?

Jens Wait a moment, I'll go get the TV guide. Let's see ... there's a comedy on a private station. A quiz show ... Oh, there's a "Tatort" on the first channel!

Iwona What is a "Tatort"?

Jens It's a crime series. Each Sunday a case from another German state is shown ...

Martina Where does it take place today?

Jens What are the odds! Today the Berlin detectives are investigating!

Pierre Sounds good. What do you think, Iwona?

Iwona Yes, sure.

Jens Well, you can go and sit on the couch already. Shall we have some wine?

Pierre Of course!

Jens Red or white?

Iwona Red wine, please.

Pierre Yes, for me too.

Vocabulary

⊙ 3/12

essen	eat
Fall, Fälle *m*	case
fantastisch	great, fantastic
Fernseher, – *m*	television
Film, -e *m*	film, movie
im Fernsehen kommen	be on TV
kochen	cook
Kommissar, -e *m*	detective
lecker	delicious, tasty
Lust haben	be up for sth.
meinen	think, mean
Moment, -e *m*	moment
Natürlich!	Of course!
normalerweise	usually
Programm, -e *n*	programme, channel
Radio, -s *n*	radio
Sender, – *m*	channel, station
Sendung, -en *f*	broadcast, show, programme
So ein Zufall!	What are the odds!
Zufall, Zufälle *m*	coincidence, chance

Colours	
blau	blue
braun	brown
gelb	yellow
grün	green
rot	red
schwarz	black
weiß	white

Genres	
Actionfilm, -e *m*	action movie
Drama, Dramen *n*	drama
Komödie, -n *f*	comedy
Krimi, -s *m*	crime series, detective story
Nachrichten (only *Pl*)	news
Quizsendung, -en *f*	quiz show
Serie, -n *f*	series
Thriller, – *m*	thriller

Media	
DVD, DVDs *f*	DVD
Fernsehen (only *Sg*) *n*	television, TV
Radio (only *Sg*) *n*	radio
Zeitschrift, -en *f*	magazine, journal
Zeitung, -en *f*	newspaper

Grammar and means of expression

Modal verbs in present and past tense ▸ *§8.6*

Modal verbs change the sense of a sentence to a certain mode: These modes are, for example, duty, advice, order and so on.

The first table is a repetition of all the modal verbs you already know.
And the second table shows all new **Präteritum** forms.

Modal verbs in the present tense					
	müssen must/ have to	sollen shall/are to	wollen want	können can	dürfen may/might
ich	muss	soll	will	kann	darf
du	musst	sollst	willst	kannst	darfst
er/sie/es	muss	soll	will	kann	darf
wir	müssen	sollen	wollen	können	dürfen
ihr	müsst	sollt	wollt	könnt	dürft
sie/Sie	müssen	sollen	wollen	können	dürfen

Modal verbs in the Präteritum					
	müssen must/ have to	sollen shall/are to	wollen want	können can	dürfen may
ich	musste	sollte	wollte	konnte	durfte
du	musstest	solltest	wolltest	konntest	durftest
er/sie/es	musste	sollte	wollte	konnte	durfte
wir	mussten	sollten	wollten	konnten	durften
ihr	musstet	solltet	wolltet	konntet	durftet
sie/Sie	mussten	sollten	wollten	konnten	durften

Be careful with the negation:
Du musst nicht ... means *You needn't .../you don't have to ...*
Du darfst nicht ... means *You mustn't ...*

1/40 **1 Listen to the dialogue on the CD and answer the questions.**

1. Wer will ins Kino?	a) ☐ Martina	b) ☐ Jens
2. Was ist „Insomnia"?	a) ☐ Thriller	b) ☐ Komödie
3. Wo kommt „Insomnia"?	a) ☐ Fernsehen	b) ☐ Kino
4. Kommt eine Komödie im Fernsehen?	a) ☐ Ja	b) ☐ Nein
5. Wer sucht den Film „Rush Hour 3" aus?	a) ☐ Martina	b) ☐ Jens
6. Wie findet Jens „Rush Hour 3"?	a) ☐ Gut	b) ☐ Schlecht

2 Go to the websites listed below (or maybe you have a printed TV guide) and search for the information you need to answer the questions.

ARD (www.daserste.de):

1. Welche Sendung kommt normalerweise um 20 Uhr?

2. Um wie viel Uhr beginnt der Tatort?

ZDF (www.zdf.de):

3. Um wie viel Uhr kommt normalerweise das „heute journal"?

4. Und welches Genre ist das „heute journal"?

Deutsche Welle (www.dw-world.de):

5. Wie oft am Tag kommt das „Journal" auf DW-TV Europe?

1/41 **3 Listen to the questions on the CD and reply after the beep with one of the answers from the box. Afterwards you'll hear the right answer.**

> Heute spielt er in Hamburg.   Heute Abend gibt es einen Actionfilm.
> Um 19 Uhr.   Nein, ich will lieber lesen.

Kulturtipp Media

A good approach to German media
is **Deutsche Welle** or **DW**. They offer
radio and TV (both via internet too –
either live or as podcasts) and plenty of
additional services (like German lessons,
information about Germany) on the
internet – often suitable even for begin-
ners. **DW** is a part of the **öffentlich-
rechtliche Rundfunkanstalten** *broadcasting corporations regulated by public
law* (e.g. like the BBC), their prominent
members being **ARD** (**das Erste** *the first
channel*) and **ZDF** (**das Zweite** *the
second (channel)*. Additionally there
are a lot of private broadcasting
corporations on the radio and TV.

There are some nationwide newspapers. Maybe you've already seen or heard of
Frankfurter Allgemeine Zeitung, **Süddeutsche Zeitung**, **Die Welt** or **Bild**. If you need
local information like the cinema program or flat advertisements then look for the
town's local newspaper.

....

What can you already do?

☺ ☺ ☹

▪ talk about TV programme	☐	☐	☐ ▸*Ü1, Ü2, Ü3*
▪ search and present short information	☐	☐	☐ ▸*Ü2*
▪ talk about mass media	☐	☐	☐ ▸*Ü1*

One more part is nearly finished now and you've even left the confines of this book
to gather information. Now that you know the websites of ARD and ZDF: check their
programme guide! You'll find something interesting or a film you'd like to see, for
sure. Watch TV and listen to the radio to get the German language in your ear!
And now have fun with more exercises in the next lesson ...

Repeat and practise

Here you repeat

- numbers and time
- sports, hobbies and leisure time
- daily routine

1 Fill the missing verb forms in the table. Be careful with the second and third person in the singular, they conjugate irregularly. Use the short grammar in the appendix for help.

	fahren	essen	schlafen	fernsehen	geben
ich				sehe fern	
du		isst			
er/sie/es					gibt
wir					
ihr			schlaft		
sie/Sie	fahren				

2 A typical day in the life of Jens. You can see the times below and what he does at that time. Write his daily routine in a few easy sentences. Use the less formal time where possible.

1. 7.30 (*aufstehen*) ....
2. 8.00 (*in die Arbeit fahren*) ....
3. 12.45 (*zu Mittag essen*) ....
4. 18.15 (*nach Hause kommen*) ....

....

◉ 2/1 🎧 **3** Listen to the CD. Now fill in the gaps on your shopping list.

Markt:
1. .... *Tomaten*
2. 1 ....
3. .... *Kilo* ....
4. .... *Bananen*
5. *0,5 kg* ....

Supermarkt:
6. *400 g* ....
7. .... *Flaschen* ....
8. 1 .... *Milch*

4 One word is missing in each line. Choose the right one from the box. Be careful, there are two extra words which you don't need.

> unten   Zucchini   Brot   Tüte   Wasser   faulenzen
> Fleisch   rot   Zeitschrift   joggen

1. Tomate, Paprika, Gurke, ...
2. klettern, schwimmen, spielen, ...
3. Schinken, Wurst, Hähnchen, ...
4. Dose, Becher, Packung, ...
5. vorne, hinten, oben, ...
6. Radio, Fernsehen, Zeitung, ...
7. braun, gelb, blau, ...
8. Cola, Saft, Bier, ...

5 Transform the advice into imperative sentences.

1. Du könntest dein Zimmer aufräumen.

....

2. Ihr solltet mehr Sport machen.

....

3. Sie sollten mit dem Kunden reden.

....

4. Sie könnten einen Kaffee trinken gehen.

....

5. Du solltest deinen Freund besuchen.

....

6. Ihr könntet eine Stadtrundfahrt machen.

....

6 Complete the sentences with a personal pronoun in the right form.

1. Gib der Frau bitte das Obst.   Gib .... bitte das Obst.

2. Martina ist Lehrerin.   .... ist Lehrerin.

3. Ich bringe dem Kunden einen Kaffee.   Ich bringe .... dem Kunden.

4. Ich bringe dem Kunden einen Kaffee.   Ich bringe .... einen Kaffee.

5. Pierre gibt Iwona eine Orange.   .... gibt Iwona eine Orange.

6. Pierre gibt Iwona eine Orange.   Pierre gibt .... Iwona.

7 One word does not match the others. Find it and cross it out.

1. Krimi, Fernsehen, Thriller, Komödie, Drama
2. abspülen, aufräumen, fegen, aufstehen, staubsaugen
3. Orange, Apfel, Pfirsich, Banane, Gurke
4. Stuhl, Schrank, Tisch, Zimmer, Regal
5. Salat, Saft, Nudeln, Reis, Suppe
6. Rad fahren, Tennis spielen, Müll wegbringen, Judo machen, schwimmen

8 Read the following text. Choose the right article from the box and fill in the gaps. (— is the *Nullartikel*).

ein   eine   dem   —   einen   —   den   —   einen   —   das   ein

Iwona ist auf _____ (1.) Markt. Sie möchte _____ (2.) Obst und _____ (3.) Gemüse kaufen. Nach dem Einkauf will Iwona etwas essen. Sie geht in _____ (4.) Café. Dort isst sie _____ (5.) Stück Kuchen und trinkt _____ (6.) Kaffee. Später will sie noch in _____ (7.) Supermarkt gehen. Dort muss sie _____ (8.) Flasche Wein und _____ (9.) Brot kaufen. Am Nachmittag möchte sie _____ (10.) Freunde treffen. Mit _____ (11.) Freunden geht sie dann in _____ (12.) Mauermuseum.

⊙ 2/2   **9** Listen to the CD and complete the sentences with the information you hear.

1. Klaus ist _____ .
2. Sie waren zusammen _____ .
3. Klaus' Eltern wohnen _____ .
4. Klaus wohnt _____ .
5. Martina und Klaus gehen _____ .
6. Aber lieber machen sie _____ .
7. Klaus spielt _____ .
8. Am Abend _____ und _____ .

10 Write the following numbers as words.

1. 357 _____
2. 812 _____
3. 1001 _____
4. 2010 _____
5. 9999 _____

11 *Trennbare Verben*. Read the text and write down the verbs with separable prefixes in their infinitive.

> Was unternimmt Iwona am Wochenende? Am Wochenende leiht sie ein Fahrrad aus. Martina und Jens nehmen sie auf eine Radtour mit. Sie fahren an den Wannsee außerhalb von Berlin. Dort schwimmen sie auch. Nach der Radtour kauft Iwona im Supermarkt ein. Am Abend geht sie auf eine Party. Vor der Party räumt sie auf und spült ab. Danach kommt sie nach Hause und sieht noch fern. Um halb eins in der Nacht geht sie ins Bett und schläft.

1. _____   3. _____   5. _____

2. _____   4. _____   6. _____

12 Now write the text from the previous exercise again using modal verbs. Use the modal verbs in brackets but put them in the appropriate present tense form.

Was *soll Iwona am Wochenende unternehmen?* _____ (sollen)

1. Am Wochenende _____ . (können)

2. Martina und Jens _____ . (wollen)

3. Sie _____ . (wollen)

4. Dort _____ . (können)

5. Nach der Radtour _____ . (müssen)

6. Am Abend _____ . (wollen)

7. Vor der Party _____ . (müssen)

8. Danach kommt sie nach Hause und _____ . (wollen)

9. Um halb eins in der Nacht _____ . (möcht-)

13 Read the shopping list. How would you tell a salesman what you want?

> *Einkaufen:*
> *3 Paprika, 0,5 kg Tomaten, 1 kg Weintrauben, 2 Gurken,*
> *1 Flasche Saft, 2 Gläser Honig, 1 Becher Sahne, 200 g Wurst*

14 Transform the sentences into Präteritum

1. Iwona will nicht an der Straße joggen.

_____

2. Ich soll etwas im Internet suchen.

_____

3. Wir haben viel Freizeit.

....

4. Ihr könnt alles auf dem Markt kaufen.

....

5. Du musst den Müll wegbringen.

....

6. Das Museum ist interessant.

....

⊙ 2/3 🎧 **15** Read the times below and listen to the CD. Repeat each time of day after the beep. Then search for it in the list and put the correct number in the box. Two times are extra.

☐ 0.40 Uhr   ☐ 4.30 Uhr   ☐ 5.15 Uhr   ☐ 9.15 Uhr   ☐ 13.00 Uhr   ☐13.15 Uhr
☐ 15.30 Uhr ☐ 15.45 Uhr ☐ 16.30 Uhr ☐ 16.45 Uhr ☐ 21.20 Uhr   ☐ 23.30 Uhr

16 Complete the sentences. Use the preposition and object given in brackets but put the object in the appropriate form (accusative/dative). Be careful with the article!

1. Pierre geht .... (vor – das Haus)
2. Die Lampe steht .... (auf – der Tisch)
3. Die Orangen liegen ....
   (hinter – die Pfirsiche (plural!))
4. Der Teller liegt ....
   (zwischen – das Messer und die Gabel)
5. Jens stellt einen Stuhl .... (an – der Tisch)
6. Die Jacke ist .... (in – der Schrank)
7. Pierre sitzt .... (neben – seine Schwestern (plural!))
8. Martina setzt sich .... (auf – das Sofa)
9. Iwona stellt die Gläser .... (in – das Regal)

17 How are you? Fill in the missing dative pronouns. Look who answers and use the appropriate pronouns.

1. Wie geht es a) .... ? – Iwona und Pierre: b) .... geht es gut!

2. Wie geht es a) .... ? – Martina: b) Danke, es geht .... gut.

3. Wie geht es a) .... ? – Frau Schneider: b) Na ja, ... geht es nicht so gut.

18 Read the sentences and questions. Listen to the dialogue on the CD and ⊙ 2/4
complete or answer them.

1. Wo war Pierre gestern?
   a) ☐ Auf einer Präsentation.   b) ☐ In der Arbeit.   c) ☐ Im Deutschkurs.

2. Der Deutschkurs gestern war ...
   a) ☐ sehr interessant.   b) ☐ schlecht.   c) ☐ cool.

3. Martina hatte eine Präsentation über ...
   a) ☐ Goethe.   b) ☐ Freizeit.   c) ☐ Partys.

4. Wann ist die Party?
   a) ☐ Heute.   b) ☐ Morgen.   c) ☐ Übermorgen.

5. Und um wie viel Uhr beginnt sie?
   a) ☐ 18 Uhr.   b) ☐ 19 Uhr.   c) ☐ 20 Uhr.

6. Was macht Pierre heute noch?
   a) ☐ Arbeiten.   b) ☐ Freunde treffen.   c) ☐ Schlafen.

19 Complete the crossword. The letters show the solution.

1. spoon   3. eat   5. cup   7. drink   9. side dish   11. napkin
2. plate   4. main dish   6. glass   8. fork   10. knife   12. dessert

Solution (a–j): _____

Intermediate test 2

1 Fill in the gaps with the words from the box.

> nach Hause Tschüs möchten Kartoffeln Ermäßigung
> ihnen Glas lecker einem muss Spaziergang kauft
> Apfelschorle interessanter Wurst aufräumen

Iwona und Pierre sind in _____ (1.) Restaurant. Der Kellner gibt _____ (2.)

die Speisekarten. Später kommt er und fragt: „Was _____ (3.) Sie bestellen?"

Iwona bestellt ein Schnitzel mit Pommes frites und eine _____ (4.). Pierre

möchte den Fisch mit Gemüse und _____ (5.). Zu trinken bestellt er ein

_____ (6.) Wasser. Das Essen ist sehr _____ (7.). Nach dem Essen machen

die beiden einen _____ (8.) in der Stadt. Sie gehen in eine Ausstellung. Iwona

_____ (9.) die Eintrittskarten. Es gibt keine _____ (10.) für Studenten und

die Ausstellung ist nicht interessant! Das Museum gestern war _____ (11.) ...

Pierre braucht jetzt noch Lebensmittel und Iwona _____ (12.) auch etwas

einkaufen. Sie gehen in einen Supermarkt. Pierre kauft Milchprodukte und

_____ (13.), Iwona kauft Getränke. „Was machst du jetzt, Pierre?", fragt Iwona.

Pierre sagt: „Ich gehe _____ (14.). Ich muss noch _____ (15.)."

„O. K. _____ (16.)!", sagt Iwona. Iwona geht noch nicht nach Hause. Sie trifft

__/16 sich noch mit Kollegen.

2 Connect the English phrases with their German translations. One has no
translation – add it please.

1. Never mind.   a) Viel Spaß!
2. My apologies.   b) Das macht nichts.
3. The bill, please.   c) Herzlichen Glückwunsch!
4. What's the matter?   d) Das tut mir leid.
5. Sorry!   e) Herzlich willkommen.
6. Happy birthday!   f) Was ist los?
7. Have fun!   g) Entschuldigung!
__/8 8. Welcome.   h) _____

3 Listen to the short messages on your voicemail. Who does what and when? ⊙ 2/5
Complete the table.

	What?	When?
Iwona		
Kathrin		
Pierre		_/6

4 Look at the table in the picture and fill in the gaps using prepositions and articles.

1. Der Teller ist .... Gabel und .... Messer.

2. Die Gabel liegt links .... Teller.

3. Der Löffel liegt .... Teller.

4. Die Serviette ist .... Teller.

5. Die Speisekarte steht .... Flasche. _/5

5 Complete the answers using a personal pronoun in the correct form.

1. Gibt Claudia ihrem Vater ein Stück Kuchen? – Ja, sie gibt .... ein Stück Kuchen.

2. Leiht Iwona ein Fahrrad aus? – Ja, sie leiht .... am Wochenende aus.

3. Wie geht es deiner Mutter? – Es geht .... gut!

4. Besucht dich dein Onkel? Nein, ... besucht mich nicht.

5. Wohin stellt Jens den Stuhl? – Er stellt .... an den Tisch. _/5

6 Which announcement matches who? There is one extra person.

a)

KinoMaxx
Tipp: Der neue Thriller mit **Robert DeNiro**.
Heute um **20 Uhr** im **KinoMaxx**.

b)

Heute im Sonderangebot:
Frische Schnitzel, 100 g nur **1,99 Euro**

c)

Stadtrundfahrten.
Jeden Tag um 15 Uhr am Alexanderplatz.
Anmelden unter **030/235**...

d)

Wer will mit uns joggen?
Wer hat Lust? Schick eine
E-Mail an **joggen@**...

1. Pierre möchte die Stadt sehen. ☐
2. Martina muss Fleisch einkaufen. ☐
3. Jens geht auf eine Geburtstagsparty. ☐
4. Kathrin möchte wieder mehr Sport machen. ☐
5. Iwona will einen Film sehen. ☐

__/4

7 Fill in the gaps with the verbs from the first sentences. Decide whether you need the present or past tense.

1. Gestern wollte ich schwimmen. Heute _____ ich klettern.

2. Pierre ist Student. Jens und Martina _____ Studenten.

3. Pierre, Iwona und Martina haben Geschwister. Jens _____ keine Geschwister.

4. Wir müssen jetzt einkaufen. Gestern _____ wir aufräumen.

5. Du hattest gestern keine Lust! Und heute _____ du auch keine Lust?!

6. Gestern durftest du nicht fernsehen. Aber heute _____ du.

__/6

__/50

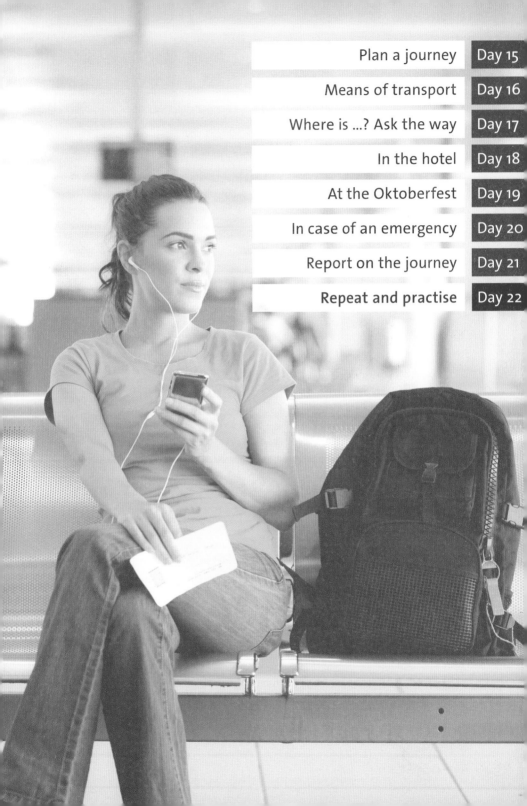

| # Plan a journey

In this lesson you will learn

- to make suggestions and to talk about plans
- to gather information about a hotel and to book a room online
- ordinal numbers, dates and months

⊙ 2/6 Wohin wollen wir fahren?

Iwona und Pierre machen Pläne für ein freies Wochenende.

Iwona	Pierre, der 3. Oktober ist ein Feiertag in Deutschland und wir haben ein langes Wochenende. Wollen wir wegfahren?
Pierre	Gern! Ich wollte immer mal nach Köln. Wir können dort zum Beispiel den Dom besichtigen oder in ein Museum gehen ... Was hältst du davon?
Iwona	Tut mir leid, Pierre, aber ich war schon in Köln. Ich habe eine bessere Idee: Wir fahren nach München und gehen auf das Oktoberfest. Was meinst du dazu?
Pierre	Ja, die Idee ist toll! München wollte ich mir auch ansehen.
Iwona	Am besten fahren wir am 2. Oktober am Nachmittag, denn dann haben wir fast drei ganze Tage Zeit für München.
Pierre	Gut. Wo wollen wir übernachten? In einer Jugendherberge?
Iwona	Eine Jugendherberge ist billiger, aber nicht sehr komfortabel. Wir suchen erst im Internet nach einem günstigen Hotel. Wie findest du den Vorschlag?
Pierre	Der Vorschlag gefällt mir. Das machen wir so. Im Notfall können wir immer noch in der Jugendherberge übernachten ... Also, dann sind wir vom 2. bis 5. Oktober in München, ja?
Iwona	Genau.
Pierre	Gut. Ich suche mal ein paar Angebote und wir können uns dann für ein Hotel entscheiden.

Dialogue questions

Mark with a cross:

	right	wrong
1. Pierre will am 3. Oktober in Berlin sein.	☐	☐
2. Iwona war schon in Köln.	☐	☐
3. Die Fahrt nach München ist Iwonas Idee.	☐	☐
4. Iwona will in einer Jugendherberge übernachten.	☐	☐

Where do we want to go to?

Iwona and Pierre make plans for a free weekend.

Iwona Pierre, 3 October is a holiday in Germany and we have a long weekend. Shall we go away on a trip?

Pierre Sure! I've always wanted to go to Cologne. We could visit the cathedral for instance or a museum ... What do you think?

Iwona I'm sorry, Pierre, but I've already been to Cologne. I have a better idea: Let's go to Munich and, to the Oktoberfest. What do you think?

Pierre Yes, that's a great idea! I wanted to see Munich too.

Iwona Best we go on 2 October in the afternoon, because then we have almost three full days for Munich.

Pierre Fine. Where do you think we should stay? In a youth hostel?

Iwona A youth hostel is cheaper, but not very comfortable. Let's search for an inexpensive hotel on the internet first. What do you think?

Pierre Sounds good. Let's do it. If need be we can always stay in a youth hostel ... Well, then we're in Munich from 2 to 5 October, right?

Iwona Exactly.

Pierre Good. I'll look for a few offers and then we can decide about the hotel.

⊙ 3/13

Angebot, -e *n*	offer
ansehen	see, view
billig	cheap, inexpensive
bleiben	stay
Dom, -e *m*	cathedral
ein paar	(a) few
entscheiden	decide
fahren	go, ride, drive
fast	almost, nearly
Feiertag, -e *m*	holiday
finden	here: think
gefallen	appeal, please
günstig	low priced
Hotel, -s *n*	hotel
Idee, -n *f*	idea
im Notfall	if need be
Jugend-herberge, -n *f*	youth hostel
komfortabel	comfortable
Notfall, -fälle *m*	emergency
Plan, Pläne *m*	plan
planen	plan
Reise, -n *f*	journey, trip, tour
übernachten	stay/spend the night
Vorschlag, Vor-schläge *m*	proposition, suggestion
vorschlagen	propose, suggest
Was hältst du davon?	What do you think?
wegfahren	go away (on a trip)

Hotel

Anreise (*mostly Sg*) *f*	arrival
Abreise (*mostly Sg*) *f*	departure
Übernachtung, -en *f*	overnight stay
inklusive (*short* inkl.)	inclusive
Doppelzimmer (*short* DZ), – *n*	double room
Einzelzimmer (*short* EZ), – *n*	single room
Dusche, -n *f*	shower
WC, WCs *n*	WC, toilet
Rezeption, -en *f*	reception, front desk
Bett, -en *n*	bed
Doppelbett, -en *n*	double bed

Months

Januar *m*	January
Februar *m*	February
März *m*	March
April *m*	April
Mai *m*	May
Juni *m*	June
Juli *m*	July
August *m*	August
September *m*	September
Oktober *m*	October
November *m*	November
Dezember *m*	December

Seasons

Frühling *m*	spring
Sommer *m*	summer
Herbst *m*	autumn
Winter *m*	winter

Grammar and means of expression

Coordinating conjunctions ▸ §9

With the coordinating conjunctions **und** *and*, **oder** *or*, **aber** *but*, **denn** *for/because* you can connect two or more main clauses. The word order in both connected sentences stays the same: verb in the second position (the conjunction does not count!). If the subject and/or verb are the same in both sentences you can omit them (not possible with **denn**!).

Der 3. Oktober ist ein Feiertag **und** wir haben ein langes Wochenende.
3 October is a holiday in Germany and we have a long weekend.
Wir können den Dom besichtigen **oder** (wir können) in ein Museum gehen.
We could visit the cathedral for instance or a museum.

Temporal prepositions ▸ §5.4

Check the following table for the most common temporal prepositions and when you need them.

um at	**am** in, on	**im** in
Time: **Wir treffen uns um 14 Uhr.** We meet at 2 p.m.	Daytime: **Am** Morgen frühstücke ich. In the morning I eat breakfast.	Months: Das Oktoberfest ist **im** September. The Oktoberfest is in September.
	Weekdays and dates: Ich fahre **am** Dienstag nach München. I go to Munich on Tuesday. Wir fahren **am** 2. Oktober. We go on 2 October.	Seasons: Das Oktoberfest ist **im** Herbst. The Oktoberfest is in autumn.

Ordinal numbers

When talking about dates you need ordinal numbers. In German, when written as a number, they always have a full stop.
Up to 19. you just add **-te** as an ending (with the exceptions: 1. erste, 3. dritte, 7. siebte, 8. achte). All numbers above (when the cardinal number ends with **-zig**) get the ending -ste: 110. – hundert**zehn** + **te** = hunderzehnte; 93. – dreiundneun**zig** + **ste** = dreiundneunzigste.

⊙ 2/7 🎧 **1** Listen to the dates on the CD. The months are written below but the day is missing. Write the ordinal numbers in the gaps.

1. .... Januar   4. .... April   7. .... Juli   10. .... Oktober
2. .... Februar   5. .... Mai   8. .... August 11. .... November
3. .... März   6. .... Juni   9. .... September 12. .... Dezember

💬 **2** Read the sentences and find the appropriate replies in the box. Say them loud.

> Nein, ich muss an dem Tag arbeiten.
> Mir gefällt dein Vorschlag.   Ich finde Ihre Idee gut.

1. Wohin fahren wir? Mein Vorschlag ist Hamburg.
2. Was halten Sie von einer Reise nach Frankreich?
3. Können wir am 6. Oktober fahren?

📖 **3** Read the short information about a hotel and answer the questions.

> Verbringen Sie Ihren Urlaub in unserem komfortablen Hotel. Wir bieten Ihnen 18 Doppelzimmer und 6 Einzelzimmer mit Dusche und WC und zusätzlich TV und Radio. Pro Person und Nacht kostet das Einzelzimmer 55 Euro, das Doppelzimmer 45 Euro. Das Frühstück ist inklusive. Sie können erst am Abend anreisen? Kein Problem! Die Rezeption ist immer offen und eine Anreise auch nach 20 Uhr ist möglich!

1. Wie viel kosten zwei Nächte in einem Einzelzimmer? .... Euro.
2. Gibt es eine Dusche im Zimmer?   ☐ Ja. ☐ Nein.
3. Ist eine Anreise um 21 Uhr möglich?   ☐ Ja. ☐ Nein.
4. Wie viele Zimmer hat das Hotel? .... Zimmer.

⊙ 2/8 🎧 **4** Look at the booking form and listen to the short dialogue on the CD to gather the information needed. Then fill in the form.

Anreise: .... – Abreise: ....
Erwachsene: .... – Kinder: ....
Einzelzimmer ☐ Doppelzimmer ☐
Inkl. Frühstück?   Nein ☐ Ja ☐ (+ 7,00 EUR)

Kulturtipp The Oktoberfest in Munich

You've probably heard of the Oktoberfest already and that's no big surprise, because it's one of the events Germany is famous for. It takes place from late September to early October and is the travelling destination for lots of tourists from all over the world.

In the first years from 1810 on it was more of a sporting event with a big horse race. That changed in the late 19th century and the Oktoberfest became what it is today when they started to sell beer in 1880. And today it's most famous attraction is still beer. Over 6 million people come to the Oktoberfest and consume almost 7 million litres of beer in the big **Festzelte** *festival tents*.

Other culinary delicacies are **Hendl** *roast chicken*, **Haxn** *pork knuckle*, **Würstl** *sausage* and **Brezn** *pretzel* and many more...

In the 20th century more and more rides were added to the Oktoberfest. Today's attractions are the big wheel with its height of 48 metres or the world's largest portable roller coaster with five loops, among others.

....

What can you already do?

☺ ☺ ☹

- make suggestions and talk about plans ▸ *Ü2*
- gather information about a hotel ▸ *Ü3*
- book a room ▸ *Ü4*
- understand dates, months and ordinal numbers ▸ *Ü1*

Means of transport

In this lesson you will learn

- to read a timetable
- to look for a train connection on the internet
- about means of transport, especially trains

⊙ 2/9 **Wie kommen wir nach München?**

Jetzt müssen die beiden nur noch das geeignete Verkehrsmittel finden.

Pierre	Gut. Die Zimmer sind gebucht. Aber wie kommen wir nach München? Mit dem Flugzeug?
Iwona	Ich glaube nicht, dass wir einen guten Flug bekommen, aber wir prüfen das im Internet. Ich denke, dass wir am besten mit dem Auto oder dem Zug fahren.
Pierre	Dann bin ich für den Zug! Das ist besser, weil wir dann nicht im Stau stehen und auch keine Parkplätze suchen müssen.
Iwona	Ja, du hast recht. Aber lass uns erst noch nach einem Flug suchen.
Pierre	O. K. Hmm ... Nein, die Flüge sind zu teuer und die Zeit passt nicht. Wir fahren also mit dem Zug!
Iwona	Ja, dann geh auf die Webseite der Bahn und such uns eine Verbindung nach München!
Pierre	In Ordnung. Also: Von Berlin ... nach München. Hinfahrt ... am 2.10. und Rückfahrt ... am 5.10. Zweite Klasse ... zwei Erwachsene. Um wie viel Uhr wollen wir am Donnerstag hier abfahren?
Iwona	Vielleicht starten wir so, dass wir um 20 Uhr in München ankommen. Wie lange dauert die Fahrt?
Pierre	Moment ... die Fahrt dauert ungefähr 6 Stunden. Dann müssen wir um 14 Uhr hier abfahren.
Iwona	Das ist O. K.
Pierre	Gut, das passt mir auch. Oh, sieh mal: Wir können die Fahrkarten gleich online buchen und auch noch ausdrucken. Soll ich uns Sitzplätze reservieren? Das kostet zwei Euro mehr ... Hast du eine Kreditkarte?

Dialogue questions

Cross out the wrong answer.

1. Pierre und Iwona *fahren | fliegen* nach München.
2. Sie reisen in der *ersten | zweiten* Klasse.
3. Die Fahrt nach München dauert *sechs | vierzehn* Stunden.
4. Pierre kauft die Fahrkarten *am Schalter | online*.

How to get to Munich?

Now the two just have to find the right means of transport.

Pierre   OK. The rooms are booked. But how do we get to Munich? By plane?

Iwona   I don't think that we will be able to get a good flight, but we can check it on the internet. I think, the best would be we driving by car or taking the train.

Pierre   Then I prefer the train! It's better because we won't get caught up in a traffic jam and won't have to look for parking spaces.

Iwona   Yes, you're right. But let's still look for a flight first.

Pierre   OK. Hmm ... No, the flights are too expensive and the time is wrong. We'll go by train then!

Iwona   Yes, so go to the website of the railway company and look for a connection to Munich!

Pierre   All right. Well: From Berlin ... to Munich. Journey there ... on 2.10. and return journey ... on 5.10. Second class ... two adults. When do you want to depart?

Iwona   Maybe we should set off in order to arrive in Munich at 8 p.m. How long does the journey take?

Pierre   Just a moment ... the journey takes about 6 hours. So we have to leave here at 2 p.m.

Iwona   That's OK.

Pierre   Good, fine by me. Oh, look: We can book the tickets immediately online and print them too. Should I book seats for us? That costs two Euro more ... Do you have a credit card?

Vocabulary

⊙ 3/14

(aus)drucken	print
Auto, -s *n*	car
Bahn, -en *f*	train, railway
buchen	book
Das passt mir!	Fine by me!
dauern	take
denken	think
erst	first
Erwachsene, -n *f+m*	adult, grown-up
Fahrt, -en *f*	journey, trip, drive
Flug, Flüge *m*	flight
Flugzeug, -e *n*	plane
für etwas sein	favour, prefer
gleich	immediately
im Stau stehen	get caught up in a traffic jam
In Ordnung!	All right!
kommen	here: get to
Kreditkarte, -n *f*	credit card
lass uns	let's
Moment!	Just a moment!
nach	to
still	noch
Parkplatz, -plätze *m*	parking space
prüfen	check
recht haben	be right
reisen	travel
reservieren	book, retain
Sieh mal!	Look!
Sitzplatz, -plätze *m*	seat
Stau, -s *m*	traffic jam
suchen	search, look for
Verkehrsmittel, – *n*	means of transport
von	from
Zug, Züge *m*	train

Around the station

Bahnhof, -höfe *m*	station
Gleis, -e *n*	rails
Bahnsteig, -e *m*	platform
Abfahrt (*mostly Sg*) *f*	departure
abfahren	depart
Ankunft (*mostly Sg*) *f*	arrival
ankommen	arrive
2. Klasse (*only Sg*) *f*	second class
Regionalzug, -züge *m*	regional train
einsteigen	board, get on
umsteigen	change
aussteigen	alight, get off
Fahrplan, -pläne *m*	timetable
Fahrkarte, -n *f*	ticket
(Fahrkarten-) Schalter, – *m*	ticket office
einfache Fahrt	one-way (ticket)
Hinfahrt, -en *f*	journey there
Rückfahrt, -en *f*	return journey
pünktlich	punctual
Verspätung, -en *f*	delay

Grammar and means of expression

Subordinate clauses with *dass* and *weil* ▸ *§9*

Dass *that* and **weil** *because* are subordinating conjunctions – unlike the coordinating conjunctions you've learned in the previous lesson. The big difference is the word order in the subordinate clause:
It's always conjunction first and (conjugated) verb last.

Dass usually stands after certain verbs like **glauben** *believe*, **denken** *think*, **meinen** *mean*, **sagen** *say*, **wissen** *know*:
Ich **glaube** nicht, **dass** wir einen guten Flug bekommen.
I don't think that we will be able to get a good flight.

If you want to give a reason or a cause you can use **weil**. You can use **denn** for the same purpose and you've noticed already that the translation for **denn** and **weil** is both "because".
But be careful: First, the word order is different! And second, you can always use **weil** (much like with "because", you can, for example, say or write the subordinate clause first), but **denn** is only possible **between** two coordinated main clauses.

1 Read the extract from the timetable of Berlin Hbf and answer the questions below.

Abfahrt	Zug	Reiseziel	Gleis
16:29	EC 47	Frankfurt (Oder) 17:30 – Warszawa Centralna 22:06 – **Warszawa Wschodnia 22:18**	11
16:32	ICE 875	Göttingen 18:53 – Frankfurt (Main) Hbf 20:44 – Freiburg (Breisgau) Hbf 23:09 – **Basel SBB 23:55**	14
16:36	EC 179	Dresden Hbf 18:52 – Praha-Holesovice 21:16 – **Praha hl. n. 21:27**	2

1. Auf welchem Gleis fährt der Zug nach Freiburg ab? Gleis ....
2. Wann fährt der EC nach Frankfurt ab? ....
3. Wohin fährt der ICE? ....
4. Wann ist der EC 179 in Dresden? ....

2 Pierre wants to look up the train connection on the internet. Help him fill in the form. Find the information needed in this lesson's dialogue.

☐ Einfache Fahrt ☐ Hin- und Rückfahrt
Von: .... , Nach: ....
Hinfahrt am: .... , Uhrzeit: .... ☐ Abfahrt ☐ Ankunft
Rückfahrt am: .... , Uhrzeit: 15.30 ☒ Abfahrt ☐ Ankunft

3 Bring the sentences in the correct order. Be careful with the subordinated clauses.

1. lieber / weil / Ich / schneller / fahre / er / mit dem ICE / ist / .

....

2. die Regionalbahn / Ich / dass / zu langsam / denke / ist / .

....

3. fahren / Iwona / wollen / Pierre / nach München / und / .

....

4. ist / Pierre / ein Flug / dass / zu teuer / sagt / .

....

Kulturtipp Travelling in Germany

The (mostly) well built **Autobahnen** *motorways* allow for fast travel throughout Germany. But often you have to cope with traffic jams, especially at the beginning and end of holidays and on long weekends (keep in mind that different **Bundesländer** can have different dates for holidays). An alternative are **Billigflieger** *no-frills airlines* between the big cities – be careful, because not all fly to the main airports but to other ones often quite a distance away from the city.

Travelling by train is often considered more expensive, but **die Deutsche Bahn** (**DB** and often simply **die Bahn**, the German railway company) has some special offers worth considering: e.g. the **Schönes-Wochenende-Ticket** allows up to 5 persons to travel on Saturday or Sunday throughout Germany, but limited to **Nahverkehrszüge** *commuter trains*. Check the **Bahn**'s web page for other offers!

Abbreviations around the train		
RB	Regionalbahn *f*	a regional train that stops at every station
RE	Regional-Express *m*	a regional train that stops at most stations
ICE	Intercity-Express *m*	high-speed train in Germany
IC	Intercity *m*	fast train between major German cities
EC	Eurocity *m*	fast train between major European cities
Hbf	Hauptbahnhof *m*	main station
Bf	Bahnhof *m*	station

What can you already do?

☺ ☺ ☹

- read a timetable ▸ Ü1
- look for train connections ▸ Ü2
- know means of transport ▸ Ü3

Where is ...? Ask the way

In this lesson you will learn

- to approach strangers and ask for help
- to ask the way
- to give and understand directions

⊙ 2/10 **Zum Hotel**

Iwona und Pierre sind am Bahnhof in München angekommen.

Pierre	Hurra! Endlich in München.
	Jetzt müssen wir nur noch den Weg zum Hotel finden.
Iwona	Auf der Webseite steht ja „nur 10 Minuten vom Bahnhof".
	Wir fragen einfach jemanden. Entschuldigen Sie bitte.
Passantin	Ja?
Iwona	Können Sie uns vielleicht sagen, wo wir das Hotel München finden?
Passantin	In welcher Straße ist das denn?
Pierre	In der Schillerstraße.
Passantin	Ah ja, das ist ganz einfach. Gehen Sie dort vorne rechts, am Bahnhof vorbei bis zu der Kreuzung und geradeaus über die Kreuzung. Dann sind Sie schon in der Schillerstraße.
	Am Ende der Straße ist das Hotel.
Iwona	Also hier rechts und dann immer geradeaus?
Passantin	Ja, genau!
Pierre	Das finden wir! Vielen Dank.
Passantin	Gern geschehen. Schönen Aufenthalt in München!
Iwona	Danke. Auf Wiedersehen.
Pierre	Na, das ist wirklich einfach und nicht weit.
Iwona	Stimmt, lass uns gehen. Sieh mal, das dort ist sicher die Kreuzung ...

Dialogue questions

Mark the right answer.

1. Wen fragt Iwona?
   a) ☐ Einen Mann.   b) ☐ Eine Frau.
2. Wie heißt das Hotel?
   a) ☐ München.   b) ☐ Schiller.
3. Wo ist das Hotel?
   a) ☐ Direkt am Bahnhof.   b) ☐ 10 Minuten vom Bahnhof.
4. Wie erreichen Iwona und Pierre das Hotel?
   a) ☐ Sie fahren mit dem Bus. b) ☐ Sie gehen.

To the hotel

Iwona and Pierre have arrived at the station in Munich.

Pierre	Hooray! Finally in Munich. Now we just have to find the hotel.
Iwona	On the website it said "only 10 minutes from the station". Let's just ask someone. Excuse me, please.
Passerby	Yes?
Iwona	Could you tell us where we can find the hotel München?
Passerby	What street is it on?
Pierre	On Schiller street.
Passerby	Ah yes, that's quite easy. There, up ahead, turn right, go past the station to the crossroads and straight on over the crossroads. Then you're already in Schiller street. The hotel's at the end of the street.
Iwona	So here right and then just straight on?
Passerby	Yes, exactly!
Pierre	We'll find it! Thank you very much.
Passerby	You're welcome. Have a nice stay in Munich!
Iwona	Thanks. Goodbye.
Pierre	Well, that's really easy and not far.
Iwona	True, let's go. Look, there, that's surely the crossroads ...

◉ 3/15

Aufenthalt, -e *m*	stay
einfach	just, simply
einmal	once
Ende, -n *n*	end
endlich	finally
entschuldigen	excuse
Entschuldigen Sie.	Excuse me.
Entschuldigung.	Sorry./Excuse me.
helfen	help
Hurra!	Hooray!
keinmal	not once, never
Passant *m*/ Passantin *f*, Passanten	passerby
schön	nice, beautiful
Stimmt!	True!
weit	far
welcher, welche, welches	which, what
wirklich	really

Directions

abbiegen	turn
die nächste/erste Straße	the next/first street/road
die zweite/ dritte/... Straße	the second/third/... street/road
dort	there
dort hinten	back there
dort vorne	there up ahead
geradeaus	straight on
hier	(right) here
Kurve, -n *f*	turn
links	left
nehmen	take
rechts	right
sich halten	keep
vorbeigehen	pass

Basic buildings and landmarks

Ampel, -n *f*	traffic light
Baustelle, -n *f*	road works, construction site
Bushaltestelle, -n *f*	bus stop
Einbahnstraße, -n *f*	one-way street
Haltestelle, -n *f*	stop
Hochhaus, -häuser *n*	high-rise building
Kirche, -n *f*	church
Kreuzung, -en *f*	crossroads
Post (*only Sg*) *f*	post (office)
Straßenbahn- haltestelle, -n *f*	tram stop
Zebrastreifen, – *m*	zebra crossing

Grammar and means of expression

Subordinate clauses with interrogative pronouns ▸ §9

All interrogative pronouns that you used until now for 'wh' questions only,
can also be used as subordinating conjunctions. The rules are the same as for
subordinate clauses with **dass** *that* and **weil** *because*: the conjunctions come
first and the verb last.
It's a way to transform a question into a subordinate clause, used after certain
verbs like:

sagen	say
wissen	know
fragen	ask
schreiben	write

Wo finden wir das Hotel? *Where can we find the hotel?*
Können Sie uns sagen, **wo** wir das Hotel finden?
Could you tell us, where we can find the hotel?

Prepositions with the dative ▸ §5.2

In part 2 of this book you learned the prepositions that can have either dative or
accusative. But there are also prepositions that always have the following noun in
the same case. Nouns after the prepositions in the table are always in the dative
case – like in the dialogue:
Wir müssen den Weg **zum** Hotel finden. *We have to find the way to the hotel.*
Das sind 10 Minuten **vom** Bahnhof. *It's 10 minutes from the station.*

aus	from
von	from, of
nach	to, toward, past, after
zu	to, toward
bei	at, by, next to
mit	with
seit	since, for

Here again the prepositions **von**, **zu** and **bei** are merged with the article **dem** of
masculine and neuter nouns to **vom**, **zum** and **beim**. Additionally **zu** merges with **der**
of feminine dative nouns to **zur**.

1 Read the situations below. Then find the appropriate sentences in the box and say them out loud.

> Können Sie mir bitte sagen, wo der Bahnhof ist?
> Entschuldigen Sie, ich suche das Theater.   Entschuldigen Sie bitte.
> Wissen Sie, wo die Schillerstraße ist?   Können Sie mir vielleicht helfen?

1. You want to stop a passerby politely.
2. You ask a passerby if he could help you.
3. Your train is leaving soon, but you can't remember the way to the station.
4. You need directions to a certain street.
5. You're going to see "Romeo and Juliet". If only you knew the way …

 2 Look at the pictures and then write short directions. Start at the arrow and go to the X.

1.
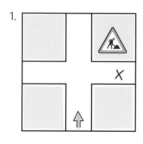

3.
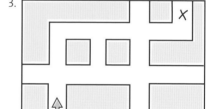

2.
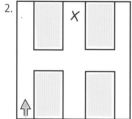

4.
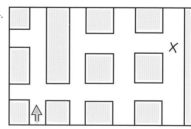

1. ....

2. ....

3. ....

4. ....

Kulturtipp
Munich's sights

Like Berlin, Munich has so much to offer but time is short:

In the historic city centre is **der Marienplatz**, the central square, and not far from it **die Frauenkirche**, its full name "Cathedral of Our Blessed Lady" and considered the town's greatest landmark.

Still in the city centre you can visit the **Viktualienmarkt**, a huge market with a wide variety of all kinds of food, which is constantly open (except for Sundays and holidays).

On a sunny day **der Englische Garten** *the English Garden*, one of the world's biggest parks, is good for walks, sport or just sitting in a **Biergarten** *beer garden* to enjoy a **Weißbier** *wheat beer* (literally *white beer*) and a **Brezn** *pretzel*.

And if you're a museum fan then don't forget to pay a visit to **das Deutsche Museum** *the German Museum*, the world's biggest museum of technology and science with a lot of interactive exhibits for children and grown-up children.

....

What can you already do?

☺ ☺ ☹

■ approach strangers and passersby and ask for help			▶*Ü1*
■ ask the way			▶*Ü1*
■ give directions			▶*Ü2*

So, now you're more than halfway through the book. How's it going? Good, we hope. If you have the feeling that it's getting more difficult now, don't get discouraged. If you can't solve an exercise, repeat the lesson and have a look in the solution in the appendix – you'll learn a lot in that way too!

In the hotel

In this lesson you will learn

- to deal with the check-in at a hotel
- to fill in forms with your personal data
- about services in a hotel

◉ 2/11 **Beim Einchecken**

Nach der Ankunft im Hotel müssen die beiden einchecken.

Hotelangestellter	Grüß Gott, wie kann ich Ihnen helfen?
Pierre	Mein Name ist Pierre Dupont und das ist Iwona Nowak. Wir haben online zwei Zimmer reserviert.
Hotelangestellter	Haben Sie die Bestätigung der Buchung dabei?
Pierre	Ja. Hier bitte.
Hotelangestellter	Vielen Dank. Einen Moment bitte ... Nowak und Dupont ... ah ja, hier. Wir haben die Zimmer 211 und 212 für Sie hergerichtet. Ich bräuchte noch Ihre Personalausweise oder Reisepässe, bitte.
Iwona	Bitte schön.
Hotelangestellter	Danke. Hier sind Ihre Schlüssel. Ihre Zimmer sind im zweiten Stock. Dort links ist der Aufzug und die Treppe. Der Speiseraum ist dort rechts. Frühstück gibt es von 6.30 Uhr bis 10 Uhr. Haben Sie noch irgendwelche Fragen?
Iwona	Ja, wann müssen wir am Sonntag das Zimmer verlassen?
Hotelangestellter	Sie haben bis 12 Uhr mittags Zeit auszuchecken. Ah, und ich möchte Sie bitten, dass Sie noch diese Formulare ausfüllen. Sie können das auf dem Zimmer machen und sie später hier abgeben.
Iwona	Gut. Auf Wiedersehen. Ich möchte mich kurz waschen und frisch machen. Ich beeile mich. Gehen wir dann in die Stadt?
Pierre	Ja, gern!

Dialogue questions

Mark with a cross:

	right	wrong
1. Pierre hat die Buchungsbestätigung dabei.	☐	☐
2. Der Speiseraum ist rechts von der Rezeption.	☐	☐
3. Um 9 Uhr gibt es noch Frühstück.	☐	☐
4. Pierre möchte nicht mehr in die Stadt.	☐	☐

Checking in

After arriving at the hotel, the two have to check in.

Hotel clerk	Good evening, how may I help you?
Pierre	My name is Pierre Dupont and this is Iwona Nowak. We booked two rooms online.
Hotel clerk	Do you have the booking confirmation with you?
Pierre	Yes. Here you are.
Hotel clerk	Thank you. Just a moment, please ... Nowak and Dupont ... ah yes, here. We've prepared rooms 211 and 212 for you. I need your ID cards or passports, please.
Iwona	Here you go.
Hotel clerk	Thanks. Here are your keys. Your rooms are on the second floor. There on the left are the elevator and the stairs. The dining room is there on the right. Breakfast is from 6.30 to 10 o'clock. Do you have any questions?
Iwona	Yes, when do we have to leave the rooms on Sunday?
Hotel clerk	You have time to check out until noon. Ah, and I'd like to ask you to fill in these forms. You can do it in your rooms and return them later.
Iwona	Fine. Goodbye. I'd like to wash myself and freshen up. I'll hurry. Shall we go to the city then?
Pierre	Yes, I'd love to!

Vocabulary

⊙ 3/16

abgeben	deliver
angenehm	pleasant
Aufzug, Aufzüge *m*	elevator
auschecken	check out
ausfüllen	fill in
Bestätigung, -en *f*	confirmation
Buchung, -en *f*	booking
einchecken	check in
Formular, -e *n*	form
herrichten	prepare
irgendwelche	any
kostenlos	(for) free
Personalausweis, -e *m*	ID card
Reisepass, -pässe *m*	passport
Schlüssel, – *m*	key
sich beeilen	hurry
sich frisch machen	freshen up
sich waschen	wash (oneself)
Stock, – *m*/ Stockwerk, -e *n*/ Etage, -n *f*	floor, level
Treppe, -n *f*	stairs
verlassen	leave

Personal data	
Nachname, -n *m*	last name
Titel, – *m*	(academic) title
Postleitzahl, -en *f* (*often short* PLZ)	postal code
Telefon, -e *n* (*often short* Tel.)	telephone
geschäftlich	business
Geburtsdatum, -daten *n*	date of birth
Anrede, -n *f*	title (Herr Mr or Frau Ms)
Hausnummer, -n *f* (*often short* Haus-Nr.)	house number
Wohnort, -e *m*	residence
privat	private
Mobiltelefon, -e *n*	mobile phone
Staats- angehörigkeit, -en *f*	nationality

Hotel services	
(Mini)Bar, -s *f*	bar
Schwimmbad, -bäder *n*	swimming pool
Radverleih, -e *m*	bike rental
Zimmerservice, -s *m*	room service
Sauna, Saunen *f*	sauna
Filmverleih, -e *m*	film rental

Grammar and means of expression

Reflexive verbs ▸ §8.8

Maybe you wondered why some verbs in the vocabulary sections in the previous lessons had the word **sich**. **Sich** means *oneself* and indicates that the subject and the object are the same ("reflexive"). In German reflexive verbs are used much more frequently than in English and often the English translation is not reflexive – as in the following example:

Ich beeile **mich**. *I'll hurry.*

Iwona macht **sich** frisch. *Iwona will freshen up.*

Often the same verb can be used reflexively and not reflexively. (In this case **sich** is put in brackets in the vocabulary.)

Take the verb **waschen** *wash* for example:

You can wash yourself:

Ich wasche **mich**. *I wash myself.*

Or you can wash another person or something:

Ich wasche **meinen Bruder/ihn/mein Kind/das Gemüse**.

I wash my brother/him/my child/the vegetables.

In all cases we have an accusative object, that in the first example is identical to the subject (I – myself).

The reflexive pronouns in nominative, accusative						
	Sg			Pl		
Nom.	ich	du	er/sie/es	wir	ihr	sie/Sie
Acc.	mich	dich	sich	uns	euch	sich

Nationalities

We introduced a few languages in Day 11 (▸ *Day 11*). The nationalities are generally the same like the languages – but since they are adjectives, they start with a lowercase letter. You'll see they most often end with **-isch** – but there is no general rule as how to build the form. Best is, you look up the German word for your own nationality and language and remember it! Some commonly used nationalities are in the table below.

deutsch	German	britisch	British
polnisch	Polish	US-amerikanisch	American
russisch	Russian	japanisch	Japanese

1 Fill in the form with your personal data.

Anrede:	☐ Herr ☐ Frau
Titel: _____, Vorname: _____, Nachname: _____	
Straße, Haus-Nr.: _____	
PLZ: _____, Wohnort: _____	
Land: _____, Staatsangehörigkeit: _____	
Tel.: _____, Mobiltelefon: _____	

2 Martina and Jens arrived at their hotel, but the dialogue at the reception got mixed up. Can you put it back in its original order?

1. **Hotelangestellter**   Darf ich bitte noch Ihren Personalausweis sehen?
2. **Hotelangestellter**   Und wie ist Ihr Name?
3. **Hotelangestellter**   Danke. Sie haben Zimmer 103, im ersten Stock. Hier ist Ihr Schlüssel. Haben Sie noch Fragen?
4. **Hotelangestellter**   Guten Tag, was kann ich für Sie tun?
5. **Hotelangestellter**   Ich wünsche Ihnen einen angenehmen Aufenthalt. Auf Wiedersehen.
6. **Jens**   Guten Tag, wir haben ein Zimmer reserviert.
7. **Jens**   Ja, hier ist er, bitte.
8. **Jens**   Nein. Auf Wiedersehen.
9. **Jens**   Schubert, Jens Schubert.

Correct order: _____

⊙ 2/12 **3** Jens discovered a leaflet with additional hotel services. Read the questions below and listen to his conversation with Martina. Then briefly answer the questions.

1. Wie viel kostet die Sauna? _____

2. Wo kann man etwas trinken? _____

3. Was kann man in dem Hotel ausleihen? _____

4. Welche kostenlosen Services gibt es? _____

Kulturtipp Bread

Even in smaller villages with no other shops you'll probably find a **Bäckerei** *baker's shop*. Those shops often open as early as 6 a.m. and close again at 6 p.m. – some are closed for a lunch break and some are even open on Sunday morning.

Entering a **Bäckerei** you might be overwhelmed with the choice of bread and other bakery products. Most German breads are rather dark and made from rye and sourdough instead of wheat and yeast. But it's also possible to get your favourite French baguette or Italian ciabatta.

Besides bread you can choose from a wide variety of **Brötchen** *bread rolls* (all with different names and forms in different regions: **die Semmel** in Bavaria, **die Schrippe** in Northern Germany and many, many more) and sweet pastries and cakes.

....

What can you already do?

☺ ☻ ☹

- deal with the check in   ▸ *Ü2*
- fill in a form   ▸ *Ü1*
- know about hotel services   ▸ *Ü3*

At the Oktoberfest

In this lesson you will learn

- to talk about the weather
- to understand short weather forecasts
- to write a simple SMS

 2/13 **Auf zum Riesenrad!**

Dann kommen Iwona und Pierre endlich auch auf dem Oktoberfest an.

Iwona   Wir haben echt Glück mit dem Wetter! Es ist richtig warm und sonnig!

Pierre   Ja! Komm, wir fahren erst einmal mit dem Riesenrad ... dann können wir alles von oben sehen.

Iwona   Das ist eine gute Idee! Aber mit der Achterbahn möchte ich auch fahren.

Pierre   Na klar! Dann auf zum Riesenrad!

Einige Zeit später

Iwona   Das war großartig.

Pierre   Das stimmt! Iwona, es ist jetzt schon nach vier und ich habe Hunger. Wollen wir etwas essen gehen?

Iwona   Ja, gern, ich habe auch Hunger. Schau mal, dort gibt es Bratwurst. Hast du darauf Lust?

Pierre   Hmm, ich weiß noch nicht. Lass uns vielleicht schauen, was es sonst noch gibt.

Iwona   Möchtest du in eins dieser großen Festzelte?

Pierre   Nein, lieber nicht. Da ist es zu voll!

Iwona   Du hast recht. Lass uns hier draußen etwas Leckeres suchen. Ich schreibe nur noch schnell Martina eine SMS.

Kurze Zeit später in Berlin

Martina   Jens, hör mal. Iwona schreibt vom Oktoberfest: „Liebe Martina. Die Sonne scheint, es ist warm. Uns geht es gut, das Oktoberfest ist toll! LG Iwona & Pierre".

Jens   Na toll ... und hier regnet es!

Dialogue questions

Cross out the wrong answer.

1. Das Wetter in München ist *gut | schlecht*.
2. Pierre und Iwona fahren zuerst mit *dem Riesenrad | der Achterbahn*.
3. Pierre möchte *sehr gern | lieber nicht* in ein Festzelt.
4. *Iwona | Pierre* schreibt eine SMS an *Martina | Jens*.

To the big wheel!

Then Iwona and Pierre finally arrive at the Oktoberfest as well.

Iwona We're quite lucky with the weather! It's really warm and sunny!

Pierre Yes! Come on, let's ride the big wheel first ... then we can see everything from above.

Iwona That's a good idea! But I want to ride the roller coaster too.

Pierre Of course! Then to the big wheel!

Some time later

Iwona That was awesome.

Pierre True! Iwona, it's already past four and I'm hungry. Are we going to eat something?

Iwona I'd like that, I'm hungry too. Look, they're selling bratwurst there. Are you up for that?

Pierre Hmm, I don't know yet. Maybe let's look first, what else there is.

Iwona Do you want to go in one of those big festival tents?

Pierre No, rather not. It's too crowded in there!

Iwona You're right. Let's find something delicious out here. I'm just writing quickly an SMS to Martina.

A short time later in Berlin

Martina Jens, listen. Iwona writes from the Oktoberfest: „Dear Martina. The sun's shining, it's warm. We're fine, the Oktoberfest is great! Love Iwona & Pierre".

Jens Well great ... and here it's raining!

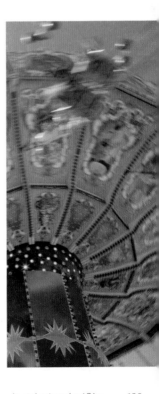

⊙ 3/17

Achterbahn, -en *f*	roller coaster
Bratwurst, -würste *f*	bratwurst
es gibt	there is/are
Fahrgeschäft, -e *n*	ride
Festzelt, -e *n*	festival tent
Hör mal!	Listen!
hungrig	hungry
Karussell, -e/-s *n*	roundabout
Komm!	Come on!
Leute (*only Pl*)	people
lieber nicht	rather not
Riesenrad, -räder *n*	big wheel
schreiben	write
simsen	text
SMS, – *f*	SMS, text (message)
sonst	else
Wetter (*only Sg*) *n*	weather
Zelt, -e *n*	tent

Common abbreviations for farewells in SMS	
hdl (hab dich lieb)	I like/love you (not necessarily for lovers but for good friends too)
bb (bye, bye/bis bald)	see you (later)
cu (see you)	see you
lg (liebe Grüße)	lové, regards (common among friends)

Weather	
bewölkt	cloudy, overcast
Eis (*only Sg*) *n*	ice
eisig	icy
Gewitter, – *n*	thunderstorm
heiß	hot
kalt	cold
kühl	chilly, cool
Nebel (*mostly Sg*) *m*	fog
neblig	foggy
Regen (*only Sg*) *m*	rain
regnen	rain
scheinen	shine
Schnee (*only Sg*) *m*	snow
schneien	snow
Sonne, -n *f*	sun
sonnig	sunny
stürmen	storm
Sturm, Stürme *m*	storm
verschneit	snowy
warm	warm
Wind, -e *m*	wind
winden	blow
Wolke, -n *f*	cloud

Grammar and means of expression

The impersonal *es* ▸ *§3.1.1*

Each sentence has to have a subject. If there's no person (or animal or thing) that acts as a subject you normally use **es** *it*.
It's like in English and you can use it – as you already know – when talking about time.
Es ist jetzt schon nach vier. *It's already after four.*
Another use is when talking about the weather – which we will show you below.

Weather

Let's have a look at an example from the dialogue:
Es ist richtig sonnig und warm. *It's really sunny and warm.*
Most expressions around the weather are similar to English expressions.
A question often asked is **"Wie ist das Wetter?"** *"How's the weather?"*. But how do you answer? You can say for example:
Das Wetter ist gut/schlecht. *The weather's fine/bad.*
Es regnet/schneit/stürmt. *It's raining/snowing/stormy.*
Es ist regnerisch/verschneit/stürmisch. *It's rainy/snowy/stormy.*
Die Sonne scheint. *The sun's shining.*
Es ist kalt/warm/heiß. *It's cold/warm/hot.*

Tips for writing SMS to your friends

Your space for a SMS is limited: But with friends, you normally know who sends and gets an SMS, so you can omit the names and use the abbreviations from the vocabulary:
Hi, bin auf dem Oktoberfest. Es ist toll! LG *Hi, I'm on the Oktoberfest. It's great! Love*
When Germans send you SMS, you'll also see that they omit from time to time certain verbs or pronouns or articles. There are no general rules as long as the message makes still sense. So, in the above example, the personal pronoun **ich** is missing, because **bin** states clearly the first person. And, lastly, it's also no problem to write the whole SMS in lowercase.

⊙ 2/14 🎧 **1** Listen to the short weather forecasts on the CD. Then write the number of each forecast next to the appropriate weather icon. One icon remains.

1. ....   3. ....   5. ....

2. ....   4. ....   6. ....

✏ **2** Write a short SMS to your friends. Try to stay under 160 characters!

1. You're at the Oktoberfest. It's great, the sun is shining and there are lots of people.

....

2. Your friend's on holiday. Ask her/him, how she/he is and how the weather is.

....

3. You're meeting your friend at the Oktoberfest. Tell her/him that you've arrived and will wait by the rollercoaster.

....

4. Your friend sent you an SMS asking about the weather. Tell her/him that it's overcast and chilly, but you like that.

....

📖 **3** Connect the sentences below with the appropriate replies.

1. Wie ist das Wetter in Hamburg?   a) Wieso? Heute regnet es nicht!
2. Schneit es bei euch?   b) Ja, es stürmt sogar!
3. Nimm einen Regenschirm mit!   c) In Hamburg regnet es und es ist kalt.
4. Ist es heute kalt?   d) Nein, es gibt keinen Schnee. Bei uns
                                              scheint die Sonne.
5. Windet es?   e) Ja, es ist bewölkt und richtig kalt.

Kulturtipp
Snack specialties

You're in Germany and you're hungry? You don't want to sit in a restaurant and you've already checked out all kinds of bread and bread rolls your bakery offers? Then it's time to taste one of the many German snacks!

There is for example **die Currywurst**. It's a hot pork sausage with curry sauce (usually ketchup with curry) that often comes with chips. It's said that it was invented in 1949 in Berlin. Additionally, there are a lot of different regional sausage specialties in the different German regions – often available for takeaway too. For example **die Thüringer Rostbratwurst** *Thuringian sausage* from Thuringia or **die Weißwurst** *weisswurst* (literally *white sausage*) from Bavaria.

Another snack is **der Döner** or **der Kebab** or **der Dönerkebab**. Brought to Berlin by Turkish immigrants, the German version in a flatbread with different salads, cabbages and sauces quickly became one of the most popular snacks in Germany.

Especially in the northern coastal region, bread rolls with fish (often **Bismarckhering** *pickled herring* with salad and onion) are common snacks too.

....

What can you already do?

☺ ☺ ☹

▪ talk about the weather	■ ■ ■	► *Ü2, Ü3*
▪ understand weather forecasts	■ ■ ■	► *Ü1*
▪ write an SMS in German	■ ■ ■	► *Ü2*

In case of an emergency

In this lesson you will learn

- to talk about illness and health
- to give a short accident report
- about body parts

⊙ 2/15 Pierre beim Arzt

Krankenschwester	Herr Dupont. Waren Sie schon einmal bei uns in Behandlung?
Pierre	Nein, das ist das erste Mal.
Krankenschwester	Gut, dann brauche ich Ihre Versicherungskarte, bitte. Und füllen Sie bitte diesen kurzen Fragebogen mit Ihren persönlichen Daten und Informationen zu Allergien und so weiter aus.
Pierre	O. K., hier ist meine Karte.
Krankenschwester	Danke, dann können Sie dort im Wartebereich Platz nehmen und den Fragebogen ausfüllen. Wir rufen Sie dann auf.
Arzt	*(im Behandlungsraum)* Herr Dupont, was tut Ihnen denn weh?
Pierre	Hier am Knöchel schmerzt es beim Auftreten. Ich kann kaum gehen.
Arzt	Was haben Sie denn gemacht? Wie haben Sie sich verletzt?
Pierre	Wir haben ein Museum besichtigt. Auf der Treppe beim Ausgang habe ich eine Stufe übersehen. Dann bin ich ausgerutscht, hingefallen und mit dem Fuß umgeknickt. Zuerst konnte ich noch gehen, aber dann hat es nach ein paar Minuten so wehgetan, dass ich nicht mehr gehen konnte.
Arzt	Hmm ... ja, da ist eine starke Schwellung am Knöchel. Zuerst müssen wir den Fuß röntgen. Dann sehen wir, ob sie ihn gebrochen haben oder nicht. Sonst ist aber alles in Ordnung?
Pierre	Ja.
Arzt	Das ist gut. Warten Sie hier, ich hole einen Pfleger, der Sie zum Röntgen bringt.

Dialogue questions

Mark the right answer.

1. Wie oft war Pierre schon in diesem Krankenhaus?
   a) ☐ Keinmal.   b) ☐ Einmal.
2. Wo hat Pierre Schmerzen?
   a) ☐ Am Fuß.   b) ☐ An der Hand.
3. Wo ist der Unfall passiert?
   a) ☐ Im Krankenhaus.   b) ☐ Im Museum.
4. Wer bringt Pierre zum Röntgen?
   a) ☐ Eine Krankenschwester.   b) ☐ Ein Pfleger.

Pierre goes to see the doctor

Nurse   Mister Dupont. Have you already been treated here before?
Pierre   No, it's the first time.
Nurse   Well, then I need your health insurance card, please. And please fill in this short questionnaire with your personal data and information about allergies and so on.
Pierre   OK, here's my card.
Nurse   Thank you, you can take a seat in the waiting area then and fill in the questionnaire. We'll call you when the doctor will see you.

Doctor   *(in the surgery)* Mister Dupont, where does it hurt?
Pierre   It hurts here in my ankle when I tread on it. I can hardly walk.
Doctor   What have you done? How did you harm yourself?
Pierre   We visited a museum. On the stairs at the exit I missed a step. Then I slipped, fell over and twisted my ankle. At first I still could walk, but then after a few minutes it hurt so much, that I couldn't walk anymore.
Doctor   Hmm ... yes, there's a heavy swelling around your ankle. We'll have to x-ray the foot first. Then we'll see, whether you've broken it or not. But everything else is OK?
Pierre   Yes.
Doctor   That's good. Wait here, I'll get a male nurse, who'll take you for the X-ray.

⊙ 3/18

sich verletzen	hurt (oneself), injure
Arzt, Ärzte *m*	(male) doctor
Ärztin, -nen *f*	(female) doctor
aufrufen	call
auftreten	tread
ausrutschen	slip
behandeln	treat
Behandlung, -en *f*	treatment
einmal	once
Fragebogen, – *m*	questionnaire
hinfallen	fall over
kaum	hardly
Krankenhaus, -häuser *n*	hospital
Kranken-schwester, -n *f*	nurse
Mal, -e *n*	time
umknicken	twist
nicht mehr	not anymore
Pfleger, – *m*	male nurse
Platz nehmen	have a seat
röntgen	x-ray
schon	already, yet
sonst	else
Stufe, -n *f*	stair step
übersehen	overlook
Wartebereich, -e *m*	waiting area
Wartezimmer, – *n*	waiting room
wehtun, schmerzen	hurt

Body parts

Arm, -e *m*	arm
Bauch, Bäuche *m*	stomach, belly
Bein, -e *n*	leg
Fuß, Füße *m*	foot
Gelenk, -e *n*	joint
Hals, Hälse *m*	neck, throat
Hand, Hände *f*	hand
Knöchel, – *m*	ankle
Knochen, – *m*	bone
Kopf, Köpfe *m*	head
Nase, -n *f*	nose
Ohr, -en *n*	ear
Rücken, – *m*	back

Health and illness

(sich) etwas brechen	break
Allergie, -n *f*	allergy
Erkältung, -en *f*	cold
Fieber (*only Sg*) *n*	fever
gesund	healthy
Gesundheit (*only Sg*) *f*	health
Grippe (*only Sg*) *f*	flu
husten	cough
krank	ill
Krankheit, -en *f*	illness
niesen	sneeze
Schmerz, -en *m*	pain
sich gut/schlecht fühlen	feel good/bad
Verletzung, -en *f*	injury

Grammar and means of expression

Perfekt – haben or *sein*? ▸ *§8.2*

You've learned a past tense (the **Präteritum**) already and now it's time to learn another one: the **Perfekt**.

If you're talking about the past you use mostly the **Perfekt** in spoken language. However, as we've already said in the lessons with the **Präteritum**, **haben** and **sein** (as main verbs!) and the modal verbs are still used in **Präteritum**, even in spoken language.

The **Perfekt** is a compound tense built similar to the English present perfect, i.e. you have an auxiliary verb (**haben** or **sein** in present tense ▸ *Day 4*) and the past participle of the main verb. Be careful, though, because the use of German **Perfekt** and the English present perfect differs!

Now, grammatical questions get a bit philosophical, for the question is: to have or to be?

Most German verbs build their **Perfekt** with **haben**:

Was **haben** Sie denn gemacht? *What have you done?*

Wir **haben** ein Museum besichtigt. *We have visited a museum.*

But some verbs have **sein**:

Dann **bin** ich ausgerutscht. *Then I've slipped.*

As a general rule most verbs of movement (like **gehen** *go*, **fahren** *drive*, **ausrutschen** *slip*, **hinfallen** *fall over*) and change of state (like **einschlafen** *fall asleep*, **werden** *become*) build the **Perfekt** with **sein**.

As for the word order: the auxiliary verb (i.e. **haben** or **sein**) is the conjugated verb and therefore stands in the second position. The past participle stands in the last position in the sentence.

Dann **bin** ich ausgerutscht. *Then I slipped.*

Es **hat** so wehgetan. *It hurt so much.*

1 If a certain part of your body hurts, you can sometimes use a composite noun of this part and *-schmerzen* or *-weh*. Write a short sentence about what hurts.

die Gelenkschmerzen – *Meine Gelenke tun weh./Meine Gelenke schmerzen.*

1. das Bauchweh – _____

2. die Zahnschmerzen – _____

3. das Halsweh – _____

4. die Ohrenschmerzen – _____

5. die Kopfschmerzen – _____

⊙ 2/16 🎧 **2** Listen to the CD. You hear some statements about health that help you fill in the gaps. One term from the box is not used.

Rückenschmerzen	gesund	eine Verletzung	eine Erkältung
eine Allergie	eine Grippe	gebrochen	krank

1. Martina hat _____ .
2. Jens hat _____ .
3. Johannes' Fuß ist _____ .
4. Pierre hat _____ .
5. Iwona hat _____ .
6. Peter hat _____ am Arm.
7. Claudia ist _____ .

3 Read the short text. Then give a short accident report as if that had happened to you. Where needed, use Perfekt with the past participles from the box.

ausgewichen	gehört	umgedreht	hingefallen	gefahren
bewegt	wehgetan	gesehen	gegangen	ausgerutscht

Heute ist Freitag, der 13. März. Julia geht im Park spazieren. Julia hört ein Fahrrad kommen und dreht sich um. Ein Mann auf einem Fahrrad fährt sehr schnell in ihre Richtung. Er sieht Julia nicht. Im letzten Moment kann der Mann ausweichen*. Aber Julia rutscht aus und fällt hin. Ihre rechte Hand tut weh und sie kann sie nicht mehr bewegen.

* ausweichen *dodge*

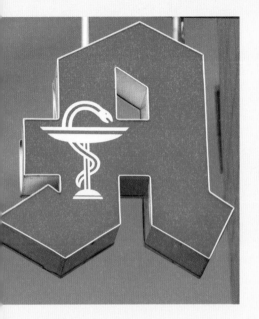

Kulturtipp German health care system

If you're in Germany for a short stay you probably have travel health insurance. If you stay longer to work or study in Germany, you must have health insurance. Usually, as an employee, you and your employer share the cost for health insurance in one of the **gesetzliche Krankenkassen** *government health insurance companies*. If you're self-employed, you have to choose a private insurance company.

You get your medicine in one of the many **Apotheken** *pharmacies*, usually marked with a big red, gothic type A.

What can you already do?

☺ ☻ ☹

- talk about illness and health   ■ ■ ■ ► *Ü1, Ü2*
- give a short accident report   ■ ■ ■ ► *Ü3*
- know body parts   ■ ■ ■ ► *Ü1, Ü2*

Have you been to Germany already? Not yet? Could we whet your appetite to visit Munich for instance or one of the other cities worth seeing? From the language point of view you should be perfectly able to enjoy your stay there!
If you're going to work in Germany or with Germans, just complete this part of the book and then we'll teach you the basics concerning work and business.

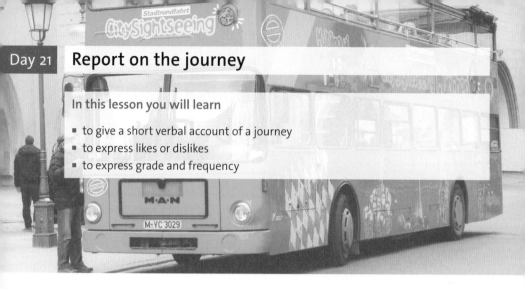

Report on the journey

In this lesson you will learn

- to give a short verbal account of a journey
- to express likes or dislikes
- to express grade and frequency

⊚ 2/17 **Zurück in Berlin**

Zurück in Berlin treffen sich Iwona und Pierre mit Martina und Jens in einem Café.

Martina Mensch, Pierre ... Was ist denn mit deinem Fuß passiert?

Pierre Ich bin ausgerutscht, als ich aus dem Museum gegangen bin.
Wenn es wieder besser ist, muss ich hier wieder zum Arzt zur Kontrolle.

Jens Oje, das ist schlimm. Aber wie war euer Ausflug? Hattet ihr trotzdem schöne Tage?

Martina Erzählt doch bitte!

Iwona Ja, wir hatten schöne Tage in München und Pierres Unfall war erst am Samstag. Wir sind am Donnerstag mit dem Zug nach München gefahren. Aber die Fahrt war etwas langweilig.

Pierre Als wir dann in München waren, sind wir zuerst zum Hotel gegangen und haben eingecheckt. Dann haben wir noch etwas im Stadtzentrum gegessen und sind früh ins Bett gegangen.

Iwona Und am Freitag sind wir früh aufgestanden. Zuerst haben wir eine kleine Stadtrundfahrt gemacht. Das hat mir sehr gefallen. Nach dem Mittagessen sind wir dann auf das Oktoberfest gegangen.

Pierre Das war echt toll. So ein großes Volksfest habe ich noch nicht erlebt!

Iwona Ja, ich auch nicht. Aber es war sehr voll. Das hat mir nicht so gefallen. Am Samstag waren wir im Englischen Garten und in einem Museum und – nach Pierres Unfall – im Krankenhaus!

Dialogue questions

Answer the questions briefly.

1. An welchem Tag war Pierres Unfall?

2. Was haben Iwona und Pierre in München zuerst gemacht?

3. Was hat Iwona in München gefallen?

4. Wann waren Pierre und Iwona auf dem Oktoberfest? Am Vormittag oder Nachmittag?

Back in Berlin

Back in Berlin Iwona and Pierre meet Martina and Jens in a café.

Martina Blimey, Pierre ... What has happened to your foot?

Pierre I slipped, when leaving the museum. When it's better again, I'll have to see the doctor here for checkup.

Jens Oh dear, that's bad. But how was your trip? Did you have nice days anyway?

Martina Tell us, please!

Iwona Yes, we've had nice days in Munich and Pierre's accident was not until Saturday. We went to Munich by train on Thursday. But the journey was a bit boring.

Pierre When we were in Munich, we went to the hotel first and checked in. Then we ate something in the city centre and went to bed early.

Iwona And on Friday we got up early. First we went on a short sightseeing tour. I liked that very much. After lunch we went to the Oktoberfest.

Pierre That was really terrific. I haven't experienced such a big fair in my life!

Iwona Yes, neither have I. But it was very crowded. I didn't like that very much. On Saturday we were in the English Garden and in a museum and – after Pierre's accident – in the hospital!

⊙ 3/19

Das finde ich gut/ schlecht.	I think that's good/bad.
Das gefällt mir (nicht).	I (don't) like that.
eintönig	monotonous
erzählen	tell
gefallen	like
informativ	informative
interessant	interesting
Kontrolle, -n f	checkup
langweilig	boring
Mensch!/ Meine Güte!	Blimey!
Oje!	Oh dear!
passieren	happen
schlimm	bad
spannend	fascinating
trotzdem	anyway
Unfall, Unfälle m	accident
Volksfest, -e n	fair
voll	crowded

Adverbs of grade

gar nicht/ überhaupt nicht	not at all
nicht so (sehr)	not that much, not very much
etwas	somewhat, a little
total	totally
wenig	little
ein bisschen	a bit
sehr	very

Temporal adverbs of order

zuerst	(at) first
zuletzt, zum Schluss	lastly
dann, danach	then

Temporal adverbs of frequency

immer	always
manchmal, ab und zu	sometimes
nie	never
oft, häufig	often
selten	rarely

Grammar and means of expression

Perfekt – the past participle ▸ *§8.2*

How to build the past participle? For most verbs it's easy, because you have the infinitive as a base for the participle. This is the case with the so called regular verbs. With the irregular verbs, you have to learn the forms with the verb tables in the appendix.

For a general overview over the regular verbs look at the following table:

verb type	infinitive	transformation	past participle	rule
"normal"	machen	**ge** + mache̶n̶ + **t**	gemacht	For regular verbs without a prefix you add **ge**- prefix, omit -**en** ending and put -**t** instead (-**et** if it ends on **t** or **d**)
	warten	**ge** + warte̶n̶ + **et**	gewartet	
non-separable prefix	verletzen	verletze̶n̶ + **t**	verletzt	Just keep the prefix, ending the same as above.
separable prefix	einchecken	ein + **ge** + checke̶n̶ + **t**	eingecheckt	-**ge**- is put in between, right after the prefix, ending the same as above.

The rules regarding the prefixes are also valid for the irregular forms! The past participle of regular verbs always ends with -**t**, that of irregular verbs always with -**en**!

Temporal subordinate clauses with *wenn* and *als* ▸ *§9*

Both conjunctions are translated as "when" in English. You use them, when you want to specify a certain point in time. If referring to a one-time event in the past, you use **als**, in all other cases **wenn**.
Ich bin ausgerutscht, **als** ich aus dem Museum gegangen bin.
I slipped, when leaving the museum.
Wenn es wieder besser ist, muss ich hier wieder zum Arzt.
When it's better again, I'll have to see the doctor here.

1 Put the adverbs from the box on the scales. Decide which word belongs to which scale and sort them accordingly starting with the least.

ein bisschen   immer   sehr   total   wenig   nie
gar nicht   etwas   oft   manchmal   nicht so   selten

Grade:
1. ....   5. ....
2. ....   6. ....
3. ....   7. ....
4. ....

Frequency:
1. ....   4. ....
2. ....   5. ....
3. ....

⊙ 2/18 **2** Listen to the account of Martina's and Jens' journey. Who liked (☺) and who didn't like (☹) what? Write the names on the appropriate line.

	☺	☹
1. Prag	....	....
2. die Fahrt	....	....
3. die Innenstadt	....	....
4. die Kirchen	....	....
5. die Burg	....	....
6. die Läden	....	....
7. der Urlaub	....	....

3 Tell your friend what you've seen on your weekend trip and whether you liked it or not. Use the past tense.

Museum: *Ich war im Museum. Das hat mir nicht so gefallen. Das war langweilig.*
1. Ausstellung: ....
2. Kirche: ....
3. Spaziergang: ....
4. Zugfahrt: ....
5. Markt: ....
6. Restaurant: ....

Kulturtipp
Tourism in Germany

Over 50% of the foreigners that come to Germany each year, come on holiday. Most visitors are from Europe, but a great number are from the U.S.A. and a growing number from the far east, especially China.

City breaks are very popular, with Berlin and Munich being the top destinations. Another common way to spend the holidays in Germany are round trips through the country. It's no surprise that, for most, the main reason to come to Germany are the country's sights. But there are also travellers who come to Germany for holidays in the country-side, to relax and enjoy the nature. And Germany has a lot to offer: A lot of interesting cities with a long history, castles and palaces, mountains, big forests and nature reserves, lakes, the northern coastal region and much more ... So everyone can find their favourite spot!

What can you already do?

☺ ☺ ☹

- give an account of a journey ▸ *Ü3*
- express likes or dislikes ▸ *Ü2, Ü3*
- express grade and frequency ▸ *Ü1*

Repeat and practise

Here you repeat

- talking about the weather
- understanding directions
- talking about plans
- the topic of health and illnesses

1 Build the past participles of the verbs in the box and then sort them into the table depending on their auxiliary verb used in *Perfekt*.

| regnen ansehen ausfüllen ausrutschen einchecken fahren finden gefallen gehen hinfallen husten machen niesen planen sagen schmerzen übernachten übersehen verletzen wegfahren wehtun schneien |

haben

sein

2 Which word does not belong here? Cross out the wrong one.

1. Nase, Bauch, Kopf, Halsweh, Rücken
2. Bahnhof, Gleis, Bahnsteig, Fahrkarte, Baustelle
3. Kopfweh, Grippe, Gesundheit, Verletzung, Allergie
4. Zug, Sitzplatz, Flugzeug, Auto, Straßenbahn
5. Bratwurst, Riesenrad, Karussell, Fahrgeschäft, Achterbahn
6. eisig, wenig, sonnig, neblig, windig

3 Fill in the gaps with the appropriate forms of *haben* or *sein*.

Gestern _____ (1.) ich einkaufen gegangen. Im Supermarkt _____ (2.) ich ein-

en Freund getroffen. Ich _____ (3.) meine Einkäufe bezahlt und wir _____ (4.)

zusammen in ein Café gegangen. Im Café _____ (5.) ich ein Stück Torte bestellt

und eine große Tasse Cappuccino. Mein Freund _____ (6.) Apfelkuchen bestellt

und ein Glas Cola. Wir _____ (7.) viel geredet. Danach _____ (8.) wir noch einen

Spaziergang durch die Stadt gemacht. Wir _____ (9.) auch auf den Marktplatz

gegangen. Dort _____ (10.) gerade Wochenmarkt. Mein Freund _____ (11.)

noch frisches Obst gekauft. Dann _____ (12.) wir uns verabschiedet und ich

_____ (13.) die Straßenbahn genommen und _____ (14.) nach Hause gefahren.

4 Listen to the CD. You'll hear five people giving directions. Follow the   ⊙ 2/19
directions and write down what building is at the end of each route.

1. _____

2. _____

3. _____

4. _____

5. _____

5 Fill in the gaps with the correct prepositions.

1. _____ Sommer ist es oft sehr heiß.

2. Wir treffen uns _____ 14 Uhr im Café am Marktplatz.

3. _____ 4. Mai habe ich Geburtstag.

4. Ich habe _____ Mai Geburtstag.

5. Wann treffen wir uns? – _____ a) Donnerstag, _____ b) 17 Uhr.

6. _____ a) Vormittag arbeite ich und _____ b) Nachmittag lerne ich Deutsch.

6 Put the sentences in the Perfekt in the correct order.

1. Iwona / sind / einkaufen / Pierre / und / gestern / gegangen / .

   ....

2. du / gemacht / die Aufgabe / richtig / hast / !

   ....

3. Martina / wann / eingecheckt / im Hotel / hat / ?

   ....

4. gesehen / hast / in München / was / du / ?

   ....

5. ich / nach Hamburg / gefahren / bin / gestern / .

   ....

◉ 2/20 **7** Read the phrases in the box and then listen to the CD. You will hear some questions. Choose the correct answer from the box (one is not used) and say it out loud after the beep. You can hear the correct answer after the next beep.

> Nicht direkt. Wir müssen noch 5 Minuten laufen.   Am besten nehmen wir den Bus.
> Nein, am Samstag wollen wir eine Radtour machen.   Um 19.30 Uhr.
> Im Sommer fahren wir Fahrrad.   Am Mittwoch, den 3. Juli.

8 Read the sentences and insert the missing reflexive pronouns.

1. Es ist 13 Uhr und der Zug fährt um 13.14 Uhr ab. Wir müssen .... beeilen!
2. Frau Gerber, wie fühlen Sie .... ? a) – Ach, heute fühle ich
   .... b) nicht gut!
3. Möchtest du noch etwas trinken? Dort stehen Getränke und du darfst
   .... einfach bedienen.
4. Iwona und Pierre gehen noch in die Stadt. Aber zuerst will Iwona
   .... waschen.
5. Mensch, was ist passiert? Wie habt ihr .... verletzt?

◉ 2/21 **9** Read the sentences below and then listen to the weather reports. Mark:

	right	wrong
1. In Köln regnet es.	☐	☐
2. Das Wetter in Hamburg ist schön.	☐	☐
3. In München regnet es am Vormittag.	☐	☐
4. In Berlin ist es warm.	☐	☐
5. In Stuttgart ist es kalt.	☐	☐

10 Complete the sentences with *und*, *oder*, *aber* or *denn*.

1. Ich gehe gern ins Kino, _____ ich mag Filme.
2. Pierre hat zwei Schwestern, _____ keinen Bruder.
3. Iwonas Eltern haben eine Tochter _____ einen Sohn.
4. Fahren Iwona und Pierre nach München _____ nach Köln?
5. Martina ist Deutschlehrerin _____ Jens ist Informatiker.
6. Ich bin krank, _____ ich gehe nicht zum Arzt!
7. Martina geht zum Arzt, _____ sie ist krank.

11 Read the questions below. Then listen to the announcements at the station ⊙ 2/22 and answer the questions.

1. Wie viel Verspätung hat der Zug nach München?

_____

2. Woher kommt der Zug an Gleis 3?

_____

3. Wohin fährt der Regionalexpress?

_____

4. Welcher Zug fährt nach Hamburg?

_____

5. Auf welchem Gleis fährt der Zug nach Potsdam ab?

_____

6. Wohin fährt der ICE?

_____

12 Describe the typical German weather for each season. Use adverbs of frequency too.

Frühling: _____

Sommer: _____

Herbst: _____

Winter: _____

🗨 **13** Read about Iwona's plans for next summer. Write down your own plans in 5 or 6 sentences following her example. Then present your plans to a friend.

> Im Sommer möchte ich nach Italien fahren, am liebsten nach Rom. Dort will ich das Kolosseum* sehen und den Petersdom** besichtigen. Aber zuerst will ich eine Stadtrundfahrt machen. Und dann möchte ich in ein Café gehen und Espresso trinken. Ich mache auch einen Spaziergang in der Stadt. Das finde ich toll!

* das Kolosseum *Colosseum*
** der Petersdom *St. Peter's Basilica*

....
....
....
....
....
....
....

📖 **14** Find the generic term for the lexical fields below.

1. .... : Ohren, Beine, Hände
2. .... : Karussell, Achterbahn, Riesenrad
3. .... : ICE, Regionalbahn, Intercity
4. .... : Sonne, Regen, Schnee
5. .... : Schalter, Gleis, Fahrplan
6. .... : Röntgen, Pfleger, Behandlungsraum
7. .... : Grippe, Erkältung, Halsschmerzen

📝 **15** Complete the sentences with *wenn* or *als*.

1. .... ich auf dem Oktoberfest war, bin ich Karussell gefahren.

2. Im Sommer stehe ich morgens auf, ... die Sonne aufgeht.

3. .... a) ich ein Kind war, habe ich immer eine Schokolade bekommen,

   .... b) ich mit meiner Mutter einkaufen war.

4. .... ich auf dem Oktoberfest bin, will ich mit der Achterbahn fahren.

5. Ich muss wieder zum Arzt, ... mein Fieber bleibt.

16 Imagine you have the following illnesses. Describe the symptoms or how you feel briefly. Exercise 2 in lesson 20 can help you.

| Grippe   Allergie   Erkältung   Halsweh   Verletzung am Knöchel |

....

....

....

....

....

....

....

....

17 Complete the crossword. The grey fields show the solution.

1. flu
2. sneeze
3. sore throat
4. stomach
5. cold

6. hand
7. bone
8. illness
9. fever
10. cough

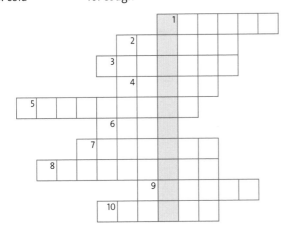

Solution: ....

Intermediate test 3

1 Read the text and fill in the gaps with the correct word from the box. Make sure to use the appropriate forms (e.g. plural).

> immer   Englisch   Jugendherberge   ein Fahrradverleih   sind   für
> haben   sich   Stockwerk   Bett   morgens   wir   Doppelzimmer
> wollen   Sehenswürdigkeit   sprechen   denn   fragen

Willkommen in unserer _____ (1.)!
Suchen Sie eine günstige Übernachtung? Dann _____ (2.) Sie hier genau
richtig! Wir _____ (3.) 10 Einzelzimmer und 20 _____ (4.).
Und für Gruppen haben wir auch Zimmer mit 4–10 _____ (5.). Duschen
und WCs finden Sie auf jedem _____ (6.).
_____ (7.) gibt es Frühstück und Sie können auch ein kleines Essen
_____ (8.) den Tag mitnehmen.
_____ (9.) haben auch verschiedene Sportangebote: einen Fußballplatz,
Tischtennisplatten*, _____ (10.).
_____ (11.) Sie die Stadt besichtigen? Unser Team hilft Ihnen
_____ (12.) gerne: _____ (13.) Sie nach dem Weg, nach
_____ (14.), nach Verkehrsmitteln ... Sie sprechen nicht Deutsch? Das ist
kein Problem, _____ (15.) mit uns können Sie _____ (16.),
Französisch, Spanisch und Italienisch _____ (17.)!
Wir freuen _____ (18.) auf Ihren Besuch!

___/18   * die Tischtennisplatte *table tennis table*

2 Read the text from the previous exercise again and mark if the following phrases are right or wrong.

	right	wrong
1. Übernachten in der Jugendherberge ist teuer.	☐	☐
2. In der Jugendherberge gibt es mehr als 30 Zimmer.	☐	☐
3. Es gibt auch Zimmer für 10 Personen.	☐	☐
4. In jedem Zimmer gibt es eine Dusche.	☐	☐
5. Es gibt auch Abendessen in der Jugendherberge.	☐	☐
6. Es gibt einen Sportplatz und ein Schwimmbad.	☐	☐
7. Das Team hilft gerne bei Fragen.	☐	☐
8. Die Leute dort sprechen auch Spanisch.	☐	☐

___/8

3 Listen to the short dialogues on the CD and find the matching situations.   ⊙ 2/23

1. Beim Arzt: _____

2. Auf dem Bahnhof: _____

3. Im Hotel: _____

4. Auf dem Oktoberfest: _____

5. Auf der Straße: _____   _/5

4 Fill in the gaps with the missing prepositions and articles. But be careful, not all words in the box are used!

> beim   zur   bei   nach   zu   mit dem
> nach   seit dem   mit   aus   mit der

1. Ich bin _____ England.

2. Ich fahre morgen _____ Berlin.

3. Können Sie mir sagen, wie ich _____ Frauenkirche komme?

4. Wie fahren wir _____ a) München? _____ b) Auto oder
   _____ c) Bahn?

5. _____ Unfall habe ich oft Kopfweh.

6. Das Hotel ist direkt _____ Bahnhof.   _/8

5 Read the questions and listen to David's plans for the summer. Then mark the   ⊙ 2/24
right answer.

1. Wann geht David nach England?
   a) ☐ Am 14. Juni.   b) ☐ Am 4. Juli.   c) ☐ Am 14. Juli.
2. Wie lange bleibt David in London?
   a) ☐ 4 Tage.   b) ☐ 8 Tage.   c) ☐ 14 Tage.
3. Wohin geht David zuletzt?
   a) ☐ Nach London.   b) ☐ Nach Oxford.   c) ☐ Nach Brighton.
4. Was will David in London nicht sehen?
   a) ☐ Den Hyde Park.   b) ☐ Das British Museum.   c) ☐ Madame Tussauds.
5. Was macht David dann in Brighton?
   a) ☐ Etwas besichtigen.   b) ☐ Einkaufen.   c) ☐ Faulenzen.   _/5

6 Transform the questions into subordinate clauses.

1. Was hast du in Prag besichtigt?

   Erzähl doch mal, _____.

2. Wo ist das Hotel „Seeblick"?

   Können Sie mir bitte sagen, _____?

3. Wie haben Sie sich verletzt?

   Sagen Sie mir bitte, _____.

4. Wer hat dir geschrieben?

   Weißt du, _____?

5. Wann warst du im Urlaub?

   Ich möchte gern wissen, _____.

6. Warum hast du das gemacht?

   __/6   Kannst du mir sagen, _____?

__/50

On the phone

In this lesson you will learn

- to say hello and goodbye on the phone
- to leave messages
- to ask about people

⊙ 2/25 **Iwona am Telefon**

Iwona muss zur Vorbereitung einer Präsentation für ihre Firma einige Anrufe machen.

Frau List Firma Steigmann, List am Apparat.

Iwona Guten Tag, Iwona Nowak von der Firma Consult hier in Berlin. Kann ich bitte mit Herrn Steigmann sprechen?

Frau List Tut mir leid, aber Herr Steigmann ist heute nicht im Büro. Kann ich Ihnen vielleicht weiterhelfen?

Iwona Ja, vielleicht: Am Donnerstag nächste Woche findet bei Ihnen eine Besprechung statt. Ich bereite die Präsentation vor und habe noch ein paar Fragen. Haben Sie einen Beamer und könnten wir ihn am Donnerstag benutzen?

Frau List Ja, wir haben einen. Ich werde sicherstellen, dass niemand ihn an dem Tag benutzt. Brauchen Sie auch einen Laptop?

Iwona Nein, ich bringe selbst einen mit. Aber haben Sie vielleicht ein Whiteboard?

Frau List Nein, wir haben keins, tut mir leid. Aber wir haben ein Flipchart im Besprechungszimmer. Reicht das?

Iwona Ja, das reicht auch, vielen Dank. Gut, dann ist alles vorbereitet. Ich muss aber Herrn Steigmann persönlich auch noch einige Fragen stellen ... Können Sie ihm bitte ausrichten, dass er mich zurückrufen soll? Meine Telefonnummer ist 0154 223456678.

Frau List Gut, ich schreibe ihm eine Notiz.

Iwona Vielen Dank. Auf Wiederhören.

Frau List Auf Wiederhören.

Dialogue questions

Mark with a cross:

	right	wrong
1. Iwona ruft bei der Firma Consult an.	☐	☐
2. Herr Steigmann ist im Büro.	☐	☐
3. Iwona hat einen eigenen Laptop.	☐	☐
4. Iwona muss noch mit Herrn Steigmann sprechen.	☐	☐

Iwona on the phone

Iwona has to make a few phone calls for her company in connexion with her preparation of a presentation.

Frau List Steigmann company, List speaking.

Iwona Good morning, Iwona Nowak of Consult company here in Berlin. Could I speak to Mr Steigmann, please?

Frau List I'm sorry, but Mr Steigmann is not in the office today. Maybe I can help you with something?

Iwona Yes, please. Next Thursday in your office a meeting is taking place. I'm preparing the presentation and I have a few questions. Do you have a video projector and could I use it on Thursday?

Frau List Yes, we have one. I will make sure that nobody's going to use it on that day. Do you need a laptop too?

Iwona No, I'll bring my own. But do you have a whiteboard?

Frau List No, we haven't , I'm sorry. But we have a flip chart in the meeting room. Is that enough?

Iwona Yes, that's enough of course, thank you. Well, all's set then. But I still have to ask Mr Steigmann a few questions personally ... Could you leave him a message if he could call me back, please? My phone number is 0154 223456678.

Frau List Very well, I'll make a note.

Iwona Thank you very much. Goodbye.

Frau List Goodbye.

⊙ 3/20

Anruf, -e *m*	(telephone) call
Anrufbeantworter, – *m*	answering machine
anrufen	call, phone
Anschluss, Anschlüsse *m*	line, telephone connection
Apparat, -e *m*	here: telephone, phone
Auf Wiederhören. *(only phone)*	Goodbye.
ausrichten	leave/deliver a message
benutzen	use
Besprechung, -en *f*	meeting
Besprechungszimmer, – *n*	meeting room
Büro, -s *n*	office
erreichen	reach
Festnetzanschluss, -anschlüsse *m*	landline
Flipchart, -s *n*	flip chart
hinterlassen	leave
mitbringen	bring along
Nachricht, -en *f*	message
Notiz, -en *f*	note

Null, -en *f*	zero
Nummer, -n *f*	number
persönlich	personally
Piepston, -töne *m*	beep, pip
reichen	be enough
Rufnummer, -n *f*	phone number
sicherstellen	make sure
stattfinden	take place
Telefon, -e *n*	phone/telephone
telefonieren	call, phone, talk over the phone
Telefonnummer, -n *f*	phone number
verbinden	put through
verwählen	dial the wrong number
vorbereiten	prepare
Vorbereitung, -en *f*	preparation
wählen	dial
Whiteboard, -s *n*	whiteboard
weiterhelfen	help
zurückrufen	call back

Grammar and means of expression

Indefinite pronouns I – *einer, keiner* ▸ *§3.5.1*

You already know the indefinite article **ein** and the negation article **kein**. These pronouns look almost identical to the articles, but they are not articles because they stand alone, instead of a noun!

You saw in the dialogue that Iwona asks about a video projector.

Haben Sie einen Beamer? *Do you have a video projector?*

And Ms List answers without repeating the noun using the pronoun instead.

Ja, wir haben **einen**. *Yes, we have one.*

Iwona asks for a whiteboard too which they don't have. That's why Frau List answers:

Nein, wir haben **keins**. *No, we haven't.*

Look at the following table with the forms of the indefinite pronouns and notice differences to the articles highlighted bold.

	m	f	n	Pl
Nom.	ein**er**/kein**er**	eine/kein	ein**s**/kein**s**	–/keine
Acc.	einen/keinen	eine/keine	ein**s**/kein**s**	–/keine
Dat.	einem/keinem	ein**er**/kein**er**	einem/keinem	–/keinen

Indefinite pronouns II – *alles, alle, etwas, jemand, nichts, niemand* ▸ *§3.5.3*

These indefinite pronouns are easy to use, they are like their English counterparts. Normally they don't change because of gender or case (while not often used in spoken language, there are accusative and dative forms for **jemand** and **niemand** – see the grammar in the back). These pronouns either refer to people (**alle** *everybody*, **jemand** *someone/somebody*, **niemand** *no one/nobody*) or things (**alles** *everything*, **etwas** *something*, **nichts** *nothing*).

Be careful: If you use **alle** as a subject you need the verb in the third person plural – for all others (including **alles**) use the third person singular.

⊙ 2/26 🎧 **1** Listen to the short phone calls and answering machine messages and write down the phone numbers you hear.

1. _____   3. _____   5. _____

2. _____   4. _____   6. _____

💬 **2** Read the situations. Then choose the right German phrase from the box and say it loud.

> Kann ich etwas ausrichten?   Meine Telefonnummer ist 030 998766.
> Kann ich bitte mit Frau Meisner sprechen?   Auf Wiederhören.
> Bleiben Sie bitte am Apparat.   Rufen Sie mich bitte zurück.
> Entschuldigung, ich habe mich verwählt.   Am Apparat.
> Sagen Sie ihm bitte, dass ich angerufen habe.

1. Ask someone to call you back.
2. Say your phone number.
3. Ask for the person you want to talk with.
4. A caller asked if he could talk to you. Say that it's you speaking.
5. Ask the other to hold the line.
6. Apologise for dialing the wrong number.
7. Ask if you should deliver a message.
8. Ask to convey the message that you've called.
9. Say goodbye on the phone.

📝 **3** Fill in the gaps using indefinite pronouns.

1. Hast du einen Festnetzanschluss? – Nein, ich habe _____ . Ich habe nur ein Handy.

2. Ich bestelle einen Kuchen. Willst du auch a) _____ ? – Nein, danke.

   Ich will b) _____ .

3. Ich habe das nicht verstanden – _____ konnte es für mich übersetzen.

4. Leider habe ich _____ verstanden.

5. Kommt a) _____ mit? – Ja, b) _____ kommen mit!

6. Ist dort ein Beamer? – Nein, dort ist _____ .

Kulturtipp
Phoning home

When you need a public phone, look for the magenta coloured booths or racks. Magenta is the corporate colour of **Deutsche Telekom**, the German telecommunications company, which provides most of the public phones. To phone there you need coins, a **Telefonkarte** *telephone card*, a credit card or **a Calling-Card** *telephone card with a PIN and a landline number.* You can buy telephone cards at the post office, in **Telekom Shops** and kiosks or supermarkets.

An alternative can be a German prepaid SIM card for your mobile. By now there are lots of different providers and you can buy such cards even in discount supermarkets and chemist's shops or via internet. But be careful: Often you can't make your first call at once because by law the providers need your name and address before they can activate your card. And sometimes you can do that only online.

What can you already do?

☺ ☺ ☹

■ say hello and goodbye on the phone	☐	☐	☐	▸ *Ü1, Ü2*
■ leave messages	☐	☐	☐	▸ *Ü1, Ü2*
■ ask about people	☐	☐	☐	▸ *Ü1, Ü2*

Well, the last part of this book has begun. You have made it this far and now you can understand and say a lot. Congratulations! The rest is now a piece of cake ... enjoy the last part!

E-mails

In this lesson you will learn

- to write formal e-mails
- to understand a formal e-mail
- common salutations and valedictions

⊚ 2/27 **Pierres Pläne**

Pierre besucht Jens in seinem Büro.

Pierre Hi, Jens. Hast du kurz Zeit?

Jens Hi, Pierre. Klar, komm rein! Was gibt's denn?

Pierre Mein Praktikum ist ja bald zu Ende. Ich möchte nach meinem Abschluss gerne in Deutschland weiterarbeiten. Aber wenn ich hier bleiben will, dann muss ich mich jetzt bewerben. Kannst du mir da ein paar Tipps geben?

Jens Ja, natürlich! Was willst du denn wissen?

Pierre Eine Firma will zum Beispiel, dass ich die Bewerbung per E-Mail verschicke. Meine Bewerbung hier war per Post. Muss ich da noch etwas beachten?

Jens Eigentlich nicht. Für eine Online-Bewerbung gilt das Gleiche wie für eine auf Papier.

Pierre Aha, dann scanne ich einfach meine Zeugnisse ein und schicke sie als Anhang mit?

Jens Ja, aber es ist wichtig, dass alle deine Dateien lesen können. Wenn ein Personalchef eine Datei nicht öffnen kann, bekommst du die Stelle sicher nicht!

Pierre Stimmt, das merke ich mir!

Jens Und schau genau, was die Firma wirklich braucht. Schick keine unnötigen Dokumente! Am besten du machst eine einzelne PDF-Datei aus deinen Bewerbungsunterlagen – dann ist die E-Mail auch nicht zu groß. Hast du noch eine Frage?

Pierre Nein, das ist alles. Vielen Dank.

Jens Aber klar!

Dialogue questions

Answer the questions briefly.

1. Was will Pierre von Jens? ....

2. Was will Pierre nach dem Abschluss machen? ....

3. Wie kann Pierre seine Bewerbung verschicken? ....

4. Was macht Pierre mit seinen Zeugnissen? ....

Pierre's plans

Pierre visits Jens in his office.

Pierre   Hi, Jens. Have you got a moment?

Jens   Hi, Pierre. Sure, come on in! What's the matter?

Pierre   My internship is going to end soon. After my degree, I'd like to continue working in Germany. But if I want to stay, I have to apply for a job now. Could you give me a few tips?

Jens   Yes, of course! What do you want to know?

Pierre   One company, for instance, wants me to send my application by e-mail. My application here was by mail. Do I have to pay attention to something?

Jens   Actually, no. The same applies for an online application as for one on paper.

Pierre   I see. Then I just need to scan my certificates and send them as an attachment?

Jens   Yes, but it's important that everybody could read your files. If the personnel manager can't open a file, you won't get the job for sure!

Pierre   True, I'll keep that in mind!

Jens   And pay attention to what the company really needs. Don't send unnecessary documents! The best way is to make one single PDF file from your application documents – then also the e-mail isn't too big. Do you have some more questions?

Pierre   No, that's all. Thanks a lot.

Jens   You're welcome!

Vocabulary

3/21

Abschluss, Abschlüsse *m*	degree
arbeiten	work
Arbeitgeber, – *m*	employer
Arbeitnehmer, – *m*	employee
Arbeitsplatz, -plätze *m*	job, position
beachten	pay attention to
bewerben	apply
Bewerbung, -en *f*	job application
bleiben	stay
das Gleiche	the same
Dokument, -e *n*	document
einzeln	single
gelten	apply
öffnen	open
per	by
Personalchef, -s *m*	personnel manager
Planung, -en *f*	planning
Post *(only Sg) f*	mail
scannen	scan
Stelle, -n *f*	job
Stellenanzeige, -n *f*	job advertisement
unnötig	unnecessary
Unterlagen *(only Pl)*	documents
weiterarbeiten	continue working
wichtig	important
Zeugnis, -se *n*	certificate
zu Ende sein	to end

E-mails	
Absender, – *m*	sender
an	to
Anhang, Anhänge *m*	attachment
Antwort, -en *f*	reply, answer
antworten	reply, answer
Betreff, -e *m*	subject
E-Mail-Adresse, -n *f*	e-mail address
Empfänger, – *m*	recipient
Posteingang, -eingänge *m*	in-box
schicken	send
senden	send
verschicken	send
von	from
weiterleiten	forward

Grammar and means of expression

Conditional clauses ‣ §9

Conditional clauses are subordinate clauses that usually begin with **wenn** *if* and state a condition. The main clause contains the outcome if the condition comes true.
For the word order let's look at the example:
Wenn ich hier bleiben will, (dann) muss ich mich jetzt bewerben.
If I want to stay, I have to apply for a job now.

You can swap the order of main and subordinate clause:
Ich muss mich bewerben, **wenn** ich hier bleiben will.
The word order in the conditional clause is clear: conjunction first and verb last.
In the first example the subordinate clause (including the optional **dann**) takes the first position in the main clause – that's why the verb is now positioned before the subject.

Writing a formal e-mail (or letter)

If you don't know who will receive the e-mail you use the salutation
Sehr geehrte Damen und Herren, ... *Dear Madam or Sir, ...*
You can also write **Guten Tag** or even **Hallo**, but that's already less formal.
However, for formal correspondence it's always better to address the recipient personally by name:
Sehr geehrte Frau Nowak, ... *Dear Ms Nowak, ...*
Guten Tag, Herr Dupont, ...
Not limited to private mails is the use of **Liebe/r Frau/Herr** ... *Dear Ms/Mr* or **Hallo Frau/Herr ...**, but you should use it only if there's a friendly relationship between you and the recipient.
The valediction does not differ whether you know the recipient's name or not.
The formal standard for all kinds of formal correspondence is:
Mit freundlichen Grüßen *Yours sincerely/faithfully*
A more familiar valediction (for all recipients you address with **Liebe/r**) can be the following:
Es grüßt Sie herzlich
Herzliche/Liebe Grüße *Best/Kind regards*

Exercises

1 Read Iwona's e-mail and fill in the gaps with the words/phrases from the box. Not all words/phrases are used!

> anrufen Besprechung Fragen geplant Hallo Liebe mich mir
> Mit freundlichen Grüßen schicken Sehr geehrte Sie telefoniert
> Tschüs weil wenn wir zwei

Neue E-Mail

An:

Kopie:

Betreff: Planung der ....(1.) am Donnerstag, 23.4

Von:

.... (2.) Frau List,

wir haben ja vor ein paar Tagen .... (3.). Gestern habe ich mit Herrn Steigmann gesprochen und ich soll Ihnen noch die Details zur Besprechung .... (4.). Ich komme mit .... (5.) Kollegen. Wir haben zwei Präsentationen .... (6.): eine Präsentation dauert etwa 30 Minuten, die andere etwa 60. Am Schluss ist noch Zeit für .... (7.) und Antworten. Wenn Sie noch Fragen zur Planung haben, dann schicken .... (8.) mir eine E-Mail oder rufen Sie .... (9.) an.

.... (10.)

Iwona Nowak

2 Read the e-mail above again and answer the questions.

1. Was soll Iwona Frau List schicken? ....
2. Wie viele Personen von Consult gehen zur Firma Steigmann? ....
3. Was soll Frau List machen, wenn sie Fragen hat? ....

3 Write the following sentences in one using *wenn*.

1. Ich esse etwas. Ich habe Hunger.

....

2. Wir fahren nach München. Wir gehen auf das Oktoberfest.

....

3. Ich rufe dich an. Du gibst mir deine Telefonnummer.

....

Kulturtipp German (formal) e-mail style

Regarding form and orthography, Germans can be quite picky – and that concerns e-mails too (or at least formal and business e-mails). So even brief e-mails normally have the formal salutation and valediction. Just think about an e-mail like a letter and write it with equal care.

And give the e-mail's subject a thought or two, too! If the recipient gets hundred or more e-mails a day a concise subject is more than important.

Before you send your German e-mail, don't forget to run a spell check or – for important e-mails like a job application – give it to a German native speaker to read it.

Since e-mail is a form of communication not unlike a personal talk, more or less the same rules apply. If you're writing your first formal e-mails and you don't know the recipients yet, it's never a problem if you're rather formal in the beginning. If the correspondence continues you'll see how the others write and you can adapt to their style and formulations.

As long as you don't yet know the habits, it's better not to use acronyms (like ASAP or BTW – yes, those can be used in Germany too) or smiles and emoticons.

What can you already do?

	☺ ☺ ☹	
■ write formal e-mails	▢ ▢ ▢	▸ *Ü1*
■ understand formal e-mails	▢ ▢ ▢	▸ *Ü2*
■ know common salutations and valedictions	▢ ▢ ▢	▸ *Ü1*

Making appointments

In this lesson you will learn

- to make appointments
- to agree to appointments and to decline
- date, time, days

⊙ 2/28 **Wann haben Sie denn Zeit?**

Pierre sitzt in seinem Büro als auf einmal sein Handy klingelt ...

Pierre	Pierre Dupont.
Herr Maler	Maler, von der Firma Gleisser, Hamburg. Tag, Herr Dupont. Sie haben sich bei uns beworben – ist das richtig?
Pierre	Ja, das stimmt.
Herr Maler	Vor mir liegt Ihre Bewerbung, die mir sehr gut gefallen hat. Wir möchten Sie gerne zu einem persönlichen Gespräch einladen.
Pierre	Oh, das ist toll!
Herr Maler	Herr Dupont, wann haben Sie denn Zeit, zu uns zu kommen? Welcher Tag passt Ihnen denn am besten?
Pierre	Hmm ... am besten passt mir Donnerstag oder Freitag. Da habe ich nachmittags fast immer Zeit.
Herr Maler	Gut. Wie ist dann Donnerstag, der 18.5.?
Pierre	Der 18. Mai? Einen Moment, bitte ... Nein, tut mir leid, ausgerechnet da habe ich schon einen Zahnarzttermin ...
Herr Maler	Und einen Tag später, am Freitag?
Pierre	Ja, Freitag, der 19., ist gut. Da habe ich keine Termine!
Herr Maler	Wunderbar! Geht 15 Uhr?
Pierre	Ja, das ist kein Problem!
Herr Maler	Gut, kommen sie dann direkt in mein Büro, das im ersten Stock liegt. Sie können aber auch an der Rezeption fragen. Dort sind Mitarbeiter, die Ihnen gern den Weg erklären! Wir sehen uns in zwei Wochen, Herr Dupont.
Pierre	Ja, ich freue mich darauf. Auf Wiederhören.

Dialogue questions

Cross out the wrong answer.

1. Die Firma *Maler* | *Gleisser* ruft Pierre an.
2. Herr Maler lädt Pierre zu *Kaffee und Kuchen* | *einem Bewerbungsgespräch* ein.
3. Am 18.5. hat Pierre *ein Bewerbungsgespräch* | *einen Zahnarzttermin*.
4. Pierre soll *an der Rezeption warten* | *direkt ins Büro gehen*.

When do you have time?

Pierre is sitting in his office when his mobile suddenly rings ...

Pierre	Pierre Dupont.
Mr Maler	Maler, of Gleisser company, Hamburg. Good morning, Mr Dupont. You did apply for a job with us – is that correct?
Pierre	Yes, that's correct.
Mr Maler	Your job application, which I liked very much, is lying in front of me. We would like to invite you to a personal interview.
Pierre	Oh, that's great!
Mr Maler	Mr Dupont, when do you have time to come to us? Which day suits you best?
Pierre	Hmm ... Thursday or Friday suits me best. Then I have nearly always time in the afternoon.
Mr Maler	Well. How about Thursday, on 18th May then?
Pierre	On 18th May? One moment, please ... No, I'm sorry, I have an appointment with my dentist then.
Mr Maler	And one day later, on Friday?
Pierre	Yes, Friday 19th is good. I have no appointments on that day!
Mr Maler	Marvelous! Will 3 p.m. be fine?
Pierre	Yes, that'll be fine!
Mr Maler	Great. Please come directly to my office then, which is on the first floor. You can ask at the reception too. There is personnel who will gladly give you directions! We'll meet in two weeks, Mr Dupont.
Pierre	Yes, I'm looking forward to it. Goodbye.

Vocabulary

anbieten	offer
Bewerbungsgespräch, -e n	job interview
Buch, Bücher n	book
Büro, -s n	office
direkt	directly
einen Termin vereinbaren	make an appointment
einladen	invite
frei halten	keep free
frei	free
Freitagnachmittag, -e m	Friday afternoon
Ich freue mich darauf.	I'm looking forward to it.
Jahreszeit, -en f	season
Kein Problem!	No Problem!
leider	unfortunately
Mitarbeiter Pl	personnel
nachmittags	in the afternoon
passen	fit, suit
persönlich	personal
plötzlich	suddenly
richtig	correct, right
Termin, -e m	appointment

Terminkalender, – m	diary
Verabredung, -en f	appointment, date, rendezvous
Zahnarzt, -ärzte m	dentist
Zeit haben	have time

Learning tip I

When saying the year in German you don't use a preposition:
2012 fahre ich nach Frankreich.
In 2012 I'm going to go to France.

Learning tip II

To specify a time of day (like afternoon) on a certain day of the week (like Friday), you build a compound noun: **der Freitagnachmittag** or **der Montagmorgen.**

Days

Montag m	Monday
Dienstag m	Tuesday
Mittwoch m	Wednesday
Donnerstag m	Thursday
Freitag m	Friday
Samstag/ Sonnabend m	Saturday
Sonntag m	Sunday

Grammar and means of expression

Relative clauses ▸ §3.4

Relative clauses are subordinate clauses that specify a noun. The relative pronouns
are **der**, **die**, **das** *who/which/that* – they replace the noun in the subordinate clause.
Thereby, their number and gender match the related noun:
Vor mir liegt **Ihre Bewerbung**, **die** mir sehr gut gefallen hat.
Your job application, which I liked very much, is lying in front of me.
Here, the relative pronoun is the subject in the subordinate clause and therefore its
case is nominative.

The forms of the relative pronouns are the same as of the definite articles – with one
exception: the dative plural relative pronoun is **denen** (whereas the article is **den**)!
Wir geben **den** Kindern Bonbons.
We give the children sweets.
Da sind die Kinder, **denen** wir Bonbons geben.
There are the children, whom we give sweets.

These examples show that the relative pronoun isn't always the subject. In fact,
a relative pronoun can be any kind of object in the subordinate clause.
Die Wohnung, **in der** ich wohne, ist klein.
The flat, in which I live, is small.
In the previous two examples the relative pronoun is not the subject, but a dative
object or an object with a preposition that requires dative.

Interrogative articles ▸ §6.2

Welcher Tag passt Ihnen am besten? *Which day suits you best?*
With **welcher**, **welche**, **welches** (*Pl* **welche**) *which/what* you can ask about a person
or thing from a group. If you want to ask about the type of a thing or the nature
of a person you use **was für ein/eine** *what* (*Pl* **was für**). See the difference in the
examples:
Was für ein Buch kaufst du? – Einen Thriller.
What (kind of) book are you buying? – A thriller.
Welches Buch kaufst du? – Harry Potter.
Which book are you buying? – Harry Potter.

⊙ 2/29 🎧 **1** Read the questions below. Then listen to the short dialogues on the CD and answer the questions.

1. An welchem Tag hat die Frau Zeit?   ☐ Am 4.3.   ☐ Am 4.5.   ☐ Am 14.5.

2. a) In welchem Monat liegt der Termin? ....

   b) Um wie viel Uhr ist der Termin? ....

3. a) Um wie viel Uhr soll der Mann kommen?   ☐ Um 4 Uhr.   ☐ Um 16 Uhr.

   b) Hat er zu diesem Termin Zeit? ....

4. An welchem Tag, in welchem Monat und Jahr und um wie viel Uhr ist der Termin?

   ....

5. Um wie viel Uhr fährt der Zug ab? ....

📝 **2** Answer each question with one possible answer from the box. Some questions may have multiple answers and some answers fit to more than one question.

> An diesem Tag habe ich keine Zeit.   Ja, das passt mir gut.
> Am Montag.   Tut mir leid. Leider nicht.   Im Juli.   Am Mittwoch um 16 Uhr.
> Ich habe meinen Terminkalender leider nicht hier.

1. Wann haben Sie Zeit? ....
2. Haben Sie am Freitag einen freien Termin? ....
3. Können Sie am Dienstag zu mir kommen? ....
4. Haben Sie am 17.8. Zeit? ....
5. Wann können wir uns treffen? ....
6. An welchem Tag passt es Ihnen? ....

📝 **3** Fill in the gaps using the appropriate relative pronoun.

1. Meine Schwester, ... in Berlin studiert, hat einen Sohn.
2. Gibst du mir bitte den Beamer, ... dort im Schrank steht?
3. Der Film, ... ich ausgeliehen habe, ist echt spannend!
4. Pierre, ... Jens viele Tipps gegeben hat, bewirbt sich bei einer deutschen Firma.
5. Iwona und Pierre, ... schon gut Deutsch sprechen, fahren nach München.

Kulturtipp
German punctuality

One of the characteristics often attributed to Germans is punctuality. However in private life it depends on an individual person. For ones it's very important, while others don't care very much. It may even be that the contact with other cultures in our globalized world made the Germans a bit more relaxed and tolerant regarding (un-) punctuality!?

But no matter how one's personal attitude is, punctuality really matters in business life. Here, even minutes can influence the mood of your colleagues and seniors. If you're going to be late (after all, it's not always your fault, isn't it?), then it's always good to give a brief call, especially if you've got an appointment.

In private life, it's usually OK to be late for 10–15 minutes (and not call).

If you're travelling by train or using buses and trams, you're probably soon going to realize that delays can occur (and those who value punctuality can get quite angry because of that and rant about the decay of values ...). But generally trains are quite punctual – so try not to be late (particularly when you bought a special offer train ticket for a particular train).

....

What can you already do?

	🙂 😐 ☹	
■ make appointments	▢ ▢ ▢	▸ Ü1, Ü2
■ agree to appointments or decline	▢ ▢ ▢	▸ Ü1, Ü2
■ speak about date, time and days	▢ ▢ ▢	▸ Ü1, Ü2

Making contacts

In this lesson you will learn

- to talk about clothes and networks
- to prepare for a job interview

⊙ 2/30 Gute Nachrichten

Jens sitzt in der Kantine beim Mittagessen. Da kommt Pierre dazu.

Pierre Hallo Jens! Eben hat einer von der Firma angerufen, bei der ich mich beworben habe.

Jens Hi Pierre, setz dich doch! Und? Was hat er gesagt?

Pierre Er hat mich zu einem Gespräch eingeladen! Ich bin schon richtig nervös.

Jens Ich gratuliere! Wann ist denn der Termin?

Pierre In zwei Wochen.

Jens Ach, das ist genug Zeit. Im Internet findet man viele Ratgeber zum Thema Bewerbungsgespräch – zum Beispiel auf fast jeder Webseite mit Stellenanzeigen.

Pierre Steht da auch, was ich anziehen soll?

Jens Sicher! Am besten ist wohl ein Anzug, aber lies das in den Ratgebern nach.

Pierre O. K., mache ich.

Jens Ach, ich wollte dir auch noch einen Tipp geben. Bist du schon Mitglied in einem Business-Netzwerk im Internet?

Pierre Nein.

Jens Ich finde das heute ziemlich wichtig. So kann man ganz einfach mit ehemaligen Kollegen in Kontakt bleiben und auch leicht neue Kontakte knüpfen. Und vielleicht ergibt sich ja auch der ein oder andere neue Job!

Pierre Verstehe! Und wo melde ich mich da an?

Jens Zum einen gibt es da LinkedIn, das ist das weltweit größte Netzwerk dieser Art. In Deutschland und Europa ist aber auch Xing sehr populär. Viele Kollegen hier sind dort Mitglied – ich auch! Wenn du willst, kann ich dir eine Einladung schicken.

Pierre Ja, mach das bitte.

Dialogue questions

Mark with a cross:

	right	wrong
1. Jens ist in seinem Büro als Pierre kommt.	☐	☐
2. Pierre soll im Internet nach Ratgebern suchen.	☐	☐
3. Pierre ist Mitglied bei LinkedIn.	☐	☐

Good news

Jens is sitting in the canteen at lunch. Then Pierre arrives.

Pierre Hello Jens! A moment ago I had a call from someone from the company I applied to.

Jens Hi Pierre, do sit down! And? What did they say?

Pierre They invited me to an interview! I'm really nervous already.

Jens Congratulations! When's the appointment?

Pierre In two weeks.

Jens Oh, there is enough time. You'll find many guides on the internet dealing with job interviews – for instance nearly on every website with job advertisements.

Pierre Is there also anything said about how I should dress?

Jens Sure! A suit will probably be the best, but you'd better read those guides.

Pierre O. K., I'll do.

Jens Oh, and I wanted to give you a tip, too. Are you already a member of a business network on the internet?

Pierre No.

Jens I think it's pretty important today. You can really easily keep in touch with former colleagues and make new contacts. So the one or other new job might come along!

Pierre I see! And where do I register?

Jens On one hand, there's LinkedIn, that's the world's biggest network of this kind. But in Germany and Europe Xing's very popular too. A lot of our colleagues are members of it – and me too! If you want I can send you an invitation.

Pierre Yes, please do that.

Vocabulary

anmelden	register
anziehen	dress
Art, -en *f*	kind, type
auffällig	flashy
ausziehen	undress
bunt	colourful
eben	a moment ago
ehemalig	former
elegant	elegant
genug	enough
gepflegt	neat, groomed
Gespräch, -e *n*	conversation, talk
gratulieren	congratulate
in Kontakt bleiben	stay in touch
Kleidung *f* (*only Sg*)	clothes
Kleidungsstück, -e *n*	piece of clothing
Kontakt, -e *m*	contact
Kontakte knüpfen	to make new contacts
locker, sportlich	casual
Mitglied, -er *n*	member
nervös	nervous
Netzwerk, -e *n*	network
passend, geeignet	suitable
pflegen	maintain
populär	popular
Ratgeber, – *m*	guide
schick	chic, fashionable
Schmuck (*only Sg*) *m*	jewellery
Thema, Themen *n*	topic
Verstehe!	I see!, I get it!
verteilen	distribute
Visitenkarte, -n *f*	business card
Voraussetzung, -en *f*	requirement
wohl	probably
ziemlich	pretty, quite
zurückhaltend	conservative

Clothes

Anzug, Anzüge *m*	suit
Bluse, -n *f*	blouse
Handschuh, -e *m*	glove
Hemd, -en *n*	shirt
Hose, -n *f*	trousers
Hosenanzug, -anzüge *m*	pantsuit
Hut, Hüte *m*	hat
Jacke, -n *f*	jacket, (shorter) coat
Jackett, -s *n*	jacket, suit jacket
Jeans, – *f*	jeans
Kleid, -er *n*	dress
Kostüm, -e *n*	female suit
Krawatte, -n *f*	tie
Mantel, Mäntel *m*	(longer) coat
Mütze, -n *f*	cap
Pullover, – *m*	jumper, sweater
Rock, Röcke *m*	skirt
Schal, -s *m*	scarf
Schuh, -e *m*	shoe
Socke, -n *f*	sock
T-Shirt, -s *n*	T-shirt
Unterwäsche (*only Sg*) *f*	underwear

Grammar and means of expression

The indefinite pronoun *man* ► *§3.5.1*

There's another indefinite pronoun in German: **man** *one/they/you*. It substitutes one or more unspecified persons. It's always the subject of the sentence and the referring verb is always in third person singular.
Im Internet findet **man** viele Ratgeber. *You'll find many guides on the internet.*
For accusative or dative objects you use the suitable forms of the indefinite pronoun **einer**.

Other articles ► *§2.2*

There are some words in German that are used like articles, i.e. before a noun. They are used to state more or less definite quantities or partial quantities. All of them can be used as pronouns as well, that is without the noun – but only if it's clear what you're referring to.
You saw some of them in the dialogue:
Im Internet findet man **viele** Ratgeber. *You'll find many guides on the internet.*
Auf fast **jeder** Webseite. *Nearly on every website.*
Or as a pronoun:

► Ich suche einen Ratgeber.	◄ Im Internet findest du **viele**.
► *I'm looking for a guide.*	◄ *You'll find many on the internet.*

The most important of these articles/pronouns are:
jeder, jede, jedes (no *Pl*, endings are similar to the indefinite pronoun **einer**)
each/every/any
beide (*only Pl*) *both*
alle (*only Pl*) *all*
viele (*only Pl*) *many/a lot of*
mehrere (*only Pl*) *several*
einige, manche (*only Pl*) *some*

And also the following articles/pronouns which don't change with gender or case:
etwas, ein wenig (*only Sg* and only with mass nouns) *some, a little bit of*
viel (*only Sg* and only with mass nouns) *much*
ein paar (*only Pl*) *a few, a couple of*

Exercises

 1 Read the text from a job interview guide and answer the questions (multiple answers are possible).

Die richtige Kleidung ist eine wichtige Voraussetzung für ein gelungenes Bewerbungsgespräch. „Passend und authentisch" soll die Kleidung sein, liest man oft. Gemeint ist: passend zum zukünftigen Beruf und passend zu einem selbst! Wichtig ist, dass man sich selbst in seiner Kleidung wohlfühlt. Denn wenn nicht, merken das die anderen gleich. Auch sollte man darauf achten, dass die Kleidung nicht ablenkt. Ihr zukünftiger Arbeitgeber sollte sich während des Gesprächs nicht ständig Gedanken wegen Ihrer bunten Krawatte oder einer auffälligen Brosche* machen müssen. Treten Sie zurückhaltend, aber gepflegt auf – dann sind Sie auf der sicheren Seite!

1. Was ist wichtig für ein Bewerbungsgespräch?
   a) ☐ Richtige Kleidung.   b) ☐ Passende Kleidung.   c) ☐ Sportliche Kleidung.
2. Was ist an der Kleidung für ein Bewerbungsgespräch wichtig?
   a) ☐ Dass man sich darin wohlfühlt.
   b) ☐ Dass sie zum Beruf passt.
   c) ☐ Dass sie andere Menschen ablenkt.
3. Wie soll die Krawatte sein?
   a) ☐ Auffällig.   b) ☐ Zurückhaltend.   c) ☐ Bunt.
4. Welches Kleidungsstück ist gut geeignet für ein Bewerbungsgespräch?
   a) ☐ Jackett.   b) ☐ T-Shirt.   c) ☐ Hemd.
* die Brosche *brooch*

⊙ 2/31 🎧 **2 Pierre and Iwona are talking about networks and contacts. Listen to their conversation on the CD and mark the right answer.**

	right	wrong
1. Iwona ist nur in einem Netzwerk Mitglied.	☐	☐
2. Iwona findet Netzwerke nicht wichtig.	☐	☐
3. Pierre hat keinen direkten Kontakt mit Kunden.	☐	☐
4. Iwona geht auf Veranstaltungen. Dort pflegt sie ihre Kontakte.	☐	☐
5. Pierre ist Mitglied in einem Business-Netzwerk.	☐	☐
6. Iwona ist schon seit vielen Jahren Mitglied bei Xing.	☐	☐

Kulturtipp My German job interview

Did you receive an invitation to a job interview? Congratulations! But now it's important to prepare accordingly.

First you need to collect as much information about the company as possible. Try to gather all information in German (even if the company has a website in your native language or English). Thus you won't have to translate it later and you will already have the right terminology.

One good method to prepare to the interview is to make a mind map. Write down the information you've gathered. Also write down any questions you might get asked and, of course, questions which you would like to ask. Then ask a German friend to look it over and correct if necessary. That's the base for your next step: Practise your job interview in a role play – preferably also with a German friend. And keep in mind that you're not supposed to just sit and answer, ask the questions you've prepared. It's a good sign to show some initiative – all the more since you're talking in a foreign language!

Now, fingers crossed and good luck!

....

What can you already do?

	☺	☺	☹	
■ talk about clothes	■	■	■	▸Ü1
■ prepare for a job interview	■	■	■	▸Ü1
■ talk about networking	■	■	■	▸Ü2

Meetings

In this lesson you will learn

- to welcome the members of a meeting
- to moderate a meeting
- about presentations and presentation media

◉ 2/32 **Noch Fragen?**

Die Besprechung, die Iwona organisiert hat, beginnt.

Iwona Guten Tag, mein Name ist Iwona Nowak und ich möchte Sie ganz herzlich zu dieser Besprechung begrüßen! Mein Kollege Herr Theus stellt Ihnen jetzt das Programm für heute vor.

Herr Theus Ja, als ersten Tagesordnungspunkt haben wir eine kurze Präsentation zum aktuellen Geschäftsbericht vorbereitet. Im Anschluss sagt Herr Steigmann ein paar Worte zur Situation in der Firma. Dann machen wir eine Pause. Danach ist Frau Nowaks Präsentation zu den zukünftigen Strategien an der Reihe und dann bespricht Frau Klein noch die Planung und das weitere Vorgehen mit Ihnen. Kommen wir also zum ersten Punkt ...

Herr Theus und Herr Steigmann halten ihre Vorträge. Nach der Pause fährt Iwona fort.

Iwona So, ich hoffe, Sie haben die Pause genossen. Ich will in meiner Präsentation die neuen Strategien ansprechen ...

Iwona hält ihre Präsentation.

Iwona Gibt es noch Fragen?

Teilnehmer Ja. Gibt es die Möglichkeit für uns, dass wir die Dinge, die Sie genannt haben, noch einmal nachlesen?

Iwona Ja, wir schicken Ihnen eine Zusammenfassung per E-Mail.

Teilnehmer Ah, gut. Vielen Dank.

Iwona Gern. Weitere Fragen?

Die Teilnehmer stellen noch einige weitere Fragen.

Iwona Gut, ich denke, dass wir alles Wichtige angesprochen und Ihre Fragen beantwortet haben. Ich möchte Ihnen für die Aufmerksamkeit danken und wünsche uns allen weiterhin gute Zusammenarbeit und eine erfolgreiche Zukunft. Vielen Dank und auf Wiedersehen!

Dialogue questions

Mark the right answer.

1. Wie heißt Iwonas Kollegin?   a) ☐ Frau Klein.   b) ☐ Frau Theus.
2. Wer spricht zuerst?   a) ☐ Herr Steigmann.   b) ☐ Frau Klein.
3. Worüber spricht Frau Klein?   a) ☐ Die Strategien.   b) ☐ Die Planung.
4. Wie gibt es die Zusammenfassung?   a) ☐ Als Handout.   b) ☐ Als E-Mail.

Any questions?

The meeting which Iwona organized begins.

Iwona   Good morning, my name is Iwona Nowak and I would like to cordially welcome you to this meeting! My colleague Mr Theus is now going to present the programme for today.

Mr Theus   Well, as the first topic we prepared a short presentation of the current report on the company. Next Mr Steigmann is going to say a few words about the situation in the company. Then we will have a break. After that there will be Ms Nowak's turn to present future strategies and finally Ms Klein is going to discuss with you the planning and further actions. Let's proceed thus to the first topic ...

Mr Theus and Mr Steigmann make their speeches. After the break Iwona continues.

Iwona   Well, I hope you've enjoyed the break. I'd like to speak about the new strategies now ...

Iwona conducts her presentation.

Iwona   Are there any questions?

Member   Yes. Is there a possibility for us to read about those things you've mentioned once again?

Iwona   Yes, we e-mail a summary to you.

Member   Oh, well. Thank you very much.

Iwona   You're welcome. Are there any other questions?

The members ask some more questions.

Iwona   Well, I think that we have addressed all important topics and answered your questions. I'd like to thank you for your attention and also I wish us good cooperation and a successful future. Thank you very much and goodbye!

Vocabulary

3/24

aktuell	current
alles Wichtige	all important topics
also	thus
an der Reihe sein	to be so.'s turn to ...
ansprechen	address
Aufmerksamkeit *(only Sg) f*	attention
beantworten	answer
begrüßen	welcome
besprechen	talk, discuss
Dame, -n *f*	lady, madam
Ding, -e *n*	thing
einen Vortrag halten	make a speech
erfolgreich	successful
es geht um	it's about
fortfahren	continue
Frage, -n *f*	question
genießen	enjoy
Geschäftsbericht, -e *m*	company report
Herr, -en *m*	sir, mister
herzlich	dearly, cordially
heutig	today's
im Anschluss	subsequently
im Folgenden	in the following
Moderation, -en *f*	moderation
moderieren	moderate
Möglichkeit, -en *f*	possibility
nennen	mention
noch einmal	once again
Pause, -n *f*	break

Programm, -e *n*	programme
Punkt, -e *m*	here: topic, point
Situation, -en *f*	situation
Strategie, -n *f*	strategy
Tagesordnungs- punkt, -e *m*	topic
vorstellen	present
Vortrag, Vorträge *m*	speech
Wand, Wände *f*	wall
weiterhin	furthermore, also
zukünftig	future
Zukunft *(only Sg) f*	future
Zusammenarbeit *(only Sg) f*	cooperation
Zusammen- fassung, -en *f*	summary

Presentations	
Einleitung, -en *f*	introduction
Hauptteil, -e *m*	main part/section
Schluss, Schlüsse *m*	conclusion
Diskussion, -en *f*	discussion
Handzettel, – *m*; Handout, -s *n*	handout
Tageslichtprojek- tor, Overhead- projektor, -en *m*	overhead projector
Medium, Medien *n*	medium

Grammar and means of expression

Adjectives I ▸ §6

There are two possible positions of adjectives. The one you have already used is after the verb **sein**. For example:

Das Museum ist interessant. *The museum is interesting.*

In this position the adjective does not change its form because of case, gender or number.

Now let us have a look at the adjectives positioned before nouns, where they have to be declined. That's what a lot of students consider really difficult to learn, but there really is nothing to fear. For now it's essential to understand what it's about – you can use in most cases the adjective after **sein**. But we'll do some exercises with adjectives here and there will be more than enough possibilities to practise once you start your B1 German class later! So let's just cut the preamble and jump right in at the deep end:

The declined form of the adjectives differs according to the article you used – let's start with the definite article:

Ich will **die** neue**n** Strategien ansprechen. – *I'd like to speak about the new strategies.*
Danach ist Frau Nowaks Präsentation zu **den** zukünftigen Strategien an der Reihe. *After that it's Ms Nowak's turn to present future strategies.*

Now in this position (before the noun) after the definite article, the adjective gets **-e** or **-en** as an ending according to the noun's case, gender and number as you can see in the table.

	m (e.g. Plan)	f (e.g. Frage)	n (e.g. Buch)	Pl (e.g. Strategien)
Nom.	der neue	die neue	das neue	die neuen
Acc.	den neuen	die neue	das neue	die neuen
Dat.	dem neuen	der neuen	dem neuen	den neuen

Exercises

⊙ 2/33 🎧 **1** Listen to the CD. You'll hear the phrases below. Fill in the gaps and repeat each sentence after the beep.

Guten Tag, _____ (1.) Herren. – Ich _____ (2.) zur heutigen

Besprechung. – Ich möchte kurz _____ (3.). – In der Präsentation

_____ (4.) neue Strategien. – Gibt es noch _____ (5.)? –

Dann sind alle Fragen _____ (6.). – Vielen Dank _____ (7.).

– Auf _____ (8.).

📖 **2** You have received an e-mail about the presentations for the next meeting. Read the e-mail and answer the questions.

Neue E-Mail

Guten Tag,

wie am Telefon besprochen, sende ich Ihnen die Planung für die Besprechung. Herr Maier präsentiert um 9.15 Uhr den Geschäftsbericht 2009. Um 10 Uhr ist Frau Leser an der Reihe. Sie spricht von der Firmenentwicklung* in den letzten Jahren. Von 10.45 Uhr bis 11 Uhr ist eine Pause. Danach hält Frau Berger ihren Vortrag zum Thema „Neue Strategien für die Zukunft". Herr Maier braucht um 9 Uhr einen Beamer und Frau Leser braucht für ihren Vortrag einen Tageslichtprojektor. Vielen Dank!
Mit freundlichen Grüßen
I. Schmitz

---

1. Das Thema von Herrn Maiers Präsentation? _____
2. Wann beginnt Frau Bergers Vortrag? _____
3. Wer spricht von der Firmenentwicklung? _____
4. Wer braucht einen Tageslichtprojektor? _____
* die Firmenentwicklung *the company's development*

✏️ **3** Write the sentences again by placing the adjective before the noun.

1. Das Buch ist langweilig. _____
2. Der Anzug ist schick. _____
3. Die Hemden sind weiß. _____
4. Die Schuhe sind sportlich. _____

Kulturtipp
Body language

Germans are often perceived as cold and closed. One reason might be that the body language of German people – especially in a professional environment – is not so distinctive. But that depends on your point of view: analyses showed that there is more or less a decline where body language and contacts get more extensive from north to south.

In Germany you normally keep some distance (about an arm's length) to people you're not familiar with, like colleagues at work. The standard greeting is a handshake (pecks on the cheeks are possible only in familiar surroundings). It's uncommon to touch others during a conversation, except for the handshakes or maybe a motivating or praising backslapping. But don't give your superiors a backslap – they may only come from someone higher in the hierarchy.

Of course all that can be very different among close friends!

What can you already do?

	☺	☺	☹	
▪ welcome the members of a meeting	□	□	□	‣*Ü1*
▪ present a topic	□	□	□	‣*Ü1*
▪ moderate a meeting	□	□	□	‣*Ü1*
▪ talk about presentations and presentation media	□	□	□	‣*Ü2*

Draw the balance

In this lesson you will learn

- to praise and criticise others
- to receive praise or criticism
- to have a conversation with colleagues and seniors

⊙ 2/34 **Gut gemacht!**

Nach der Besprechung bittet Frau Klein Iwona zu sich in ihr Büro.

Frau Klein   Frau Nowak, ich möchte Sie loben. Die Präsentation war wirklich hervorragend. Das haben Sie ganz toll gemacht!

Iwona   Vielen Dank, Frau Klein. Ich habe mich auch lange darauf vorbereitet. Das war das erste größere Projekt auf Deutsch, deshalb war ich ganz schön nervös ...

Frau Klein   Ja? Das hat man Ihnen aber nicht angemerkt. Und auch sprachlich war das einwandfrei. Sie haben in der kurzen Zeit hier wirklich gut Deutsch gelernt.

Iwona   Stimmt, ich bin selbst zufrieden. Ich habe aber auch eine sehr gute Lehrerin!

Frau Klein   Ich bin jedenfalls froh, dass Sie in meiner Abteilung sind.

Iwona   Ich arbeite sehr gern in Ihrer Abteilung. Das angenehme Klima und die netten Kollegen erleichtern die Arbeit sehr!

Frau Klein   Dann hoffe ich, dass Sie noch eine Weile bei uns bleiben. Wenn Sie im nächsten Quartal auch so gute Leistung bringen, dann können wir bald über eine Beförderung sprechen.

Iwona   Vielen Dank. Die Arbeit macht mir einfach Spaß und das motiviert mich auch.

Frau Klein   Das merkt man, Frau Nowak. Nun gut, ich freue mich schon auf das nächste Projekt, das Sie übernehmen.

Iwona   Ja, ich auch!

Dialogue questions

Answer the questions briefly.

1. Wie findet Frau Klein Iwonas Präsentation? ....

2. Warum war Iwona nervös vor dem Projekt? ....

3. Wie findet Iwona ihre Kollegen? ....

4. Worauf freut sich Frau Klein? ....

Well done!

After the meeting Ms Klein asks Iwona to join her in her office.

Ms Klein   Ms Nowak, I want to praise you. The presentation was really excellent. You've done great!

Iwona   Thank you, Ms Klein. I had been preparing for it for a long time. That was the first bigger project in German, that's why I was pretty nervous ...

Ms Klein   Oh, really? Nobody noticed. And also it was flawless as far as the language is concerned. You learnt German really well in such a short time.

Iwona   That's true, I'm satisfied with myself. But I have a very good teacher, too!

Ms Klein   Anyway, I'm glad that you're in my department.

Iwona   I like working in your department. A pleasant atmosphere and nice colleagues make the work very easy!

Ms Klein   Then I hope that you will stay with us for a while. If you perform so well in the next quarter too, we soon can talk about a promotion.

Iwona   Thank you very much. I have pleasure doing the work and that motivates me too.

Ms Klein   I have noticed it, Ms Nowak. Very well, I'm already looking forward to the next project you're going to take on.

Iwona   So do I!

Vocabulary

3/25

Abteilung, -en *f*	department
angenehm	kind
anmerken	notice
bald	soon
Beförderung, -en *f*	promotion
deshalb	therefore, that's why
Deutsch *(only Sg) n*	(the language) German
einwandfrei	flawless
erleichtern	to make ... easy
froh	glad
ganz schön	pretty
ganz	here: quite
Gern geschehen.	You're welcome.
Gut gemacht!	Well done!
hervorragend	excellent
hoffen	hope
Ich auch.	So do I.
jedenfalls	anyway
Leistung bringen	perform
Leistung, -en *f*	performance
merken	notice
nett	nice
Projekt, -e *n*	project
selbst	oneself
sich freuen	look forward to
Spaß, Späße *m*	fun
sprachlich	linguistic
übernehmen	take over
Verhalten *(only Sg) n*	behaviour
Weile *(only Sg) f*	while
zufrieden	satisfied

Praise and criticise

auf etwas achten	mind, pay attention
beim nächsten Mal	next time
eine Bitte haben	have a favour to ask
Kritik, -en *f*	criticism
kritisieren	criticise
Lob *(only Sg) n*	praise
loben	praise
motivieren	motivate
üblich	common
unüblich	uncommon, not common
vermeiden	avoid

Learning tip

The plural ending of all feminine nouns ending with **-ung**, **-keit**, **-heit**, **-tion** is **-en**, e.g. **Leistung, Leistungen**.

Grammar and means of expression

Adjectives II ► §6

Now let's focus our attention on adjectives positioned before a noun with an indefinite article. Here there are more different endings.
Let's look at the table first:

	m (e.g. Plan)	f (e.g. Frage)	n (e.g. Buch)	Pl (e.g. Strategien)
Nom.	ein neuer	eine neue	ein neues	– neue
Acc.	einen neuen	eine neue	ein neues	– neue
Dat.	einem neuen	einer neuen	einem neuen	– neuen

Martina ist eine gut**e** Lehrerin. *Martina is a good teacher.*
Iwona hat eine gut**e** Lehrerin. *Iwona has a good teacher.*
Iwona ist mit einer gut**en** Lehrerin befreundet. *Iwona is friends with a good teacher.*
Iwona hat gut**e** Lehrerinnen. *Iwona has good teachers.*

Refer to the grammar in the appendix to see how adjectives are declined with other articles or possessive pronouns you learned (like **mein**, **jeder** or **viele**).

deshalb and *darum* ► §9

There are some words in German that look and are used like coordinating conjunctions (you remember: like **und**, **oder**, **aber**). Two such words probably most often used are **deshalb** *therefore/thus/hence* and **darum** *therefore/that is why* and they state a result:
Der Vortrag ist auf Deutsch, **deshalb/darum** bin ich nervös.
The speech is in German, therefore I am nervous.
Vice versa, to state the cause you can use **denn** or **weil** as you already know:
Ich bin nervös, denn der Vortrag ist auf Deutsch.
I am nervous, for the speech is in German.
The special thing about **deshalb** and **darum** is that they are full constituents and that's why in the examples above the verb follows directly **deshalb** – and not the subject like after **denn**.

1 Read the situations below. Then choose the appropriate phrase from the box and say it loud.

> Dieses Verhalten ist hier unüblich.   Vermeiden Sie bitte die Anrede mit Du.   Ich habe eine Bitte: Seien Sie bitte etwas pünktlicher. Das war hervorragend.   Ihre Präsentation war etwas kurz.   Achten Sie beim nächsten Mal bitte auf die Zeit.   Das haben Sie gut gemacht.

Tell your colleague ...
1. that he should pay more attention to the timing.
2. that it was excellent.
3. that her presentation was a bit brief.
4. that he should avoid the informal language.
5. that this behaviour is not common here.
6. that she has done well.
7. that you'd ask him to be a bit more punctual.

2 Fill in the gaps with the adjectives in their correct form.

1. Pierre sieht einen _____ Film. (interessant)

2. Iwona liest ein _____ Buch. (langweilig)

3. Martina und Jens gehen mit _____ Freunden essen. (gut)

4. Ich habe ein _____ Auto. (schnell)

5. Das Oktoberfest ist ein _____ Volksfest. (groß)

6. Du bist ein _____ Lehrer. (toll)

○ 2/35 **3** Read the questions and listen to the conversation on the CD. Then answer the questions.

1. Wer hat den Vortrag gehalten? a) ☐ Herr Kern. b) ☐ Frau Roth.
2. Was kritisiert Herr Kern? Der Vortrag war a) ☐ zu kurz. b) ☐ zu lang.
3. Warum war der Vortrag nicht einwandfrei? a) ☐ Das Handout war zu kurz. b) ☐ Wenig Vorbereitung.
4. Wer hat die Materialien zu spät geschickt? a) ☐ Herr Kern. b) ☐ Frau Roth.
5. Wer ist der Chef? a) ☐ Herr Kern. b) ☐ Frau Roth.

Kulturtipp Intercultural misunderstandings

Do you feel bad because your boss criticised you openly? Germans are known for their directness which may be sometimes hurtful (in return a nice objective praise is a fine thing, isn't it?). But don't feel bad, it's not about you personally.

Punctuality, body contact, directness – these are only a few aspects of a whole multitude of possible intercultural misunderstandings and missteps. But – and that's true – there's nothing like "international cultural norms". And nobody can possibly expect you to fully adopt German norms and abandon your own cultural habits (but also you shouldn't ignore the habits of the culture in which you live). On the contrary: The more intercultural contacts there are in this globalized world, the more different cultures cultivate their peculiarities. And thus cultural tensions are unavoidable.

But what can you do when you happen to make someone cross because you were unpunctual, or touched the person you talked to? Talk about it: Explain your cultural habits and norms. When you know common stereotypes associated with your own culture and the culture you're now living in, it's easy to unmask them. It should then be possible to solve the problem and find an agreement.

....

What can you already do?

☺ ☺ ☹

■ praise and criticise others	☐	☐	☐	▸*Ü1, Ü3*
■ receive praise or criticism	☐	☐	☐	▸*Ü3*
■ have a conversation with colleagues and seniors	☐	☐	☐	▸*Ü3*

Job-related plans

In this lesson you will learn

- to express and talk about wishes
- to express plans and intentions for the future

⊙ 2/36 Was bringt uns die Zukunft?

Iwona, Martina, Pierre und Jens sitzen zusammen in einer Kneipe.

Martina	Schön, dass wir wieder mal alle zusammensitzen. Es ist ja wirklich viel passiert in letzter Zeit ... Pierre, du willst also nach Hamburg, ja?
Pierre	Ja! Aber zuerst findet noch das Bewerbungsgespräch statt und dann werde ich meinen Abschluss machen. Aber ich würde wirklich gern bei dieser Firma arbeiten!
Jens	Ich glaube nicht, dass das Bewerbungsgespräch ein Problem ist. Ich würde Pierre gleich einstellen!
Pierre	Danke. Hoffentlich sieht das die Firma auch so.
Martina	Das wird schon klappen, Pierre! Und du, Iwona? Ich habe gehört, dass du auch sehr erfolgreich warst.
Iwona	Oh ja. Die Präsentation war sehr gut. Und meine Chefin hat auch mein Deutsch gelobt.
Martina	Schließlich hast du eine tolle Lehrerin!
Iwona	Genau das Gleiche habe ich meiner Chefin auch gesagt. Und ich werde vielleicht auch bald eine Beförderung bekommen.
Martina	Wow, das ging ja schnell! Ich drücke dir die Daumen für deine Karriere. Dann werdet ihr beide also in naher Zukunft in Deutschland bleiben?
Iwona u. Pierre	Ja.
Martina	Das ist toll. Ich hoffe, dass wir noch viele Dinge gemeinsam unternehmen werden. Hamburg ist ja nicht so weit weg!
Pierre	Ich würde ja auch lieber in Berlin bleiben, aber hier habe ich einfach keine passende Arbeit gefunden. Aber ich liebe Berlin und werde euch oft besuchen!
Jens	Hoffentlich! Aber jetzt lasst uns doch anstoßen: Auf das, was uns die Zukunft bringen wird!

Dialogue questions

Mark with a cross:

	right	wrong
1. Pierre will lieber in Hamburg leben.	☐	☐
2. Iwona und Pierre bleiben noch in Deutschland.	☐	☐
3. Pierre will seine Freunde oft besuchen.	☐	☐
4. Martina will noch viel mit Pierre und Iwona unternehmen.	☐	☐

What does the future hold for us?

Iwona, Martina, Pierre and Jens are sitting in a pub.

Martina It's nice that we are all sitting together once again. Quite a lot has happened lately ... Pierre, you want to go to Hamburg, do you?

Pierre Yes! But first there's the job interview and then I have to graduate. I'd really like to work for this company!

Jens I don't think that the job interview is going to be a problem. I'd employ Pierre at once!

Pierre Thanks. I hope that the company will see it the same.

Martina That'll go off all right, Pierre! And how about you, Iwona? I've heard that you've been very successful, too.

Iwona Oh, yes. The presentation was very good. And my boss praised my German.

Martina After all, you had a great teacher!

Iwona I said to my boss exactly the same. And maybe I'll get a promotion soon, too.

Martina Wow, that was fast! I'll keep my fingers crossed for your career. So both of you are going to stay in Germany for the near future?

Iwona u. Pierre Yes.

Martina That's great. I hope that we will yet undertake a lot of things together. Hamburg isn't that far away!

Pierre I'd rather stay in Berlin, but I couldn't find a satisfying job. But I love Berlin and I'm going to visit you often!

Jens I hope so! But now let's chink glasses: To what the future holds for us!

3/26

anstoßen	chink glasses
arbeitslos	unemployed
auch so, ebenso	the same, likewise
Ausbildung, -en *f*	education
beruflich	job-related
Das wird schon klappen!	That'll go off all right.
den/einen Abschluss machen	graduate
die Daumen drücken	keep one's fingers crossed
einstellen	hire, employ
genau	exactly
glauben	think, believe
gleich	here: at once
hoffentlich	hopefully, I hope so
hören	hear
in letzter Zeit	lately
in naher Zukunft	in the near future

Karriere, -n *f*	career
Kneipe, -n *f*	pub, bar
mal, einmal	once
Rente, -n *f*	pension
Ruhestand *(only Sg) m*	retirement
schließlich	after all
Schulung, -en *f*	training
Studium, Studien *n*	studies
weit weg	far away
Weiterbildung, -en *f*	further education
wieder	again
Wunsch, Wünsche *m*	wish
zuhören	listen
zusammen	together

Grammar and means of expression

The auxiliary verb *werden* ▸ §8.4

Apart from **haben** and **sein** there's a third auxiliary verb in German: **werden**. You already know it as a main verb where it means *become*. The auxiliary **werden** is used in the future tense.

werden	
ich werde	wir werden
du wirst	ihr werdet
er/sie/es wird	sie/Sie werden

Futur I ▸ §8.4

You have learnt to use the present tense and temporal adverbs to talk about the future. But sometimes the present tense can be ambiguous and/or the point in time is not specified by an adverb. In these cases you can use the **Futur I**. (It's called **Futur I**, because there's also the **Futur II** which is seldom used and is not mentioned in this book.)
The forms are quite easy. You use the auxiliary **werden** and the infinitive of the verb. The word order is the same as with **Perfekt**: the conjugated form of **werden** is in the second position and the infinitive is in the last position in the main clause, and in the subordinate clause the auxiliary comes after the infinitive in the last position.
Ich **werde** euch oft besuchen. *I'm going to visit you often.*
Ich denke, dass ich euch oft besuchen **werde**. *I think that I'm going to visit you often.*

Wishes

To express (unrealisable) wishes you use **ich würde (gerne/lieber/am liebsten)** *I would (like/rather/like … best)*. For a certain plan you use the already learnt
ich werde *I will*. The already familiar form **ich will** *I want* is between those two: it states a possible wish if not already a rather certain plan.
Ich würde Pierre gleich einstellen.
I'd employ Pierre at once. (But Jens isn't the personnel manager.)
Ich würde lieber in Berlin bleiben.
I'd rather stay in Berlin. (But Pierre didn't find a satisfying job there.)

1 Fill in the gaps with the correct form of *werden* to build the future tense.

1. Ich _____ nächstes Jahr nach England fahren.

2. Er _____ nach seinem Abschluss sicher Rechtsanwalt werden.

3. Wir _____ euch im Sommer besuchen.

4. Im Winter _____ sie *(Pl)* ihren Abschluss an der Universität machen.

5. _____ ihr morgen einen Vortrag halten?

6. _____ du die E-Mail an Frau Wagner noch schreiben?

2 Imagine you've won a big bunch of money. What would you do? The phrases in the box might help you, but feel free to write your own wishes.

> nicht mehr arbeiten   eine Reise machen   noch ein Studium beginnen
> ein schnelles Auto kaufen   meinen Eltern Geschenke kaufen
> ein Haus bauen   anderen Menschen helfen

1. Ich würde _____

2. Ich würde gern _____

3. Ich würde am liebsten _____

4. _____

5. _____

6. _____

⊙ 2/37 **3** Read the different replies in the box. Then listen to the CD and say the appropriate reply after the beep. You'll hear the correct answer again after each sentence.

> Ich würde am liebsten Russisch lernen!   Ich will Lehrerin werden.
> Ich auch, aber ich habe leider keine Zeit.   Ich würde gern
> in Deutschland arbeiten.   Nein. Ich würde gern in Deutschland arbeiten,
> aber ich muss zurück nach Japan.

Kulturtipp
Further education

Well, this is the end (almost, at least). Now you're going to do the last repetition lesson and the final test … and then? You've already learnt a lot, but there is still more to learn. And it's very important to keep practising. If you're in Germany there's a way to do that: book a German class at the **VHS**, the **Volkshochschule** *folk high school*. The **VHS** is usually a municipal non-profit organization. You can not only learn and improve your language skills there but it's a place for all kinds of advanced education, art and culture, sport and health.

There are more than 2000 **Volkshochschulen** in Germany and Berlin alone has 14.

The courses there are not free but normally the fees aren't that high, like for example in private education centres, since the **VHS** doesn't have to make a profit.

What can you already do?

☺ ☺ ☹

- express and talk about wishes ⬛⬜⬛ ‣ *Ü2, Ü3*
- express plans and intentions for the future ⬛⬜⬛ ‣ *Ü1, Ü3*

You worked for a good base in the future. Of course it wasn't possible to address everything in the context of this book and some topics were dealt with only briefly. But now that you've acquired a taste for it, you won't stop, will you? We wish you all the best and lots of fun!

Here you repeat

- making appointments
- leaving messages on the phone
- writing e-mails
- talking about clothes
- stating plans for the future

 1 Which word does not belong here? Cross it out.

1. Beamer, Tageslichtprojektor, Flipchart, Dokument
2. Hemd, Schuhe, Jacke, Bluse
3. anrufen, verschicken, verwählen, telefonieren
4. Wunsch, Studium, Karriere, Ausbildung
5. Besprechung, Vortrag, Kantine, Präsentation
6. sportlich, nervös, gepflegt, elegant

2/38 🎧 **2 Listen to the short dialogues on the CD and write the number of the matching situation.**

1. Am Telefon: ....

4. Bewerbungsgespräch: ....

2. Termin vereinbaren: ....

5. Gespräch mit dem Chef: ....

3. Bei einer Präsentation: ....

3 *Welcher* or *was für ein?*

1. .... Vortrag war besser? – Der von Frau Krüger.

2. .... Film soll ich ausleihen? Einen Thriller oder einen Krimi?

3. Sieh mal, das rote Kleid dort. Und da, der braune Rock. .... soll ich nehmen?

4. ▸ Bei a) .... Firma hast du dich beworben? Bei der in Hamburg oder bei der in Berlin?
   ◂ Bei der in Hamburg!
   ▸ Und b) .... Firma ist das?
   ◂ Das ist eine kleine Consultingfirma.

4 Fill in the gaps with the adjectives. Pay attention to the gender.

> voll/die volle   schön/das schöne   langweilig/die langweilige
> jung/die jungen   zufrieden/der zufriedene
> spannend/das spannende   rot/der rote   lang/die langen

1. Das Haus ist _____ . – _____ Haus.

2. Der Pullover ist _____ . – _____ Pullover.

3. Die Kinder sind _____ . – _____ Kinder.

4. Die Präsentation ist _____ . – _____ Präsentation.

5. Das Buch ist _____ . – _____ Buch.

6. Die Vorträge sind _____ . – _____ Vorträge.

7. Der Chef ist _____ . – _____ Chef.

8. Die Kantine ist _____ . – _____ Kantine.

5 Leave messages on the answering machines of your colleagues/friends.

1. Tell Mr Beck that he should call you back. Your number is 89771.
2. Tell Ms Sander that you need a video projector for your presentation on Monday 22.
3. Ask Brian from your German class if he has free time on Friday. You could go to the cinema.
4. Tell Mr Schumacher that you sent an e-mail on Tuesday and ask if he has read the summary you sent.
5. Tell Ms Engel that the presentation takes place at 11 am and not at 9 am.

6 Match the appropriate sentence parts.

1. Ich hatte keine Zeit zur Vorbereitung,
2. Wenn Sie keine Zeit haben,
3. Der Vortrag war schlecht,
4. Ich bewerbe mich bei einer deutschen Firma,
5. Ich habe keine Zeit,
6. Die Präsentation war gut,
7. Weil ich keine Zeit zur Vorbereitung hatte,

a) deshalb war mein Chef zufrieden.
b) weil ich in Deutschland arbeiten will.
c) war der Vortrag schlecht.
d) deshalb war der Vortrag schlecht.
e) rufen Sie mich bitte kurz an.
f) denn ich hatte keine Zeit zur Vorbereitung.
g) deshalb rufe ich kurz an.

⊙ 2/39 🎧 **7** Pierre and Iwona are looking at photographs of their families. Listen to their conversation and answer the questions.

1. Welche Farbe hat der Mantel von Iwonas Großvater?
   a) ☐ Schwarz.   b) ☐ Grün.   c) ☐ Braun.
2. Wer trägt das grüne Jackett?
   a) ☐ Iwonas Vater.   b) ☐ Iwonas Bruder. c) ☐ Iwonas Onkel.
3. Welche Farbe hat der Hut von Iwonas Vater?
   a) ☐ Braun.   b) ☐ Blau.   c) ☐ Rot.
4. Wer trägt die blaue Mütze?
   a) ☐ Jean.   b) ☐ Pierre.   c) ☐ Julie.
5. Was trägt Camille?
   a) ☐ Ein blaues Kleid. b) ☐ Eine rote Mütze. c) ☐ Ein rotes Kleid.

8 Fill in the gaps with the pronouns/articles from the box.

| alles | dieser | ein | ein paar | einen | etwas | jeden |
| jemand | keiner | man | niemand | viele |

1. Wenn du den Weg nicht kennst, dann musst du _____ fragen.

2. In a) _____ Firma arbeiten b) _____ Menschen.

3. ▸ Ich suche a) _____ Tageslichtprojektor.

   ◂ Tut mir leid, aber hier ist b) _____.

4. ▸ Kennst du a) _____, der in dieser Firma arbeitet?

   ◂ Nein, ich kenne b) _____, der dort arbeitet.

5. Hier kann _____ Fahrräder ausleihen.

6. ▸ Möchtest du noch a) _____?

   ◂ Ja, kann ich bitte noch b) _____ Weintrauben bekommen?

7. ▸ Wie war der Vortrag? Hast du _____ verstanden?

   ◂ Ja, das war kein Problem.

8. ▸ Und hat dir a) _____ Kollege geholfen?

   ◂ Nein! Ich habe b) _____ gefragt, aber c) _____ wollte mir helfen!

9 Read about Pierre's plans. Then think about your own plans for the following dates and say them loud. Use *Futur I.*

1. Heute Abend schaue ich Fußball im Fernsehen.
2. Morgen gehe ich joggen.
3. Im Sommer fahre ich mit Iwona nach Polen.
4. Nächstes Jahr lerne ich Spanisch.
5. In naher Zukunft kaufe ich mir eine Wohnung.

10 What to wear? Choose 5 of the 10 clothes and combine each with one colour. Use the correct case!

ein Pullover	ein Hemd	eine Jacke	eine Hose	Schuhe
eine Mütze	ein Schal	Socken	eine Jeans	ein T-Shirt
rot	grün blau gelb	schwarz	braun weiß	

1. Heute ziehe ich _____ an.
2. Morgen ziehe ich vielleicht _____ an.
3. _____
4. _____
5. _____

11 Fill in the gaps with the words from the box.

> die   in   weil   oft   deshalb   viele   dass

Frauen und Männer _____ (1.) Deutschland sind gleichberechtigt. Das sagt das Gesetz. Aber in Wirklichkeit ist es _____ (2.) anders. Zum Beispiel verdient eine Frau in ihrem Leben im Durchschnitt weniger Geld als ein Mann. Das bedeutet nicht, _____ (3.) eine Frau für die gleiche Arbeit weniger Geld bekommt. Aber _____ (4.) Frauen arbeiten weniger, _____ (5.) sie mehr Zeit für Familie und Kinder brauchen. Es gibt in Deutschland auch nur wenige Frauen, _____ (6.) in hoch bezahlten Füh-rungspositionen* in deutschen Firmen arbeiten. Warum ist das so? Vielleicht sind diese Jobs als Manager für viele Frauen nicht interessant. Aber wir wissen das nicht genau.
Es gibt Statistiken, die sagen, dass heute viele Frauen bessere Abschlüsse haben als Männer. _____ (7.) gibt es in naher Zukunft vielleicht doch mehr Frauen, die Man-ager in deutschen Firmen werden.
* eine hoch bezahlte Führungsposition *a highly paid leadership position*

12 Read the text from exercise 11 again and cross out the wrong answers.

1. *Ein Mann | eine Frau* verdient im Durchschnitt mehr Geld.
2. Frauen arbeiten oft weniger, denn sie *brauchen Zeit für die Familie | sind keine Manager.*
3. *Viele | wenige* Frauen arbeiten in Deutschland in Führungspositionen.
4. *Männer | Frauen* haben bessere Abschlüsse.
5. Es gibt vielleicht bald *mehr | weniger* Frauen in Führungspositionen.

⊙ 2/40 **13** Listen to the CD. You'll hear questions about appointments. Cross out the date you hear and answer after the beep, repeating the date. Decide for yourself if you have time or not. A possible answer is given before the next question. Not all dates in the box are used.

> 8.12.   6.7.   3.10.   24.3.   8.9.   7.6.   13.10.   20.3.

14 Make relative clauses from the second sentence referring to the underlined noun.

Er hat einen Bruder. Sein Bruder arbeitet als Kellner.

Er hat einen Bruder, der als Kellner arbeitet.

1. Ich lese das Buch. Das Buch habe ich vor einer Woche gekauft.

....

2. Deine Schwester geht noch in die Schule. Deine Schwester ist jünger.

....

3. Ich bringe den Kindern Geschenke mit. Ich besuche die Kinder.

....

4. Meine Freunde sind toll. Ich fahre mit den Freunden in Urlaub.

....

5. Pierres Mutter lebt in Frankreich. Er denkt oft an seine Mutter.

....

6. Ich denke an meinen Bruder. Ich muss meinem Bruder noch eine E-Mail schreiben.

....

15 Complete the crossword about clothes. The grey fields show the solution.

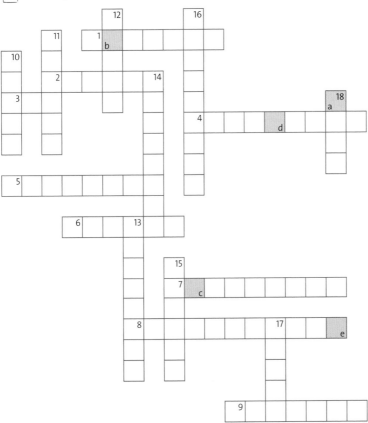

1. elegant
2. chic
3. hat
4. glove
5. neat
6. casual

7. flashy
8. underwear
9. jewellery
10. scarf
11. female dress
12. dress

13. clothes
14. tie
15. long coat
16. to dress
17. shoe
18. colourful

Solution (a–e): ....

Final test

1 Fill in the gaps with the verbs from the brackets in the right form of the present tense.

1. Er _____ mit dem Auto nach München. (fahren)
2. Morgen _____ du bei einem Freund. (schlafen)
3. Wir _____ zusammen auf das Oktoberfest. (gehen)
4. Wann _____ sie *(Sg)* ihren Vortrag? (halten)
5. Du _____ sehr schnell! (laufen)
__/6 6. Sie _____ gute Freunde. (sein)

2 Read the text and write down the infinitive of all main verbs (not the auxiliary verbs).

> Ich mache gern Sport. Am liebsten klettere und schwimme ich. Und gestern habe ich mit einem Freund zwei Stunden lang Tennis gespielt. Das war toll! Ich fahre auch gern Rad. Nur leider habe ich kein Fahrrad. Aber morgen leihe ich eins aus und mache eine Radtour. Und wenn du willst, dann nehme ich dich mit. Wie findest du das?

1. _____ 5. _____ 9. _____
2. _____ 6. _____ 10. _____
3. _____ 7. _____ 11. _____
__/12 4. _____ 8. _____ 12. _____

3 Insert the missing adjectives. Pay attention to the endings and use comparative/ superlative forms where necessary.

1. Pierre zieht für sein Bewerbungsgespräch eine a) _____ (schwarz) Hose und ein b) _____ (elegant) Jackett an.
2. Jens kann kochen, aber er ist kein a) _____ (gut) Koch. Martina ist die b) _____ (gut) Köchin.
3. Pierre fährt mit dem ICE nach Hamburg. Der ICE ist der _____ (schnell) Zug in Deutschland.
4. Iwona isst mit ihren _____ (nett) Kollegen zu Mittag.
5. Stell die a) _____ (klein) Teller doch bitte in den b) _____ (rot) Schrank neben dem c) _____ (groß) Tisch.
__/10 6. Ich gratuliere! Du hast einen _____ (toll) Vortrag gehalten!

4 Read the words and cross the odd ones out.

1. Hals, Wartezimmer, Krankenschwester, Röntgen
2. Feiertag, Freizeit, Film, Reise
3. Gast, Hobby, Party, Einladung
4. Bruder, Großvater, Onkel, Tante
5. Glas, Teller, Müll, Geschirr
6. Sprudel, Suppe, Saft, Cola

__/6

5 Listen to the short dialogues on the CD. Then write each dialogue's number next to ⊙ 2/41
the matching situation. Two situations remain unused.

1. Auf der Party: ....   3. Im Café: ....   5. Im Kino: ....
2. Beim Einkaufen: ....   4. In der Kantine: ....   6. Im Hotel: ....

__/4

6 Complete the sentences with the personal pronouns. Don't forget to use
the correct case.

1. Iwona, wann hast .... die E-Mail geschrieben?

2. Hallo Martina, hallo Jens. Ich habe ein Geschenk für ....

3. Dort steht Iwona und neben .... steht Pierre.

4. Das ist mein Freund Klaus. Ich fahre mit .... nach Polen.

5. Ich richte das aus, Herr Lang. Herr Lehmann ruft .... morgen zurück.

6. Ich esse gern frisches Obst. Am liebsten kaufe ich .... auf dem Markt.

__/6

7 Read the word snake, separate the nouns and write them in the column with
the right gender. (½ point for each correct word)

> themavortragtelefonpunktgesprächbewerbungkleidungkontakt
> bürobuchterminverabredungterminkalenderabschlussdokument
> zeugnisnachrichtabteilungverhaltenprojektausbildung
> karriererentearbeitgeber

m (der)	f (die)	n (das)
....	....	....
....	....	....
....	....	....
....	....	....
....	....	....

__/12

8 Johanna tells you about her cleaning up routine. Listen to the CD and answer the questions.

1. Wo ist das dreckige Geschirr? _____

2. Wo ist die Kleidung? _____

3. Wo stehen die sauberen Teller? _____

4. Und wo stehen die Gläser? _____

__/5 5. Wo sitzt Johanna nach dem Aufräumen? _____

9 Read the situations below. Choose the matching German phrase from the box and say it loud.

> Darf ich dir Philipp vorstellen? Wir arbeiten zusammen.
> Lass uns doch ins Kino gehen. Hallo, kommt bitte herein! Toll, dass ihr da seid.
> Das haben Sie wirklich sehr gut gemacht.
> Morgen koche ich für meine Freunde. Deshalb muss ich jetzt noch einkaufen.
> Entschuldigung, wie komme ich zum nächsten Supermarkt?

1. Welcome your friends to your party and say how great it is, that they're here.

2. Ask your way to the next supermarket.

3. Make a proposal for your evening plans.

4. Introduce your friend from work.

5. Give a reason why you have to go shopping now.

__/6 6. Praise your colleague for his/her good work.

10 Iwona and Pierre are still looking at photographs of their families.
Fill in the gaps with the missing possessive pronouns (used as articles).

> dein   deine   deinen   euren   ihre   ihrem   mein   seine   unseren

Pierre	Iwona, ist das _____ (1.) Bruder?
Iwona	Ja, das ist _____ (2.) Bruder. Neben ihm steht _____ (3.) Frau mit _____ (4.) Kind.
Pierre	Und das ist _____ (5.) Großmutter?
Iwona	Genau. Alle anderen Personen neben ihr sind _____ (6.)Kinder.
Pierre	Oh, sie hat aber viele Kinder.
Iwona	Stimmt. Pierre, das hier bist du mit _____ (7.) Schwestern, oder?
Pierre	Ja.
Iwona	Und das seid ihr mit _____ (8.) Großeltern?
Pierre	Richtig, das sind wir mit _____ (9.) Großeltern!

__/9

11 Read the extract from a networking guide. Cross out the wrong answers.

> Wenn Sie nach neuen Kontakten für Ihr persönliches Netzwerk suchen, dann ist es immer besser, nur einen oder zwei Kontakte zu knüpfen, die aber später auch von Nutzen sind*. Nur einfach viele Visitenkarten einsammeln, ist oft keine gute Idee. Gerade bei größeren Besprechungen hat man keine Zeit für mehr als ein oder zwei gute Gespräche. Deshalb ist es auch gut, wenn man vor einer Besprechung zum Beispiel im Internet schaut, welcher Teilnehmer ein interessanter Kontakt sein könnte. Und interessant ist ein beruflicher Kontakt, wenn man ähnliche Interessen hat.
> * von Nutzen sein *be of use*

1. Man sollte *immer so viele Kontakte wie möglich | nur wenige gute Kontakte* knüpfen.
2. Man sollte *mit seinem Kontakt auch kurz sprechen | von seinem Kontakt nur eine Visitenkarte nehmen.*
3. Informationen über einen neuen Kontakt sollte man *schon vor | erst auf einer* Besprechung suchen.
4. Ein interessanter Kontakt hat ähnliche *Interessen | Hobbys.*   ___/4

12 Answer the question using a pronoun instead of the underlined noun.

1. Siehst du <u>Pierre</u>? – Ja, _____ .

2. Willst du <u>ein Stück Kuchen</u>? – Nein, _____ .

3. Gebt ihr <u>den Kindern</u> Geschenke? – Ja, _____ .

4. Hast du auch <u>eine Schwester</u>? – Ja, _____ .

5. Ist <u>Martina</u> da? – Nein, _____ .

6. Ist die E-Mail von <u>deiner Schwester</u>? Nein, _____ .   ___/6

13 Listen to the conversation between Martina, Iwona and Pierre. They are talking about their plans once they've finished the German class. What are they going to do?

1. Iwona: ....
2. Pierre: ....
_/3 3. Martina: ....

14 Read the semantic fields and find the fitting generic term in the box. Not all generic terms are used.

Monate Haus Gemüse Jahreszeiten Freizeit Wetter Sommer Sport Obst

1. .... : Treppe, Aufzug, Stockwerk, Schlüssel
2. .... : Sommer, Winter, Frühling, Herbst
3. .... : Regen, Schnee, Wind, Gewitter
4. .... : Juni, Januar, Juli, August
5. .... : Tennis, Radfahren, Joggen, Judo
_/6 6. .... : Banane, Apfel, Pfirsich, Weintraube

◉ 2/44 **15** Read the answers in the box below. Then listen to the questions on the CD and say the correct answer after the beep. You'll hear the correct answer again before the next question.

> Am liebsten am Donnerstag.   Eine große Tasse Kaffee, bitte.
> Ich will Lehrer werden.
> Ich bin hingefallen und habe mich an der Hand verletzt.
_/6 Am besten mit dem Auto.   Ich glaube, dass es morgen regnen wird.

16 Match the phrases with the corresponding situation. One situation remains.

1. Die Rechnung bitte.	a) Bahnhof
2. Herzlich Willkommen!	b) Arzt
3. Was unternehmen wir heute?	c) Fernsehen
4. Ich gehe noch joggen.	d) Sport
5. Herzlichen Glückwunsch!	e) Einladung
6. Wo ist der Fahrplan?	f) Geburtstag
7. Was kommt denn heute?	g) Markt
8. Ich hätte gerne ein Kilo Bananen.	h) Freizeit
_/8	i) Restaurant

17 The articles in the text are missing. Can you fill in the gaps?

einen ein paar die seinen vielen der viel sein das viel ihrem den

Iwona und Pierre sind bald mit _____ (1.) Deutschkurs fertig.

Zum Schluss wird es _____ (2.) großen Abschlusstest geben. Deshalb müssen Pierre und Iwona noch lernen. Aber sie haben nicht _____ (3.) Zeit.

Iwona muss sich mit _____ (4.) Kunden treffen. Darum kann sie nur

_____ (5.) Stunden in _____ (6.) Woche lernen. Auch Pierre hat

_____ (7.) Arbeit: Er muss _____ (8.) Bewerbungsgespräch vorbereiten. Pierre will _____ (9.) Test gut machen, aber _____ (10.)

Bewerbungsgespräch ist wichtiger! Wir drücken ihnen _____ (11.) Daumen

für _____ (12.) Test!   ___/12

18 Read the text and answer the questions in full sentences.

Claudias Wohnung
Wir haben eine kleine Wohnung mit vier Zimmern. Im Wohnzimmer steht ein brauner Tisch mit vier schwarzen Stühlen. Es gibt auch einen weißen Schrank mit Geschirr und zwei grüne Regale mit Büchern. Unser Fernseher steht auch dort. In der Küche haben wir einen Tisch mit zwei Stühlen. Der Tisch hier ist gelb. Dort essen wir oft unser Frühstück. Das große Bett steht im Schlafzimmer. Dort steht auch unser roter Schrank, in dem wir unsere Kleidung haben. Rechts neben dem Bett steht eine rote Kommode. Dort haben wir unsere Unterwäsche. Im Bad haben wir eine Dusche, ein WC und einen kleinen weißen Schrank.

1. Wie viele Stühle hat Claudia? _____

2. Wo steht der gelbe Tisch? _____

3. Wo steht ein weißer Schrank? _____

4. Welche Farbe haben die Regale? _____

5. Welche Möbel stehen im Wohnzimmer? _____   ___/5

19 The verbs in brackets are missing in these sentences. Which is the correct position for each verb? Don't forget about the appropriate form and – where necessary – tense.

1. Wenn ihr wollt, dann _____ wir euch _____ . (helfen)

2. Ich _____ gern auf dem Markt _____ . (einkaufen)

3. Du _____ heute die Rechnung im Restaurant _____ . (bezahlen)

4. _____ Sie mir bitte _____ , wo der Bahnhof ist? (sagen, können)

5. Wir fahren am Wochenende nach Hamburg, denn _____ ich

_____ noch nicht in Hamburg _____ . (sein *Präteritum*)

6. Ich denke, dass _____ du _____ den Vortrag gestern gut

___/6 _____ . (machen *Perfekt*)

20 The following sentences got mixed up. Additionally, the verbs are still in infinitive forms. Can you put the sentences back in the correct order and the verbs in the right form and tense (and don't forget the auxiliary verbs where necessary)?

1. am Donnerstag / um 9 Uhr / ich / einen wichtigen Termin / haben (*Präsens*) / .

2. wir / einen interessanten Vortrag / halten (*Futur I*) / zusammen / .

3. du / wann / E-Mail / verschicken (*Perfekt*) / die / ?

4. jetzt / in / ein / ihr / Café / gehen (*Futur I*) / ?

5. er / einen / müssen (*Präteritum*) / erst / vereinbaren / Termin / .

6. anrufen (*Perfekt*) / wen / gestern / Sie / ?

___/6

21 Read the questions below and then listen to the phone conversation on the CD. ⊙ 2/45
Answer the questions.

1. Mit wem will Herr Meyer sprechen?
   a) ☐ Mit Herrn   b) ☐ Mit Herrn   c) ☐ Mit Herrn Thomas.
       Maurer.   Schneider.

2. Wann ist der alte Termin von Herrn Meyer?
   a) ☐ Am 7.4.,   b) ☐ Am 17.4., um   c) ☐ Am 17.4., um 11 Uhr.
       um 9.30 Uhr.   9.30 Uhr.

3. Wann ist der neue Termin?
   a) ☐ Um 4 Uhr.   b) ☐ Um 11 Uhr.   c) ☐ Um 14 Uhr.

4. Wie ist die Telefonnummer von Herrn Meyer?
   a) ☐ 0431 98223.   b) ☐ 0341 92832.   c) ☐ 0431 92833.   __/4

22 Complete the text to make sensible sentences.

Iwona ist in ihrem Büro. Heute muss sie viel _____ (1.). Zuerst schreibt sie

eine _____ (2.) an Frau Engel von der Firma Bärmann. Danach muss sie mit

Herrn Meier von der Firma Meier & Co. _____ (3.), denn sie muss ihn einige

Dinge fragen. Um 13 Uhr isst sie in der Kantine zu Mittag. Am _____ (4.) hat

sie einen Termin mit einem Kollegen. Sie müssen zusammen eine _____ (5.)

mit einem Kunden vorbereiten. Am Abend trifft sie sich mit Freunden und sie gehen in

eine _____ (6.), wo sie etwas trinken. Dann _____ (7.) sie mit dem

Bus nach Hause und geht bald ins _____ (8.) .   __/8

        __/150

Grammatical terminology

German Term	English Term	Example
Adjektiv	adjective	der nette Kollege
Adverb (Pl Adverbien)	adverb	morgen, dort
Akkusativ	accusative	Ich rufe den Mann an.
Akkusativobjekt	direct object	Ich sehe den Mann.
Artikel	article	einem Mann, meine Mutter, die Schwester
bestimmter Artikel	definite article	der Apfel, das Buch
Dativ	dative	Ich gebe den Kindern Obst.
Dativobjekt	indirect object	Ich gebe dem Mann einen Kuchen.
Deklination	declension	der Mann, den Mann, dem Mann
Demonstrativartikel	demonstrative determiner	diese Frau
Diphthong	diphthong	au, ei, eu
Fragepronomen	interrogative pronoun	Wer ist das?
Futur I	a German future tense	Ich werde nach Berlin fahren.
Hauptsatz	main clause	Ich denke, dass du gut bist.
Hilfsverb	auxiliary verb	Er hat eine E-Mail geschrieben.
Imperativ	imperative	Ruf mich an!
Infinitiv	infinitive	gehen, essen
Kardinalzahl	cardinal numeral	eins, zwei drei
Komparativ	comparative	schneller, schöner
Konjugation	conjugation	ich gehe, du gehst, er geht
Konjunktion	conjunction	und, oder, dass, weil
Konsonant	consonant	b, c, d, f, g
Modalverb	modal verb	wollen, müssen, dürfen
Nebensatz	subordinated clause	Ich denke, dass du gut bist.
Nominativ	nominative	der Mann
Ordinalzahl	ordinal numeral	Der erste April.
Partizip Perfekt	past participle	gegessen, gewartet
Perfekt	a German past tense	Ich habe dich angerufen.
Person	person	erste Person Singular: ich
Personalpronomen	personal pronoun	ich, sie, wir
Plural	plural	(zwei) Bücher
Possessivpronomen	possessive pronoun	mein Vater, seine Schwester

German Term	English Term	Example
Präposition	preposition	Er ist in einem Museum.
Präsens	the German present tense	Ich bin in Deutschland.
Präteritum	simple past	Ich war in Berlin.
Pronomen	pronoun	sie, man, alle, jemand
Relativpronomen	relative pronoun	Meine Schwester, die Kathrin heißt, ...
Singular	singular	(ein) Buch
Steigerung	comparison	schön, schöner, am schönsten
Subjekt	subject	Martina geht einkaufen.
Substantiv/Nomen	noun	das Haus, die Frage
Superlativ	superlative	am schnellsten, am schönsten
Umlaut	umlaut	ä, ö, ü
unbestimmter Artikel	indefinite article	ein Auto, eine Frau
Verb	verb	fahren, er fährt
Vokal	vowel	a, e, i, o, u

Short Grammar

§1 Nouns

Nouns in German are always written with a capital letter. All nouns have a gender and are either masculine (m), feminine (f) or neuter (n). They have a plural and there are different cases to differentiate the role of the noun in the sentence.

§1.1 Gender ▸ *Day 2*

The gender is not always logical and can differ from the natural gender of a noun – e.g. **das Mädchen** *girl* is neuter (in most cases, luckily, the gender of a person is like the natural gender, though). There are a few endings that give the gender away:

m: -ling, -ismus, -er	f: -heit, -keit, -ung, -ion	n: -chen, -lein, -(t)um

But since the exception proves the rule (e.g. **die** Mutt**er**), it's best to learn a noun right away with its definite article (▸ *§2.1*), because the definite article shows the gender! The gender of compound nouns is always that of the last part of the compound: *die* **Stadt** + *das* **Zentrum** → *das* **Stadtzentrum**.

§1.2 Plural

There are no general rules as to how to build the plural. Here too, the best advice is to learn the correct plural form together with the noun itself.

§1.3 Cases ▸ *Day 4, Day 5, Day 6*

German has four cases: **Nominativ, Genitiv, Dativ, Akkusativ**. Most nouns look the same in the different cases – it's mostly the article (▸ *§2.1*) that is declined (mostly, because nouns in the dative plural get an **-n** ending if they do not already end with **-n**).

The nominative is the case of a sentence's subject. Then there's the accusative for things or people you see, have or in general do something with and the dative is usually an object that receives something. The case of a noun depends on its role in the sentence and that role is given by the verb (or a preposition ▸ *§5*). For example the verb **sehen** *see* needs a subject (that is always needed!) that sees and an object in the accusative that is seen. Or the verb **geben** *give* needs a subject, an accusative object (what is given) and a dative object (whom is it given).

Pierre sieht den Mann. *Pierre sees the man.*

Pierre gibt dem Mann den Apfel. *Pierre gives the man the apple.*

The dative object usually stands before the accusative object.

§2 Articles

Articles are the companions of nouns. And where the noun does not so easily reveal its case or gender, the article does (especially the definite article). There are different kinds of articles in German, but all share one characteristic: they stand in front of a noun and have the same gender, case and number as the noun.

§2.1 The definite and indefinite article ▸ *Day 2, Day 5*

The definite article **der/die/das** *the* usually is used when the noun is known or it's a singular distinct person/thing. Use the indefinite article **ein/eine/ein** *a* (but also *one*) when referring to something in general or yet unknown. The use of German articles is often similar to English. The indefinite article has no plural!

	m	f	n	Pl
Nom.	der/ein	die/eine	das/ein	die/–
Acc.	den/einen	die/eine	das/ein	die/–
Dat.	dem/einem	der/einer	dem/einem	den/–

§2.2 Other articles ▸ *Day 7, Day 26*

There are some other articles in German. As said above, they all stand in front of a noun and have the same gender, case and number as that noun. Most can be used as pronouns (i.e. instead of the noun) too, so they will be explained in the next paragraph.

§2.2.1 Demonstrative determiner

The demonstrative determiner **dieser/diese/dieses** *this, that* has the same function as in English. The forms are similar to the forms of **der/die/das**.
Dieser Mann ruft **diese** Frau an. *That man calls that woman.*

§2.2.2 kein ▸ *Day 4*

kein (▸ *§4*) is the negative indefinite article and the forms are the same as those of the indefinite article. It has, however, a plural form that is **keine** in nominative and accusative and **keinen** in dative.
Kein Mensch ruft mich an. *Nobody calls me.*
Jens kauft heute **kein** Obst. *Jens buys no fruit today.*

§2.2.2 Nullartikel ▸ Day 7

Nullartikel means that there is no article. It is used for example with mass nouns of undefined quantity or professions (note that in English professions have the indefinite article!).
Ich brauche noch Milch. *I still need milk.*
Ich bin Lehrer. *I'm a teacher.*

§2.2.4 Interrogative article ▸ Day 25

There are two interrogative articles: **welcher/welche/welches?** *which?* and **was für ein/eine/ein?** *what (kind of)?* The forms of **welcher** are similar to the definite article and those of **was für ein** to the indefinite article.
Was für einen Film willst du sehen? – Einen Actionfilm.
What (kind of) film would you like to see? – An action movie.
Welches Buch willst du lesen? – Harry Potter 4.
Which book would you like to read? – Harry Potter 4.

§3 Pronouns

§3.1 Personal pronouns ▸ Day 2, Day 8

Personal pronouns can replace known persons or things, i.e. all nouns.

Declination of the personal pronouns						
Nom.	ich	du	er/sie/es	wir	ihr	sie/Sie
Acc.	mich	dich	ihn/sie/es	uns	euch	sie/Sie
Dat.	mir	dir	ihm/ihr/ihm	uns	euch	ihnen/Ihnen

Let's have a look at the verb **geben** *give*. It needs a subject (**Pierre**), a dative object (**Iwona**) and an accusative object (**einen Apfel**):
Pierre gibt Iwona einen Apfel. *Pierre gives Iwona an apple.*
Pierre gibt **ihr** den Apfel. *Pierre gives her the apple.*
If, however, the accusative object is represented by a pronoun, that pronoun stands even before the dative object (▸ §1.3):
Pierre gibt **ihn** Iwona. *Pierre gives it Iwona.*
Pierre gibt **ihn** ihr. *He gives it to her.*

The formal address **Sie** *you* always has the same form as the third person plural (**sie**). The formal address pronouns are always written with a capital **S** and are the same in singular and plural.

§3.1.1 The impersonal *es* ▸ *Day 19*

Since every sentence has to have a subject and sometimes there is no real subject, you use **es** *it*. It's mostly used with time and weather, like in English:
Es ist Viertel nach drei. *It's a quarter past three.*
Es ist sonnig. *It's sunny.*

§3.2 Possessive pronouns (used as articles)

The possessive articles are:

Personal pronouns	Possessive articles (in the nominative)	
ich	mein	my
du	dein	your
er/sie/es	sein/ihr/sein	his/her/its
wir	unser	our
ihr	euer	your
sie/Sie	ihr/Ihr	their/your

Note that the third person singular has different pronouns depending on the gender of the possessing person (or thing). Additionally, all possessive articles have to have the same gender, case and number as their related noun, i.e. the possessed person or thing. It sounds complicated but a few examples will help:
Das ist **mein** Vater. *This is my father.*
Ich gebe **meiner** Schwester ein Buch. *I give my sister a book.*
Ich fahre mit **meinen** Freunden nach München. *I go to Munich with my friends.*
Which pronoun you choose depends therefore on the possessing person or thing. The ending, though, depends on the following, related noun. Those endings are similar to the endings of the indefinite article:

	Nom.	Acc.	Dat.
Sg	mein/mein**e**/mein	mein**en**/mein**e**/mein	mein**em**/mein**er**/mein**em**
Pl	mein**e**	mein**e**	mein**en**

The other possessive articles have the same endings. Note, that if **euer** gets an ending, the **e** before the **r** is omitted:
Wo sind **eure** Freunde? *Where are your friends?*
Wir sitzen auf **eurem** Sofa. *We're sitting on your sofa.*

§3.3 Interrogative pronouns

Wer? Wen? Wem?	Wie?	Was?	Wann?	Warum?	Wo?	Wohin?	Womit?
Who? Who(m)? Who(m)?	How?	What?	When?	Why?	Where?	Where to?	With what?

§3.4 Relative pronouns ▸ *Day 25*

The relative pronouns **der/die/das** *who, which, that* are used in relative clauses. The number and gender of the relative pronoun is always the same as that of the related noun. The case of the relative pronoun depends on the role of the pronoun in the subordinate clause. It can be any kind of object!
The forms of the relative pronouns are identical to the definite article (▸ *§2.1*), with one exception: the dative of plural relative pronouns is **denen**.
Der Kunde, **dem** ich schreibe, ist wichtig. *The client, to whom I'm writing, is important.*

§3.5 Indefinite pronouns ▸ *Day 26*

§3.5.1 einer/keiner

You can use the indefinite article **ein** and the negative indefinite article **kein** as pronouns. For example in short answers.
Willst du einen Apfel? – Nein, ich will **keinen**.
Do you want an apple? – No, I don't want any.
The forms are similar to the indefinite article with following exceptions:
Nominative masculine: **ein*er*/kein*er*** and nominative/accusative neuter:
eins/keins.

§3.5.2 man

The indefinite pronoun **man** can replace any unknown or unspecified person.
It's always the subject of the sentence and the verb always has the ending for the third person singular. It's often used to paraphrase passive constructions.
Man kann in Berlin viele Sachen sehen. *One can see a lot of things in Berlin.*
Hier darf **man** nicht rauchen. *Smoking is not allowed here.*

§3.5.3 jemand/niemand ▸ *Day 23*

jemand *someone/somebody* and **niemand** *no one/nobody* have accusative and dative endings:

Nom.	Acc.	Dat.
jemand/niemand	jemand**en**/niemand**en**	jemand**em**/niemand**em**

Ich habe dort **niemanden** gesehen. *I have seen nobody there.*
Luckily in spoken language they are often not declined:
Ich habe dort **jemand** gesehen. *I have seen somebody there.*

§3.5.4 Other indefinite pronouns

German knows a lot of other pronouns that are indefinite regarding gender or number. In most cases they can be used as pronouns as well as articles. You can find an overview in (▸ *Day 23*) and (▸ *Day 26*).

§4 Negation ▸ *Day 4*

To negate single nouns you use the negative indefinite article **kein** (▸ *§2.2*). It always stands right in front of the noun.
To negate other words or a whole sentence you use **nicht** *not*.
Das Haus ist **nicht** schön. *The house is not nice.*
Ich schreibe dir **nicht**. *I am not writing to you.*
When negating a whole sentence **nicht** tends to stand as near to the end as possible (at the end of the middle field, ▸ *§10*) like in the second example.
With modal verbs **nicht** stands usually near the modal verb:
Ich will **nicht** ins Museum gehen. *I don't want to go to the museum.*

§5 Prepositions

Some verbs need an object that is neither an accusative object nor a dative object, but begins with a preposition. For example the verb **gehen** *go* needs an object that specifies the destination.
Ich gehe **in** ein Museum. *I go to a museum.*
Commonly prepositions are used for local or temporal information. Most prepositions need the following noun in a specific case. Thus it's good to learn the preposition together with a noun in the correct case. The prepositions themselves do not change!

§5.1 Prepositions with the dative or the accusative ▸ *Day 11, Day 12*

in	an	auf	über	unter	neben	zwischen	vor	hinter
in	at	on	over	beneath	by, next to	between	in front of	behind

After these prepositions the noun can be in the accusative or the dative. One of these prepositions plus a dative noun says where something is. A preposition plus an accusative noun gives a direction to somewhere.

The rule is as follows: If you ask *where?* it's the dative, and if you ask *where to?* the accusative.

Some prepositions can merge with a following definite article:

in + dem → **im**	an + dem → **am**	in + das → **ins**	an + das → **ans**

§5.2 Prepositions with the dative ▸ *Day 17*

aus	von	nach	zu	bei	mit	seit
from	from, of	to, toward, after, past	to, toward	at, by, next to	with	since, for

These prepositions are always followed by a noun in the dative. Here also the prepositions can merge:

von + dem → **vom**	zu + dem → **zum** zu + der → **zur**	bei + dem → **beim**

§5.3 Prepositions with the accusative

bis	durch	für	gegen	ohne	um
until, to	through, by	for	against, around	without	around, at

These prepositions are always followed by a noun in the accusative. They don't merge with articles!

§5.4 Temporal prepositions ▸ *Day 15*

For certain temporal statements you always use the same prepositions:

um	time	Wir treffen uns **um** 17.30 Uhr.
am	times of the day	Ich komme **am** Morgen zu dir. Wir gehen **am** Abend ins Kino.
	for days and dates	Er fährt **am** Mittwoch nach Potsdam. Sie besuchen die Eltern **am** 4. März.
im	months and seasons	**Im** Sommer ist es sehr heiß. **Im** November beginnt der Winter.

§6 Adjectives - *Day 27, Day 28*

Adjectives have the function to specify nouns. To fulfil this role they stand either in front of nouns or with the verbs **sein** *be* (or **werden** *get*).

§6.1 Adjectives with *sein* or *werden*

Adjectives in this position are not declined – which is great, isn't it? You use the adjective's basic form – the one you can find in the dictionary.
Der Apfel ist **rot**. *The apple is red.* Es wird **heiß**. *It's getting hot.*

§6.2 Adjectives in front of the noun

An adjective in front of the noun has to be declined. That means that the case, gender and number of the adjective is the same as that of the noun (and article).
The endings of the adjectives differ whether you use the definite or indefinite article.

	m (e.g. **Plan**)	f (e.g. **Frage**)	n (e.g. **Buch**)	Pl (e.g. **Strategien**)
Adjectives in front of nouns with a definite article				
Nom.	der gute	die gute	das gute	die guten
Acc.	den guten	die gute	das gute	die guten
Dat.	dem guten	der guten	dem guten	den guten
Adjectives in front of nouns with an indefinite article				
Nom.	ein guter	eine gute	ein gutes	– gute
Acc.	einen guten	eine gute	ein gutes	– gute
Dat.	einem guten	einer guten	einem guten	– guten

The declination of adjectives with other articles always follows one of these two paradigms.

Like with definite articles: the interrogative article **welcher, welche, welches** *which*, the articles **jeder, jede, jedes** *each* and **alle** *all* and the demonstrative article **dieser, dieser, dieses** *this/that*.

Dieses neue Haus ist schön. *This new house is nice.*

Er sieht **jeden** neu**en** Film. *He watches each new film.*

Like with indefinite articles: possessive articles (**mein** *my*, **dein** *your* … – but: adjectives with possessive articles have an **-en** ending in the plural!), the interrogative article **was für ein** *what* and the remaining articles from Day 26 (▸ *Day 26*).

Mein neu**er** Kollege ist Franzose. *My new colleague is a Frenchman.*

Sie haben **viele** alt**e** Weine. *They have many old wines.*

§6.3 Adjective (and adverb) comparison ▸ *Day 9*

For the comparison of adjectives with **sein** you need two suffixes: **-er** for the comparative and **-sten** (or **-esten** after d, t, s, sch, z and vowels) for the superlative. Just add them to the basic form: neu – neu**er** – am neu**esten**.

Comparative adjectives in front of a noun are built with the basic form *plus* **-er-** for comparative or **-(e)st-** for superlative *plus* the ending according to the table in (▸ *§6.2*): das neu**ere** Haus – der neu**este** Parkplatz.

Contrary to English the superlative of an adjective with **sein** has **am** in front of the adjective. In front of the noun the superlative is only used with the definite article. Most monosyllabic adjectives with **a**, **o**, **u** get the respective umlaut **ä**, **ö**, **ü** in the comparative and superlative: lang – l**ä**nger – der l**ä**ngste.

And finally there are some adjectives that are compared irregularly. The few adverbs that can be compared, are also in this list.

	Basic form	Comparative	Superlative
good	gut	besser	am besten
high	hoch	höher	am höchsten
near	nah	näher	am nächsten
much	viel	mehr	am meisten
gladly	gern	lieber	am liebsten
often	oft	öfter/häufig	am häufigsten/(*rare:* am öftesten)
soon	bald	eher	am ehesten

§7 Adverbs

Adverbs specify other words or the whole sentence. They are not declined and usually have no comparison (- §6.3). There are three big groups of adverbs:
With temporal adverbs you can say when something happens or in what order.
Ich gehe **morgen** ins Museum. *I go to the museum tomorrow.*
Danach mache ich einen Spaziergang. *Afterwards I go for a walk.*
The local adverbs determine the position or (often with prepositions) the direction.
Ich bin **hier**. *I am here.*
Gehen Sie **dort vorne** nach **rechts**. *Turn right there up ahead.*
Often you use more than one local adverb in a sentence (e.g. **dort vorne** *there up ahead*, **hinten links** *in the back left*).
Finally you can use adverbs of grade and frequency if you want to specify how much or how often you do something.
Sie mag ihren Freund **sehr**. *She likes her friend much.*
Ich telefoniere **oft** mit meiner Freundin. *I call my friend often.*

§7.1 Position in the sentence - *Day 11*

An adverb can take the first position in a sentence:
Morgen gehe ich ins Museum. *Tomorrow I go to the museum.*
If you have more than one adverb, the temporal adverbs usually come first and the local last.
Ich bin **morgen sicher dort**. *I am there tomorrow for sure.*

§8 Verbs

Verbs express actions, events or states. The basic form (which you can find in the vocabulary) is infinitive. Most verbs in the infinitive end with **-en**: geh**en**, wart**en**, hab**en**, einkauf**en** ... In sentences they show the tense and they are conjugated. That means that the verb's ending shows the person of the subject.

§8.1 Präsens - *Day 2, Day 3*

Präsens is the German simple present. Be aware that German has no progressive forms like English! So there is no grammatical way in German to differ between habitual and actual ongoing actions and events. You can use the **Präsens** to express both (differences can be made with adverbs like **immer** *always*).
Verbs have different endings according to the subject of the sentence.

	gehen go	reisen travel	warten wait	ending
ich	gehe	reise	warte	-e
du	gehst	reist	wartest	-st
er/sie/es	geht	reist	wartet	-t
wir	gehen	reisen	warten	-en
ihr	geht	reist	wartet	-t
sie/Sie	gehen	reisen	warten	-en

If the stem of the verb ends with an **s**, **ss**, **ß** or **z** the second person singular (**du**) gets only a **-t** as ending. If it ends with **t** or **d** there's an additional **-e-** between the stem and the ending in the second and third person singular (**du**, **er/sie/es**) and second person plural (**ihr**).

There are also some verbs which have irregular forms in the present tense:

	laufen walk, run	geben give	sehen see
ich	laufe	gebe	sehe
du	läufst	gibst	siehst
er/sie/es	läuft	gibt	sieht
wir	laufen	geben	sehen
ihr	lauft	gebt	seht
sie/Sie	laufen	geben	sehen

You can see, the endings are the same as those of the regular forms. But the vowels in the second and third person singular change! **a/au** become **ä/äu**, **e** becomes **i** or **ie**. Be careful, because there are only a handful of those verbs:

essen → du **isst**, er **isst**   fahren → du **fährst**, er **fährt**   lesen → du **liest**, er **liest**

As you saw above, not all verbs with **e** have this change (e.g. **gehen**).

§8.2 Perfekt ▸ Day 20, Day 21

Perfekt is the past tense that is most commonly used in spoken German. The modal verbs (▸ §8.6) and **haben** and **sein** (▸ §8.5) are mostly used in their **Präteritum** forms, though.

The structure of the German **Perfekt** (the auxiliary verb **haben** or **sein** in the Präsens plus past participle) is similar to the English present perfect – the use, however, differs. Just use the **Perfekt** for all statements about the past.

When to use **haben** and when **sein**? Most verbs of movement (like **gehen** *go*, **fahren** *drive*) or change of state (like **einschlafen** *fall asleep*) build the **Perfekt** with **sein**. The rest (which is by far the bigger part) use **haben**.

And how to build the past participle? Like in English there are regular and irregular verbs. A lot of verbs used in every day language fall into the irregular category – you will find a list of those verbs to learn and consult at the end of this grammar. The regular verbs use the infinitive as a base for the past participle. In most cases the infinitive gets the prefix **ge-** and the **-en** ending is chopped of and replaced with a **-t** (or **-et** if there's a t or d before the **-en**):

hören → ge**hö**rt	kosten → ge**kostet**

If the infinitive already has a non-separable prefix (like **ver-**, **ent-**, **be-**) this prefix stays instead and just the **-en** ending is replaced with **-(e)t**:

verletzen → verletz**t**	sich beeilen → sich beeil**t**

A separable prefix (like **mit-**, **ab-**, **aus-**) also stays but the past participle additionally gets the prefix **-ge-** right after the separable prefix. And don't forget the **-(e)t** ending.

aufhängen → auf**ge**hängt	vorstellen → vor**ge**stellt

Together, the conjugated form of **haben** or **sein** and the past participle build the **Perfekt**:

Die Äpfel **haben** 1,90 Euro **gekostet**. *The apples cost 1,90 Euro.*
Er **ist** nach Paris **gereist**. *He traveled to Paris.*
Ich **bin** zu spät zur Arbeit **gekommen**. *I've come too late to work.*

Most verbs that build the **Perfekt** with **sein** are irregular. There are only a few regular verbs with **sein**, among them **passieren** *happen* and **reisen** *travel*. However, not all irregular verbs build the **Perfekt** with **sein**!

§8.3 Präteritum

The **Präteritum** is rarely used in spoken German (which is our main goal in this book). However, there are a few verbs (**haben**, **sein** and the modal verbs) that are more often used in **Präteritum** than **Perfekt** (▸ *§8.5, §8.6*).

The list with irregular verbs after this grammar contains the **Präteritum** forms, because it's sensible to learn all forms at once. The **Präteritum** endings for regular verbs are the same as for modal verbs (▸ *Day 13*).

§8.4 Futur ▸ *Day 9, Day 29*

There are two different ways to talk about the future. You can either use the verb in the present tense and a temporal adverb (like **später** *later*, **morgen** *tomorrow* ...) or use the forms of the **Futur I**.

The **Futur I** is built with the appropriate form of **werden** and the infinitive:

Jens **geht** morgen mit Martina ins Kino. = Jens **wird** morgen mit Martina ins Kino **gehen**.

In spoken language the present tense with a temporal adverb is more common. The **Futur I**, however, is often used to underline the certainty of a future plan – like the English future with *going to*.

§8.5 haben and sein ▸ *Day 4, Day 12*

haben and **sein** are often used but conjugated irregularly:

	ich	du	er/sie/es	wir	ihr	sie/Sie
Präsens present tense						
haben	habe	hast	hat	haben	habt	haben
sein	bin	bist	ist	sind	seid	sind
Präteritum simple past						
haben	hatte	hattest	hatte	hatten	hattet	hatten
sein	war	warst	war	waren	wart	waren

Even if a text is written in **Perfekt** (▸ *§8.2*) **haben** and **sein** are usually used in their simple past forms. However, they have **Perfekt** forms too: **ich habe gehabt, du hast gehabt**, .../**ich bin gewesen, du bist gewesen**, ...

§8.6 Modal verbs ▸ *Day 5, Day 8, Day 10, Day 13*

Modal verbs are used to express wishes, necessities or prohibitions. They have a few grammatical peculiarities. Refer to Day 13 (▸ *Day 13*) for a comprehensive overview of their forms of **Präsens** and **Präteritum**. When you look at the tables you'll see that the first and third person singular (**ich, er/sie/es**) have no endings and (with the exception of **sollen**) the singular forms have a different vowel than the infinitive and plural. Modal verbs are usually combined with a verb in the infinitive. The modal verb is always the conjugated verb and therefore stands in the second position in a declarative sentence or the last in a subordinated clause (▸ *§10*).

Du **sollst** deinen Chef anrufen! *You should call your boss.*

Ich denke, dass wir uns morgen treffen **wollen**. *I think, that we want to meet tomorrow.*

Müssen *must/have to* expresses duty and necessity, often used when giving commands. Be careful with the negation: **nicht müssen** means *there's no need to*.
Sollen *shall/should* is often used for the same purposes as **müssen**. Commonly used for advice too.
Wollen *want* is used for wishes.
Können *can* expresses the possibility or ability to do something.
Dürfen *may/might* expresses permission to do something. The negation **nicht dürfen** expresses a prohibition and means *must not*.
Apart from these basic modal verbs there are some others (which are actually subjunctive forms of those above – so they have no own infinitive):

können → du könntest	sollen → Sie sollten	mögen → ich möchte

These are often considered more polite forms than the above and are used generally for the same purposes as the normal forms.
Mögen *like* itself is not a modal verb (although it conjugates like one: **ich mag, du magst, er mag, wir mögen, ihr mögt, sie mögen**), because it does not join with a verb in the infinitive but a noun. The forms **möcht-**, however, are modal verbs.
Another verb that conjugates like a modal verb is **wissen** *know*:

	ich	du	er/sie/es	wir	ihr	sie
present	weiß	weißt	weiß	wissen	wisst	wissen
past	wusste	wusstest	wusste	wussten	wusstet	wussten

The **Perfekt** forms (▸ §8.2) are **ich habe gewusst, er hat gewusst** …

§8.7 Verbs with prefixes ▸ *Day 10*

The German has a lot of verbs with prefixes. Often there is a basic verb, like **nehmen** *take*, and a lot of additional different forms with different prefixes, like **aufnehmen** *record*, **mitnehmen** *take along*, **annehmen** *accept/assume*. These verbs always conjugate in the same way as the basic form!
Most prefixes that are prepositions (like the above examples) are so called separable prefixes and the verbs are called **trennbare Verben** *verbs with separable prefixes*. That means in the present tense, the prefix is separated from the conjugated form and put at the end of the sentence:
Iwona **nimmt** Pierre ins Kino **mit**. *Iwona takes Pierre along to the cinema.*
Ich **komme** um 19.15 Uhr in Berlin **an**. *I will arrive at 19.15 in Berlin.*

Other prefixes are, for example, **ver-**, **ent-**, **be-**, **ge-**. These prefixes are never separable:

Er **ver**letzt sich. *He hurts himself.*

Wir **be**eilen uns. *We have to hurry.*

This differentiation is important for the past participle (▸ §18.2).

Note that for pronunciation these separable prefixes are always stressed (non separable prefixes are not)!

§8.8 Reflexive verbs ▸ *Day 18*

Some verbs in the vocabulary have the word **sich** added (like the two verbs from the examples above with non-separable prefixes). **Sich** is the reflexive pronoun. That means that the verb's object is identical to the subject.

The forms of the reflexive pronoun are the same as those of the personal pronouns in the accusative with the exception of the third persons in singular and plural and the formal **Sie**:

Personal pronoun (Nom.)	ich	du	er/sie/es	wir	ihr	sie/Sie
Reflexive pronoun	mich	dich	**sich**	uns	euch	**sich**

Real reflexive verbs (i.e. the object can not be different from the subject) are rare in German. Examples are **sich beeilen** *to hurry*, **sich freuen** *look forward to* or **sich treffen** *meet*. Note that these examples are not reflexive in English!

A lot of verbs can be used like reflexive verbs: e.g. **waschen** *wash.*

Ich wasche mich. *I wash myself.*

Ich wasche dich. *I wash you.*

Ich wasche meine Wäsche. *I wash my clothes.*

Wir waschen uns. *We wash ourselves./We wash each other.*

Note the ambiguity in the last example. The plural pronouns (**uns, euch, sich**) can be reflexive or mean *each other*!

§8.9 Imperative ▸ *Day 7*

The imperative is used for commands and requests, just like in English. There are three different forms:

	Declarative sentence	Imperative sentence
informal **du** *(Sg)*	Du nimmst Platz. You take a seat.	**Nimm** Platz. Take a seat.
informal **ihr** *(Pl)*	Ihr nehmt Platz. You take a seat.	**Nehmt** Platz. Take a seat.
formal **Sie** *(Sg+Pl)*	Sie nehmen Platz. You take a seat.	**Nehmen Sie** Platz. Take a seat.

You can see the English translation is always the same, but the German makes a difference depending on who you're talking to. In the imperative sentence the verb always takes the first place. For the formal address you keep the pronoun (but put it behind the verb). For the informal address the pronoun is omitted. For the informal plural the verb does not change, for the singular you leave the **-st** ending out.

§9 Conjunctions - *Day 15, Day 16, Day 17, Day 21, Day 24, Day 28*

There are two different kinds of conjunctions in German (just like in English): coordinating conjunctions and subordinating conjunctions.

A **coordinating conjunction** connects two main clauses. A coordinating conjunction is not a full sentence element and therefore the word order (▸ *§10*) of the two main clauses is not changed.

The most important coordinating conjunctions are:

und and	**oder** or	**aber** but	**denn** for/because

They are used like in English, with the exception of **denn** which can't stand at the beginning of a sentence.

Subordinating conjunctions connect a main clause with a subordinated clause. The word order in the subordinated clause is different (▸ *§10*).

dass that	**weil** because	**wenn** when	**als** when	**wenn** if

Dass stands after certain verbs (**glauben, denken, meinen, sagen, wissen** ...) in the main clause similar to the English.

Ich denke, **dass** du sehr gut Deutsch sprichst.
I think, that you speak German very well.

Wenn and **als** are temporal conjunctions. **Wenn** is used for events that keep repeating (in the past, the present or the future) – **als** is only used for singular events (or periods) in the past.

Als ich ein Kind war, bin ich oft ins Museum gegangen.
When I was a kid, I often went to the museum.
Ich gehe immer in ein Museum, **wenn** ich in Berlin bin.
I always visit a museum when I'm in Berlin.
Wenn has yet another meaning: if. It's used in conditional clauses, i.e. the subordinate clause with **wenn** states a condition and the main clause states the outcome if the condition comes true.
Wenn ich dieses Jahr nach Berlin fahre, besuche ich das Ägyptische Museum.
If I'm going to Berlin this year, I'll visit the Egyptian Museum.
Additionally you can begin subordinate clauses with interrogative pronouns.
It's a different way to express questions and stands often after verbs like **wissen, sagen, schreiben** ...
Weißt du, **wann** wir uns treffen? *Do you know, when we meet?*
Schreib ihm, **wo** er uns treffen kann! *Write him, where he can meet us.*
Deshalb *therefore/thus/hence* and **darum** *therefore/that's why* look like coordinating conjunctions and are used similarly to connect main clauses. However, they are full sentence elements and push the subject from the first position to the position after the verb.
Ich will nach Deutschland fahren, **darum** lerne ich Deutsch.
I want to go to Germany, that's why I learn German.
Subordinated clauses and coordinated main clauses with **aber** or **denn** are always separated from the main clause by a comma. The same applies for relative clauses.

§10 Word order - *Day 2, Day 5, Day 16*

The previous paragraph already described a lot of main and subordinate clauses.
Let's have a look at a normal main clause:
Ich sehe das Haus. *I see the house.*
The word order is similar to the English: subject – verb – object.
According to these constituents you separate the sentence in different positions:
The **first position**: that's where, in our example, the subject (**ich**) stands. The **second position**: that's where, in every declarative sentence, the conjugated verb stands.
The **middle field**: that's where the object (**das Haus**) stands.
You might ask, why is it called "middle field" – it's at the end of the sentence.
But look at a declarative sentence in the **Perfekt** for example:
Ich habe das Haus gesehen. *I have seen the house.*

Now there is a last position which is connected to the second position and has a place for parts of complex verbs. Together the second and last position build a brace around the sentence, the so called **Satzklammer**.

The following table shows the different word orders for different main clauses:

		1st position	2nd position	middle field	last position
Declarative sentence		Ich	gehe	in die Stadt.	
		Er	muss	das Geschirr	abspülen.
		Gestern	wollte	er in ein Museum	gehen.
		Wir	sind	gestern ins Kino	gegangen.
		In einem Jahr	wird	er nach Russland	fliegen.
Imperative sentence			Spül	das Geschirr	ab!
Wh question		Wann	fährt	der Zug?	
Coordinated main clauses		Pierre	macht	eine Stadt- rundfahrt	
	und	Iwona	geht	in eine Ausstellung.	

You can see, the second and last position are for the verb and its parts.

The conjugated part (e.g. a modal verb or the conjugated part of a verb with separable prefix) is in the second position in a main clause, the other, not conjugated part (e.g. an infinitive or a past participle) in the last.

In subordinated clauses the word order is different: all parts of the verb are always in the last position and the conjugated part comes last of all:

		1st position	2nd position	middle field	last position
Main		Wir	fahren	mit dem Zug,	
and subordinate clause	weil	wir		dann nicht im Stau	stehen.
Main		Ich	denke,		
and subordinate clause	dass	er		gestern noch lange	gearbeitet hat.
Main		Er	fragt	eine Passantin,	
and subordinate clause	wie	er		den Weg zum Hotel	finden kann.

The second position in the subordinated clauses is empty!

One word about the first position: In most cases the subject stands there. Temporal adverbs like to go there as well – in this case the subject comes first after the verb in the middle field.

But it's also possible that a whole subordinated clause stands there. Let's take a conditional clause for example:

Ich fahre nach München, wenn ich Zeit habe. *I go to Munich if I have time.*

If the main clause comes first, all is as shown above. However, like in English you can put the if-clause in front:

		1st position	2nd position	middle field	last position
Subordinate	Wenn	ich		Zeit	habe,
and main clause	(dann)		fahre	ich nach München.	
Subordinate	Weil	wir		dann nicht im Stau	stehen,
and main clause			fahren	wir mit dem Zug.	

Now the main clause starts with the verb, because the first position is occupied by the subordinate clause! And that's why the subject stands in the middle field here. That's possible for most subordinate sentences.

Irregular verbs

The forms of **Präsens**, **Präteritum**, **Perfekt** are all in the third person singular (**er/sie/es**).

	Infinitiv	Präsens	Präteritum	Perfekt
begin	**beginnen**	beginnt	begann	hat begonnen
ask, beg	**bitten**	bittet	bat	hat gebeten
stay	**bleiben**	bleibt	blieb	ist geblieben
break	**brechen**	bricht	brach	ist gebrochen
bring	**bringen**	bringt	brachte	hat gebracht
think	**denken**	denkt	dachte	hat gedacht
may	**dürfen**	darf	durfte	hat gedurft
advise	**empfehlen**	empfiehlt	empfahl	hat empfohlen
eat	**essen**	isst (ihr esst)	aß	hat gegessen
drive	**fahren**	fährt	fuhr	ist/hat gefahren
fall	**fallen**	fällt	fiel	ist gefallen
find	**finden**	findet	fand	hat gefunden
fly	**fliegen**	fliegt	flog	ist geflogen
be cold, freeze	**frieren**	friert	fror	hat gefroren
give	**geben**	gibt	gab	hat gegeben
go	**gehen**	geht	ging	ist gegangen
succeed	**gelingen**	gelingt	gelang	ist gelungen
happen	**geschehen**	geschieht	geschah	ist geschehen
win	**gewinnen**	gewinnt	gewann	hat gewonnen
have	**haben**	hat	hatte	hat gehabt
hold	**halten**	hält	hielt	hat gehalten
hang	**hängen**	hängt	hing	hat gehangen
be called	**heißen**	heißt	hieß	hat geheißen
help	**helfen**	hilft	half	hat geholfen
know	**kennen**	kennt	kannte	hat gekannt
come	**kommen**	kommt	kam	ist gekommen
can	**können**	kann	konnte	hat gekonnt
invite	**einladen**	lädt ein	lud ein	hat eingeladen
let	**lassen**	lässt	ließ	hat gelassen
run, walk	**laufen**	läuft	lief	ist gelaufen
borrow, lend	**leihen**	leiht	lieh	hat geliehen
read	**lesen**	liest	las	hat gelesen
lie	**liegen**	liegt	lag	hat gelegen
lie	**lügen**	lügt	log	hat gelogen
like	**mögen**	mag	mochte	hat gemocht

	Infinitiv	Präsens	Präteritum	Perfekt
must	**müssen**	muss	musste	hat gemusst
take	**nehmen**	nimmt	nahm	hat genommen
mention	**nennen**	nennt	nannte	hat genannt
run	**rennen**	rennt	rannte	ist gerannt
smell	**riechen**	riecht	roch	hat gerochen
shout	**rufen**	ruft	rief	hat gerufen
shine	**scheinen**	scheint	schien	hat geschienen
sleep	**schlafen**	schläft	schlief	hat geschlafen
close	**schließen**	schließt	schloss	hat geschlossen
write	**schreiben**	schreibt	schrieb	hat geschrieben
cry	**schreien**	schreit	schrie	hat geschrien
swim	**schwimmen**	schwimmt	schwamm	ist/hat geschwommen
see	**sehen**	sieht	sah	hat gesehen
be	**sein**	ist	war	ist gewesen
send	**senden**	sendet	sandte	hat gesandt
sit	**sitzen**	sitzt	saß	hat gesessen
shall	**sollen**	soll	sollte	hat gesollt
speak	**sprechen**	spricht	sprach	hat gesprochen
jump	**springen**	springt	sprang	ist gesprungen
stand	**stehen**	steht	stand	hat gestanden
die	**sterben**	stirbt	starb	ist gestorben
argue	**streiten**	streitet	stritt	hat gestritten
carry	**tragen**	trägt	trug	hat getragen
meet	**treffen**	trifft	traf	hat getroffen
drink	**trinken**	trinkt	trank	hat getrunken
do	**tun**	tut	tat	hat getan
forget	**vergessen**	vergisst	vergaß	hat vergessen
grow	**wachsen**	wächst	wuchs	ist gewachsen
wash	**waschen**	wäscht	wusch	hat gewaschen
become	**werden**	wird (du wirst)	wurde	ist geworden
throw	**werfen**	wirft	warf	hat geworfen
know	**wissen**	weiß (du weißt)	wusste	hat gewusst
want	**wollen**	will	wollte	hat gewollt

Solutions and listening texts

Day 2

Dialogue questions

    1. Martina | ~~Iwona~~ – **2.** German | ~~English.~~ – **3.** ~~19~~ | 29 – **4.** ~~Brian~~ | Susan – **5.** ~~Australia~~ | France.

1 **1.** Mein Name ist Pierre. – **2.** Ich komme aus Australien. – **3.** Yoko ist 21 Jahre alt. – **4.** Susan kommt aus England und ist 23. – **5.** Ich komme aus Polen und bin 30 Jahre alt. / Ich bin 30 Jahre alt und komme aus Polen.

2 Listening text 14, 7, 20, 3, 12, 8, 17, 5, 16, 9; *Remaining:* 2

3 **1.** Du – **2.** heißt, Sie – **3.** Ich – **4.** kommt, Er – **5.** komme

4 Listening text
    1. Guten Tag. Ich bin **Paul**. Ich bin 27 Jahre alt. Ich komme aus **Schottland**. – **2.** Hallo. Mein Name ist **Mary**. Ich bin aus **Australien**. Ich bin 24. – **3.** Guten Morgen. Mein Name ist **Lucy** und ich komme aus **den USA**. – **4.** Hi! Mein Name ist **George**. Ich bin 21 und aus **England**.

Day 3

Dialogue questions

    1. wrong – **2.** right – **3.** wrong – **4.** right – **5.** wrong

1 **1.** a) Woher kommst du? b) e.g. Ich komme aus England. – **2.** a) Wie geht es dir? b) e.g. Mir geht es gut. – **3.** a) Wo ist das? b) e.g. Das ist in der Nähe von Barcelo-na. – **4.** a) Was machst du? b) e.g. Ich studiere. / Ich arbeite in einer Firma. – **5.** a) Kommst du aus Deutschland? b) e.g. Nein, ich komme aus Polen. **6.** a) Bist du schon lange in Deutschland? b) e.g. Nein, erst seit zwei Wochen. – **7.** a) Arbeitest du hier? b) e.g. Ja, ich arbeite in einer Firma. / Nein, ich studiere hier.

2 **1.** kommt – **2.** arbeiten – **3.** kommen – **4.** arbeiten – **5.** arbeitet – **6.** kommen

3 Listening text
    1. Hallo Jens, wie geht's? – Danke gut. – **2. Woher kommst du?** – Aus Jena. – **3. Wo ist das?** – Jena ist in Thüringen. – **4. Und was machst du?** – Ich arbeite in einer Firma für Druckmaschinen.

Day 4

Dialogue questions

    1. right – **2.** wrong – **3.** right – **4.** wrong

1 **1.** ist – **2.** Seid – **3.** bin – **4.** haben – **5.** Hast

2 Possible answers
    1. Mein Name ist Iwona. – **2.** Ich komme aus Polen. – **3.** Ich bin 30 (Jahre alt). – **4.** Ja, ich habe einen Bruder. – **5.** Mein Vater ist Rechtsanwalt.
    Listening text
    1. Wie heißt du? – **2.** Woher kommst du? – **3.** Wie alt bist du? – **4.** Hast du Geschwister? – **5.** Was ist dein Vater von Beruf?

3 **1.** e) – **2.** d) – **3.** b) – **4.** a) – **5.** f) – **6.** c)

4 **1.** zwei – **2.** keinen – **3.** keine – **4.** einen – **5.** eine – **6.** drei

Day 5

1. laptop | video projector – **2.** some | no – **3.** similar | other **4.** the same as | something completely different than

1 **1.** e) – **2.** d) – **3.** c) – **4.** b) – **5.** f) – **6.** a)

2 **Listening text**
1. Entschuldigung, ich verstehe das nicht. – **2.** Kannst du das wiederholen? – **3.** Heißt es der Laptop oder das Laptop? – **4.** Garten und *garden* sind sehr ähnlich. – **5.** Dieses Wort kenne ich nicht. – **6.** Leider gibt es einige falsche Freunde.
Remaining: Das ist etwas ganz anderes.

3 **1.** a) Er muss den Satz wiederholen. b) He has to repeat the sentence. – **2.** a) Kannst du (bitte) den Beamer (bitte) holen (, bitte)? b) Can you get the video projector please? – **3.** a) Musst du viel arbeiten? – b) Do you have to work a lot? – **4.** a) Iwona muss diese Wörter nachschauen. – b) Iwona has to look up these words. – **5.** a) Wir können unseren Sohn oft besuchen. – b) We can visit our son often. – **6.** a) Ich verstehe das nicht. – b) I don't understand that. – **7.** a) Können Sie das bitte wiederholen? – b) Can (Could) you repeat please?

Day 6

1 **1.** Du arbeitest ... – **2.** Er studiert ... – **3.** Wir sind ... – **4.** Sie ist ...

2 **1.** Unsere – **2.** Mein – **3.** Ihre – **4.** Ihr – **5.** Eure – **6.** Ihr

3 Correct order: **3.** – **6.** – **5.** – **7.** – **1.** – **8.** – **2.** – **4.**

4 **a)** vier – **b)** zwei – **c)** elf – **d)** drei – **e)** zehn – **f)** sieben – **g)** acht – **h)** neun

5 **1.** a) – **2.** a) – **3.** b) – **4.** b)
Listening text
Hallo, mein Name ist Martin. Ich bin 31 Jahre alt und Deutschlehrer. Ich arbeite hier in Berlin. Ich bin seit einem Jahr in Berlin. Ich habe seit drei Jahren eine Freundin. Sie heißt Lynn. Sie ist 29 Jahre alt und kommt aus England. Sie ist schon seit fünf Jahren in Berlin. Sie ist Architektin.

6 **1.** Onkel – **2.** Geschäftsmann – **3.** Monat – **4.** Deutschland – **5.** Guten Abend – **6.** Eltern
Remaining: Auf Wiedersehen *(You use it to say goodbye, the others are to say hello.)*

7 **1.** Sie – **2.** du – **3.** du – **4.** Sie – **5.** Sie *(maybe also* du*)* – **6.** Sie

8 **1.** Das ist nicht schwer. – **2.** Martina hat keine Schwester. – **3.** Ich verstehe das nicht. – **4.** Das ist kein englisches Wort. – **5.** Du weißt es nicht. – **6.** Ich habe keinen Laptop.

9 **1.** wrong – **2.** wrong – **3.** right – **4.** wrong – **5.** right – **6.** wrong

10 **1.** Es geht. – **2.** Freut mich! – **3.** Viel Spaß! – **4.** Bis später! – **5.** Hallo!

11 **1.** Sie sehen zwei Männer. – **2.** Wir haben keine Schwester / Schwestern. – **3.** Du hast einen Sohn. – **4.** Sie hat vier Geschwister.

12 **1.** e) – **2.** c) – **3.** d) – **4.** b) – **5.** a)

13 **Possible solution**
Hallo, mein Name ist ... Ich komme aus ... Das liegt in ... Ich bin ... Jahre alt.
Ich studiere / arbeite in ... Ich habe ... Schwester / Bruder. Sie heißt / heißen ... Mein Vater ist ... von Beruf. Meine Mutter arbeitet in ...

14 **1.** Kannst du den Mann sehen? – **2.** Ich muss Deutsch lernen. – **3.** Wo arbeitest du? – **4.** Arbeitest du in einer Consultingfirma? – **5.** Wir müssen sehr viel lernen. – **6.** Sie können diese Wörter nicht verstehen.

15 Possible solution
Hallo, es geht mir gut. Ich bin schon 6 Monate in Deutschland. Ja, ich mache einen Deutschkurs. Deutsch ist schwer! Ja, ich arbeite in einer Firma. Aber ich kenne noch nicht viele Deutsche. Tschüs!

16 **1.** einen – **2.** a) Der b) einen – **3.** ein – **4.** — – **5.** a) einen b) Der c) eine d) Die

17 Listening text
1. Hallo, wie geht es dir? – **Mir geht es prima.** – **2.** Wie lange bist du schon in Deutschland? – **Ich bin seit 6 Monaten hier.** – **3.** Hast du Geschwister? – **Ja, ich habe einen Bruder.** – **4.** Was arbeiten deine Eltern? – **Mein Vater ist Rechtsanwalt. Meine Mutter ist Architektin.** – **5.** Bist du verheiratet? – **Nein, ich bin Single.** – **6.** Verstehst du alles? – **Ja, kein Problem.**

18 **1.** geht – **2.** bin (arbeite) – **3.** mache – **4.** ist – **5.** habe – **6.** heißt – **7.** kommt – **8.** ist – **9.** kenne – **10.** machst – **11.** Arbeitest (Bist)

19 Listening text
1. Guten Abend, Herr Schneider. – Ah, Herr Maier, guten Abend! *(10 pm)* – **2.** Hi, wie heißt du? – Hallo, ich bin Martin. *(possible at all times)* – **3.** Ich muss gehen! Gute Nacht. – Auf Wiedersehen und gute Nacht! *(10 pm)* – **4.** Guten Morgen und herzlich willkommen! – Vielen Dank. *(8 am)* – **5.** Guten Tag! Kann ich helfen? – Ja. Wo ist der Deutschkurs? *(2 pm, also possible at 8 am)*

20 **1.** Sie fragen Ihren Nachbarn. – **2.** Woher kommen Sie? – **3.** Arbeiten Sie viel? – **4.** Können Sie das bitte wiederholen? – **5.** Sie sind aus Deutschland.

Intermediate test 1

1 **1.** die Architektin – **2.** die Präsentation – **3.** der Garten – **4.** die Zeit – **5.** der Monat – **6.** das Restaurant – **7.** die Woche – **8.** der Dialog

2 **1.** Sie muss den Laptop holen. – **2.** Ich kann über meine Familie sprechen. – **3.** Ihr müsst den Satz wiederholen. – **4.** Müssen Sie sehr viel arbeiten?

3 **1.** right – **2.** right – **3.** wrong – **4.** wrong – **5.** wrong
Listening text

1. Mann	Verstehen Sie das, Frau Schneider?
Frau Schneider	Ja, ich verstehe alles.
2. Pierre	Kannst du das bitte wiederholen, Martina?
Martina	Ja, Gift ist „poison" auf Englisch.
3. Martina	Ihr macht das sehr gut. Ich bin sehr zufrieden!
4. Iwona	Yoko, hast du einen Bruder?
Yoko	Nein. Ich habe eine Schwester.
5. Jens	Ich muss sehr viel arbeiten. Aber ich bin glücklich.

4 **1.** Länder – **2.** Stunde – **3.** Firma – **4.** Familien – **5.** Lehrer – **6.** Sohn – **7.** Schwestern – **8.** Mütter – **9.** Haus **10.** – Restaurants

5 **1.** Woher kommen Sie? – **2.** Kannst du das (bitte) wiederholen? – **3.** Holst du (bitte) den Beamer? – **4.** Wo arbeiten Sie?

6 **1.** b) – **2.** c) – **3.** a) – **4.** c) – **5.** a)

7 **1.** Woher – **2.** Wo – **3.** Wie – **4.** Wie – **5.** Wo – **6.** Wie

8 Listening text
1. Monika Maier, guten Tag. Ich bin Rechtsanwältin. Meine Telefonnummer ist 07623 – **862274.** – **2.** Mein Name ist **Martin Schneider**. Ich arbeite in Hamburg. Ich bin **Architekt. 3.** Hallo. Ich bin **Claudia**. Ich bin Deutschlehrerin und arbeite in **Berlin**.

9   **1.** Kannst du / Können Sie mir helfen? – **2.** Ich muss den Laptop holen. – **3.** Er muss viel arbeiten. – **4.** Jens kann seine Mutter oft besuchen. – **5.** Kannst du / Können Sie diese Wörter (bitte) wiederholen (bitte)?

Evaluation

You reached .... of 50 points.

45–50   **Sehr gut!** *Very good!* Keep it up!

35–44   **Gut!** *Good!* You're on the right way.

25–34   **In Ordnung.** *OK.* You've already accomplished a lot. Repeat the exercises where you still had problems and full points won't be problem.

0–24   **Das können Sie noch besser.** *You can still do better.* But hey, it's not the end of the world! Review the lessons where you had problems and use the solutions actively: don't just correct your exercises but try to understand why the solution is correct.

Day 7

Dialogue questions

    1. wrong – **2.** wrong – **3.** wrong – **4.** right – **5.** wrong – **6.** wrong

1   **Obst:** Apfel, Banane, Birne, Orange, Pfirsich, Weintraube – **Gemüse:** Gurke, Kartoffel, Möhre (Karotte), Paprika, Tomate, Zucchini, Zwiebel – **Milchprodukte:** Butter, Joghurt, Käse, Milch, Sahne – **Anderes:** Brot, Brötchen, Ei, Fisch, Hähnchen, Fleisch, Honig, Marmelade, Müsli, Schinken, Wein, Wurst

2   **1.** b) – **2.** c) – **3.** d) – **4.** a)

3   **1.** 80 Cent pro Kilo – **2.** 1,50 Euro pro Kilo – **3.** 1,99 Euro pro Packung – **4.** 3 Euro pro Flasche

Listening text

Verehrte Kunden, heute für Sie im Sonderangebot: Kartoffeln – ein Kilo nur 80 Cent. Außerdem für Sie: frisches Obst – Birnen nur 1,50 Euro das Kilo. Im Kühlfach finden Sie Schinken: Die Packung für nur 1,99 Euro. Und als besonderes Angebot: Wein aus Frankreich – eine Flasche nur 3 Euro.

Day 8

Dialogue questions

    1. Apfelkuchen | ~~Schokoladentorte~~. – **2.** etwas | ~~keine~~ – **3.** nicht | sehr – **4.** heute | ~~morgen~~

2   **Martina:** Wasser, Fisch mit Kartoffeln – **Jens:** Bier, Schnitzel mit Pommes, die Rechnung

Listening text

Kellner	Guten Tag, was darf ich Ihnen bringen?
Martina	Guten Tag. Ich hätte gerne den Fisch und dazu Kartoffeln.
Jens	Für mich bitte das Schnitzel mit Pommes.
Kellner	Ja, natürlich. Was möchten Sie trinken?
Jens	Ich hätte gerne ein Bier.
Martina	Und ich möchte bitte ein Wasser.
Kellner	Sehr gerne. [...] Möchten Sie noch etwas?
Jens	Nein, danke. Aber bringen Sie uns bitte die Rechnung?

3   *Begin your sentences with* „**Ich hätte gerne ...**" *or* „**Ich möchte ...**". *Just be careful to use the accusative* „**einen Salat**".

Day 9

Dialogue questions

1. b) – **2.** b) – **3.** a) – **4.** a)

1 **1.** ist größer – **2.** geht lieber in ein Museum – **3.** ist besser – **4.** geht lieber ins Theater – **5.** ist interessanter – **6.** ist toller

2 **1.** Ich hätte gerne eine normale Eintrittskarte und zwei für Studenten. **2.** Ich gehe lieber einkaufen als ins Theater. **3.** Um wie viel Uhr macht das Museum zu? **4.** Gibt es eine Studentenermäßigung? **5.** Ich möchte lieber eine Stadtrundfahrt machen. **6.** Ich faulenze lieber. **7.** Was kostet eine normale Eintrittskarte?

3 **1.** 3) – **2.** 4) – **3.** 6) – **4.** 5) – **5.** 7) – **6.** 1) – **7.** 2) – **8.** –

Listening text

1. Wir treffen uns um **halb 4**. – **2.** Das Museum schließt um **18.30 Uhr**. – **3.** Es ist **Viertel nach 11**. – **4.** Mein Deutschkurs beginnt um **2**. – **5.** Martina wartet seit **Viertel vor 9**. – **6.** Es ist **9.45 Uhr**. – **7.** Um **19.15 Uhr** gehe ich auf den Fernsehturm.

Day 10

Dialogue questions

1. right – **2.** right – **3.** wrong – **4.** wrong – **5.** wrong

1 **1.** b) – **2.** e) – **3.** d) – **4.** c) – **5.** f) – **6.** a)

2 **1.** right – **2.** wrong – **3.** wrong – **4.** wrong – **5.** wrong – **6.** right

Listening text

Pierre   Am Morgen frühstücke ich nicht – ich trinke nur einen Kaffee. Dann gehe ich in die Arbeit. Zu Mittag esse ich in der Firma. Nach der Arbeit besuche ich einen Deutschkurs oder treffe mich mit Freunden.

Martina   Ich muss früh aufstehen. Aber ich mag das nicht! Dann frühstücke ich – meistens Obst oder Müsli. Ich mache Deutschkurse und komme oft erst am Abend nach Hause. Oft sehe ich dann noch fern.

Iwona   Ich stehe gern früh auf und gehe dann joggen. Ich komme oft schon am Nachmittag nach Hause. Dann gehe ich in die Stadt und kaufe ein oder treffe mich mit Freunden. Am Abend lese ich gern und gehe früh ins Bett.

3 *Orient yourself using the text in the exercise and the dialogue.*

Day 11

Dialogue questions

1. Jens hat Geburtstag. – **2.** Andreas ist der Freund von Martinas Schwester / von Kathrin. – **3.** Die Getränke stehen auf einem / dem Tisch (im Wohnzimmer). – **4.** Sie wohnt in Potsdam.

1 **1.** 3) – **2.** 5) – **3.** 4) – **4.** 1) – **5.** 2)

Listening text

1.

Frau   Hallo Jens. Ich wünsche dir alles Gute zum Geburtstag.

Jens   Danke sehr!

Frau   Hier, ich habe ein Geschenk für dich!

2.

Jens	Hi Kathrin. Hallo Andreas. Herzlich willkommen.
Kathrin	Hi Jens, danke für die Einladung.
Jens	Gern! Kommt doch herein!

3.

Jens	Martina, das ist Paul, ein Kollege von mir. Paul, das ist Martina, meine Freundin.
Paul	Hallo Martina. Freut mich dich kennenzulernen.
Martina	Freut mich auch, Paul.

4.

Frau	Wo sind denn die Getränke?
Pierre	Da, auf dem Tisch. Essen kannst du in der Küche holen.
Frau	Danke.

5.

Kathrin	Hi, wie geht's dir?
Iwona	Gut, danke.
Kathrin	Du bist aus Martinas Deutschkurs, ja?

2 **Andreas:** Toilette – **Jens:** Flur – **Kathrin:** Flur – **Martina:** Wohnzimmer – **Pierre:** Bad

3 **1.** Freut mich sehr Sie kennenzulernen. – **2.** Ich wünsche dir alles Gute zum Geburtstag. – **3.** Ich möchte euch kurz vorstellen. – **4.** Herzlich willkommen in unserer Wohnung.– **5.** Das ist mein Kollege Paul.

Day 12

Dialogue questions

1. im Wohnzimmer | in der Küche – **2.** kehrt gerne | spült gerne ab – **3.** Iwona | Pierre – **4.** sehr | nicht.

1 **Iwona:** ☺ staubsaugen, Wäsche waschen – ☹ abspülen, bügeln – **Pierre:** ☺ Müll wegbringen – ☹ aufräumen, abspülen, staubsaugen, Wäsche waschen, bügeln

Listening text

Iwona	Pierre, räumst du gerne auf?
Pierre	Nein.
Iwona	Na, das ist in Ordnung. Ich spüle dafür nicht gern ab.
Pierre	Ja, ich spüle auch nicht gern ab. In Frankreich habe ich einen Geschirrspüler.
Iwona	Das ist gut. Ich mag Staubsaugen und Wäsche waschen. Aber ich bügle nicht gern.
Pierre	Das mag ich auch alles nicht.
Iwona	Aber Pierre, du magst ja keine Hausarbeit!
Pierre	Stimmt! Oh, doch ... ich bringe gern den Müll weg!

2 **1.** Abspülen ist in Ordnung. – **2.** Was ist los? – **3.** Stell das dreckige Geschirr in den Geschirrspüler. – **4.** Das macht nichts. – **5.** Was soll ich machen? – **6.** Das tut mir leid! – **7.** Kehren mag ich nicht.

3 **1.** Regal *(article is already in "im"!)* – **2.** das Sofa – **3.** dem Stuhl – **4.** dem Tisch – **5.** den Schrank – **6.** der Kommode – **7.** der Lampe – **8.** dem Teller

Day 13

Dialogue questions

1. right – **2.** wrong – **3.** right – **4.** right

1   **1.** a) – **2.** a) – **3.** a) – **4.** b) – **5.** a) – **6.** a)

Listening text

Martina	Gehen wir ins Kino?
Jens	Ich will lieber zu Hause bleiben und einen Film im Fernsehen oder auf DVD sehen.
Martina	Was kommt denn heute Abend?
Jens	Also im Fernsehen kommt „Insomnia" – ein Thriller mit Al Pacino.
Martina	Nein, ich habe keine Lust auf einen Thriller. Kommt vielleicht eine Komödie?
Jens	Das weiß ich nicht. Ich muss erst die Fernsehzeitschrift holen. Nein, heute kommt keine Komödie.
Martina	Wollen wir vielleicht eine DVD ausleihen?
Jens	Ja, das können wir machen.
Martina	Dann suche ich einen Film im Internet aus. Okay? „Rush Hour 3" – was meinst du?
Jens	Das ist gut. Dann hole ich den Film.

2   **1.** Tagesschau – **2.** 20.15 Uhr – **3.** 21.45 Uhr – **4.** Nachrichten – **5.** 24 times (once every hour)
(June 2010)

3   Listening text
1. Hast du Lust auf einen Film? **– Nein, ich will lieber lesen. – 2.** Wo spielt der Tatort? **– Heute spielt er in Hamburg. – 3.** Um wie viel Uhr kommen die Nachrichten? **– Um 19 Uhr. – 4.** Was kommt heute Abend im Fernsehen? **– Heute Abend gibt es einen Actionfilm.**

Day 14

1   **fahren**: ich fahre, du fährst, er / sie / es fährt, wir fahren, ihr fahrt, sie / Sie fahren –
essen: ich esse, du isst, er / sie / es isst, wir essen, ihr esst, sie / Sie essen – **schlafen**: ich schlafe, du schläfst, er / sie / es schläft, wir schlafen, ihr schlaft, sie / Sie schlafen – **fernsehen**: ich sehe fern, du siehst fern, er / sie / es sieht fern, wir sehen fern, ihr seht fern, sie / Sie sehen fern – **geben**: ich gebe, du gibst, er / sie / es gibt, wir geben, ihr gebt, sie / Sie geben

2   **1.** Um halb acht steht Jens auf. – **2.** Um acht (acht Uhr) fährt er in die Arbeit. –
3. Um 12.45 isst er zu Mittag. – **4.** Um Viertel nach sechs kommt er nach Hause.

3   **1.** 5 Tomaten – **2.** 1 Zucchini – **3.** 1 Kilo Kartoffeln – **4.** 4 Bananen – **5.** 0,5 kg Äpfel –
6. 400 g Schinken – **7.** 2 Flaschen Wein – **8.** 1 Karton Milch

Listening text
So, auf dem Markt kaufe ich Gemüse und Obst. Ich möchte 5 Tomaten und 1 Zucchini kaufen – ach ja, und 1 Kilo Kartoffeln. Außerdem möchte ich noch 4 Bananen und ein halbes Kilo Äpfel kaufen. Dann gehe ich in den Supermarkt. Ich brauche 400 Gramm Schinken, 2 Flaschen Wein und 1 Karton Milch.

4   **1.** Zucchini – **2.** joggen – **3.** Fleisch – **4.** Tüte – **5.** unten – **6.** Zeitschrift – **7.** rot – **8.** Wasser

5   **1.** Räum dein Zimmer auf! – **2.** Macht mehr Sport! – **3.** Reden Sie mit dem Kunden! – **4.** Gehen Sie einen Kaffee trinken! – **5.** Besuch deinen Freund! – **6.** Macht eine Stadtrundfahrt!

6   **1.** ihr – **2.** Sie – **3.** ihn – **4.** ihm – **5.** Er – **6.** sie

7   **1.** Fernsehen – **2.** aufstehen – **3.** Gurke – **4.** Zimmer – **5.** Saft – **6.** Müll wegbringen

8   **1.** dem – **2.** — – **3.** — – **4.** ein – **5.** ein – **6.** einen – **7.** einen – **8.** eine – **9.** — – **10.** — – **11.** den – **12.** das

9 **1.** ein Freund von Martina / Martinas Freund – **2.** im Kindergarten – **3.** neben Martinas Eltern – **4.** in Hamburg – **5.** gern ins Kino – **6.** eine Radtour (oder gehen schwimmen) – **7.** gern Fußball. / am liebsten Fußball. / einmal in der Woche Fußball – **8.** sieht Klaus fern und (er) geht früh ins Bett

Listening text

Hallo, ich bin Klaus. Ich bin ein Freund von Martina. Wir waren zusammen im Kindergarten. Ich kenne sie also schon sehr lange. Meine Eltern wohnen neben Martinas Eltern – sie sind Nachbarn. Martina lebt jetzt in Berlin. Ich lebe in Hamburg. Hamburg ist eine tolle Stadt. Ich besuche Martina und ihren Freund Jens gern. Martina kommt auch oft nach Hamburg. Wir gehen gern ins Kino oder reden lang. Das macht viel Spaß. Wir machen aber lieber eine Radtour oder gehen schwimmen. Ich mache gern Sport. Am liebsten spiele ich Fußball. Aber ich bin nicht in einem Sportverein. Einmal in der Woche treffe ich mich mit Freunden und wir spielen. Am Abend sehe ich gern fern und gehe früh ins Bett.

10 **1.** dreihundertsiebenundfünfzig – **2.** achthundertzwölf – **3.** tausendeins / eintausendeins – **4.** zweitausendzehn – **5.** neuntausendneunhundertneunundneunzig

11 **1.** ausleihen – **2.** mitnehmen – **3.** einkaufen – **4.** aufräumen – **5.** abspülen – **6.** fernsehen

12 **1.** kann sie ein Fahrrad ausleihen – **2.** wollen sie auf eine Radtour mitnehmen – **3.** wollen an den Wannsee außerhalb von Berlin fahren – **4.** können sie auch schwimmen – **5.** muss Iwona im Supermarkt einkaufen – **6.** will sie auf eine Party gehen – **7.** muss sie aufräumen und abspülen – **8.** will noch fernsehen – **9.** möchte sie ins Bett gehen und schlafen

13 *Begin your sentences with* „Ich hätte gerne …" *or* „Ich möchte …". *Just be careful to use the accusative* „einen Becher Sahne". „0,5 kg" *can be* „fünfhundert Gramm" *or* „ein halbes Kilo(-gramm)".

14 **1.** Iwona wollte nicht an der Straße joggen. – **2.** Ich sollte etwas im Internet suchen. – **3.** Wir hatten viel Freizeit. – **4.** Ihr konntet alles auf dem Markt kaufen. – **5.** Du musstest den Müll wegbringen. – **6.** Das Museum war interessant.

15 0.40 Uhr: 6 – 15.30 Uhr: 2 – 4.30 Uhr: – – 15.45 Uhr: 1 – 5.15 Uhr: – – 16.30 Uhr: 5 – 9.15 Uhr: 4 – 16.45 Uhr: 7 – 13.00 Uhr: 8 – 21.20 Uhr: 3 – 13.15 Uhr: 10 – 23.30 Uhr: 9

Listening text

1. Es ist 15.45 Uhr. – **2.** Um halb 4. – **3.** Um 21.20 Uhr. – **4.** Es ist Viertel nach 9. – **5.** Um 16.30 Uhr. – **6.** Um 0.40 Uhr. – **7.** Es ist Viertel vor 5. – **8.** Es ist eins. – **9.** Um halb 12. – **10.** Um 13.15 Uhr.

16 **1.** vor das Haus – **2.** auf dem Tisch – **3.** hinter den Pfirsichen – **4.** zwischen dem Messer und der Gabel – **5.** an den Tisch – **6.** im (!) Schrank – **7.** neben seinen Schwestern – **8.** sich auf das Sofa – **9.** ins (!) Regal

17 **1.** a) euch b) Uns – **2.** a) dir b) mir – **3.** a) Ihnen b) mir

18 **1.** b) – **2.** a) – **3.** b) – **4.** b) – **5.** c) – **6.** c)

Listening text

Iwona	Hi Pierre! Wo warst du denn gestern? Du warst nicht im Deutschkurs …
Pierre	Hi Iwona. Ja, ich konnte nicht kommen. Wir mussten so viel arbeiten.
Iwona	Das macht nichts. Aber es war sehr interessant! Martina hatte eine Präsentation über Freizeit in Deutschland.
Pierre	Na ja … ich hatte keine Freizeit. Ich musste arbeiten.
Iwona	Ja. Und morgen? Hast du morgen Abend Zeit? Es gibt eine Party in der Goethestraße.
Pierre	Um wie viel Uhr beginnt die Party denn?
Iwona	Um acht.
Pierre	Ja, da habe ich Zeit. Cool.
Iwona	Und was machst du heute noch? Triffst du noch Freunde?

Pierre	Nein ... Ich gehe nur ins Bett.
Iwona	Na, dann wünsche ich dir eine gute Nacht!

19 **1.** Löffel – **2.** Teller – **3.** essen – **4.** Hauptgericht – **5.** Tasse – **6.** Glas – **7.** trinken – **8.** Gabel – **9.** Beilage – **10.** Messer – **11.** Serviette – **12.** Nachtisch
Solution: Restaurant

Intermediate test 2

1 **1.** einem – **2.** ihnen – **3.** möchten – **4.** Apfelschorle – **5.** Kartoffeln – **6.** Glas – **7.** lecker – **8.** Spaziergang – **9.** kauft – **10.** Ermäßigung – **11.** interessanter – **12.** muss – **13.** Wurst – **14.** nach Hause – **15.** aufräumen – **16.** Tschüs

2 **1.** b) – **2.** d) – **3.** h) Die Rechnung bitte. – **4.** f) – **5.** g) – **6.** c) – **7.** a) – **8.** e)

3 **Iwona:** Eintrittskarten kaufen, Viertel nach sechs / 18.15 Uhr – **Kathrin:** auf ein Konzert gehen, morgen – **Pierre:** in die Arbeit fahren, halb neun / 8.30 Uhr
Listening text

Iwona	Hier ist Iwona. Es ist Viertel nach sechs und ich will die Eintrittskarten kaufen. Hast du einen Studentenausweis? Ruf mich an!
Kathrin	Hey, ich bin's, Kathrin. Ich gehe morgen auf ein Konzert. Kommst du mit? Hast du Lust? Tschüs!
Pierre	Hi, Pierre hier. Ich fahre um halb neun in die Arbeit. Soll ich dich mitnehmen?

4 **1.** zwischen der – dem – **2.** neben dem – **3.** hinter (über) dem – **4.** auf dem – **5.** an der

5 **1.** ihm – **2.** es – **3.** ihr – **4.** er – **5.** ihn

6 **1.** c) – **2.** b) – **3.** — – **4.** d) – **5.** a)

7 **1.** will – **2.** waren – **3.** hat – **4.** mussten – **5.** hast – **6.** darfst

Evaluation

maximal:	50 points
sehr gut:	45–50
gut:	35–44
in Ordnung:	25–34

Day 15

Dialogue questions

1. wrong – **2.** right – **3.** right – **4.** wrong

1 **Listening text**
1. 1. Januar – **2.** 14. Februar – **3.** 4. März – **4.** 28. April – **5.** 12. Mai – **6.** 8. Juni – **7.** 17. Juli – **8.** 21. August – **9.** 11. September – **10.** 3. Oktober – **11.** 9. November – **12.** 24. Dezember

2 **1.** Mir gefällt dein Vorschlag. – **2.** Ich finde Ihre Idee gut. – **3.** Nein, ich muss an dem Tag arbeiten.

3 **1.** 110 Euro – **2.** Ja – **3.** Ja – **4.** 24 Zimmer

4 Anreise: 28. Juli / 28.7. – Abreise: 4. August / 4.8. – Erwachsene: 2 – Kinder: 0 – Einzelzimmer [ ] Doppelzimmer [X] – Inkl. Frühstück? Nein [ ] Ja [X]
Listening text

Jens	Martina, ich möchte das Hotel buchen. Wann fahren wir weg?
Martina	Das weißt du doch! Wir fahren am 28. Juli hier weg und bleiben bis 4. August.

Jens	Stimmt, also sieben Nächte. Wir nehmen ein Doppelzimmer, oder?
Martina	Ja, natürlich! Dachtest du, wir nehmen zwei Einzelzimmer?
Jens	Nein. Wollen wir auch im Hotel frühstücken?
Martina	Ja, ich denke das ist eine gute Idee. Dann müssen wir nicht jeden Morgen erst ein Café suchen.
Jens	Okay!

Day 16

Dialogue questions

1. fahren | ~~fliegen~~ – **2.** ~~ersten~~ | zweiten – **3.** sechs | ~~vierzehn~~ – **4.** ~~am Schalter~~ | online.

1 **1.** Gleis 14 – **2.** 16.29 Uhr – **3.** Basel – **4.** 18.52 Uhr

2 Hin- und Rückfahrt – Von: Berlin – Nach: München – Hinfahrt am: 2.10. – Uhrzeit: 14.00, Abfahrt or 20:00, Ankunft – Rückfahrt am: 5.10.

3 **1.** Ich fahre lieber mit dem ICE, weil er schneller ist. – **2.** Ich denke, dass die Regionalbahn zu langsam ist. – **3.** Iwona und Pierre wollen nach München fahren. – **4.** Pierre sagt, dass ein Flug zu teuer ist.

Day 17

Dialogue questions

1. b) – **2.** a) – **3.** b) – **4.** b)

1 **1.** Entschuldigen Sie bitte. – **2.** Können Sie mir vielleicht helfen? – **3.** Entschuldigung, wo ist der Bahnhof? – **4.** Wissen Sie, wo die Schillerstraße ist? – **5.** Entschuldigen Sie, ich suche das Theater.

2 Possible solution
1. Gehen Sie an der Kreuzung / Baustelle nach rechts. / Biegen Sie ... rechts ab. – **2.** Gehen Sie hier vorne rechts und dann die nächste Straße links. – **3.** An der Kreuzung gehen Sie geradeaus. Dann müssen Sie rechts gehen. Nehmen Sie dann die zweite Straße links. / Fahren Sie an der Kreuzung nach rechts. Dann nehmen Sie die zweite Straße links und dann rechts. – **4.** Gehen Sie hier vorne (an der Kreuzung) rechts. Dann gehen Sie die erste / zweite Straße links und gleich wieder rechts. Dann geradeaus bis ans Ende der Straße.

Day 18

Dialogue questions

1. right – **2.** right – **3.** right – **4.** wrong

2 *Correct order:* 4 – 6 – 2 – 9 – 1 – 7 – 3 – 8 – 5

3 **1.** (Die Sauna kostet) 5 Euro. – **2.** In der Bar. – **3.** Fahrräder und DVDs. – **4.** Schwimmbad und Filmverleih.
Listening text

| Jens | Schau mal, Martina. Hier ist ein Faltblatt mit zusätzlichen Services im Hotel. |
| Martina | Und was bieten sie an? |

Jens	Es gibt zum Beispiel ein Schwimmbad und eine Sauna.
	Das Schwimmbad ist kostenlos, aber die Sauna kostet 5 Euro.
Martina	Aha. Kann man hier auch etwas essen oder trinken? Oder gibt es einen Zimmerservice?
Jens	Nein, es gibt keinen Zimmerservice und auch kein Essen, nur das Frühstück. Aber es gibt eine Bar mit Getränken.
Martina	O. K., eine Bar ist gut.
Jens	Wir können auch Fahrräder ausleihen.
Martina	Das kostet sicher auch etwas, oder?
Jens	Ja, aber nicht viel: 10 Euro für einen ganzen Tag. Oh, und wir können auch kostenlos Filme auf DVD ausleihen.
Martina	Jens, Filme schauen wir uns zu Hause an, nicht im Urlaub!
Jens	Ja, du hast recht.

Day 19

Dialogue questions

1. gut | ~~schlecht~~ – **2.** dem Riesenrad | ~~der Achterbahn~~ – **3.** ~~sehr gern~~ | lieber nicht – **4.** Iwona | ~~Pierre,~~ Martina | ~~Jens.~~

1   **1.** 3) – **2.** 4) – **3.** 2) – **4.** 5) – **5.** 1) – **6.** *remaining*

Listening text

1. Am Abend sinken die Temperaturen. In der ganzen Nacht ist mit Gewittern zu rechnen. – **2.** Vor allem im Süden heute den ganzen Tag Schneefall. Die Temperaturen liegen um -5 Grad. – **3.** Heute wird es richtig warm! Die Sonne scheint den ganzen Tag und die Temperaturen steigen bis auf 28 Grad. – **4.** Im Norden scheint zwar immer wieder die Sonne, aber es bleibt den ganzen Tag bewölkt. Die Temperaturen liegen zwischen 5 und 10 Grad. – **5.** Vergessen Sie heute Ihren Regenschirm nicht! Am Nachmittag ziehen dicke Regenwolken auf und es regnet bis in die Nacht.

2   **Possible solution**

1. Hi! Ich bin auf dem Oktoberfest. Es ist toll, die Sonne scheint und es gibt viele Leute. LG – **2.** Wie geht's dir? Wie ist das Wetter (bei euch)? bb – **3.** Ich bin jetzt auf dem Oktoberfest und warte an / bei der Achterbahn. cu! – **4.** Hier ist es bewölkt und kühl. Aber ich mag das!

3   **1.** c) – **2.** d) – **3.** a) – **4.** e) – **5.** b)

Day 20

Dialogue questions

1. a) – **2.** a) – **3.** b) – **4.** b)

1   **1.** Mein Bauch tut weh. – **2.** Mein Zahn schmerzt. / Meine Zähne schmerzen. – **3.** Mein Hals tut weh. – **4.** Mein Ohr schmerzt. / Meine Ohren tun weh. – **5.** Mein Kopf schmerzt.

2   **1.** eine Allergie – **2.** eine Erkältung – **3.** gebrochen – **4.** eine Grippe – **5.** Rückenschmerzen – **6.** eine Verletzung – **7.** gesund

Listening text

| **1.** Martina | In der Nähe einer Katze muss ich immer niesen. |
| **2.** Jens | Ich fühle mich schlecht und muss viel husten. |

3. Johannes	Ich kann gar nicht mehr gehen.	
4. Pierre	Ich habe starkes Kopfweh und hohes Fieber.	
5. Iwona	Oh, mein Rücken tut so weh.	
6. Peter	Mein Arm ist stark geschwollen und schmerzt.	
7. Claudia	Also ich fühle mich so richtig gut!	

3   **Es war** Freitag, der 13. März. **Ich bin im Park spazieren gegangen. Ich habe** ein Fahrrad kommen **gehört** und **mich umgedreht.** Ein Mann auf einem Fahrrad **ist** sehr schnell in **meine** Richtung **gefahren.** Er **hat mich** nicht **gesehen.** Im letzten Moment **konnte** der Mann ausweichen. Aber **ich bin ausgerutscht** und **hingefallen. Meine** rechte Hand **hat wehgetan** und **ich konnte** sie nicht mehr bewegen.

Day 21

Dialogue questions

1. Am Samstag. – **2.** Sie sind ins/zum Hotel gegangen. – **3.** Die Stadtrundfahrt. – **4.** Am Nachmittag.

1   *Grade:* **1.** gar nicht – **2.** wenig – **3.** nicht so – **4.** ein bisschen – **5.** etwas – **6.** sehr – **7.** total – *Frequency:* **1.** nie **2.** selten **3.** manchmal **4.** oft **5.** immer

2   **1.** Prag: ☺ Martina, Jens – **2.** die Fahrt: ☹ Jens – **3.** die Innenstadt: ☺ Martina – **4.** die Kirchen: ☺ Martina, ☹ Jens – **5.** die Burg: ☺ Jens, ☹ Martina – **6.** die Läden: ☺ Martina, Jens – **7.** der Urlaub: ☺ Martina, Jens

Listening text

Martina	Wir waren ein paar Tage in Prag. Prag ist eine tolle Stadt. Der Urlaub hat mir total gefallen.
Jens	Ja, mir hat Prag auch gefallen. Aber die Fahrt war nicht so toll, denn wir sind lange im Stau gestanden.
Martina	Besonders schön finde ich die alte Innenstadt von Prag – die Häuser und Kirchen ...
Jens	Naja, die Kirchen waren etwas langweilig – das mag ich nicht so sehr. Mir hat aber die Burg gefallen. Die war total spannend!
Martina	Ach, du und deine Burgen. Ich finde, dass die Burg etwas langweilig war. Aber wir waren auch shoppen. Prag hat viele Läden. Das finde ich toll!
Jens	Ja, stimmt. Das ist interessant, fast wie im Museum. Da kann man alles finden. Ach, es war einfach ein schöner Urlaub!

3   Possible solution

1. Ich war in einer Ausstellung. Das hat mir gefallen. Das war interessant. – **2.** Ich war in einer Kirche. Das hat mir wenig gefallen. Das war eintönig. – **3.** Ich habe einen Spaziergang gemacht. Das hat mir sehr gefallen. Das war toll. – **4.** Ich bin mit dem Zug gefahren. Das hat mir gar nicht gefallen. Das war langweilig. – **5.** Ich war auf dem Markt. Das hat mir nicht so gefallen. Das war nicht interessant. – **6.** Ich war in einem Restaurant. Das hat mir total gefallen. (Das Essen war gut.)

Day 22

1   **haben**: geregnet, angesehen, ausgefüllt, eingecheckt, gefunden, gefallen, gehustet, gemacht, geniest, geplant, geschmerzt, übernachtet, übersehen, verletzt, wehgetan, geschneit – **sein**: ausgerutscht, gefahren, gegangen, hingefallen, weggefahren

2   **1.** Halsweh – **2.** Baustelle – **3.** Gesundheit – **4.** Sitzplatz – **5.** Bratwurst – **6.** wenig

3   **1.** bin – **2.** habe – **3.** habe – **4.** sind – **5.** habe – **6.** hat – **7.** haben – **8.** haben – **9.** sind –
    10. war – **11.** hat – **12.** haben – **13.** habe – **14.** bin

4   **1.** die Kirche – **2.** der Bahnhof – **3.** die Post – **4.** das Restaurant – **5.** der Supermarkt
    Listening text
    1. Fahren Sie hier vorne rechts. Am Kino biegen Sie links ab und fahren dann immer gera-
    deaus bis ans Ende der Straße. – **2.** Ah, das ist einfach. Gehen Sie einfach geradeaus. Dann
    die zweite Straße links. Dann ist es nicht mehr weit. – **3.** Hmm, am besten gehen Sie hier
    vorne links und dann die nächste Straße rechts. Dann geradeaus und die zweite Straße
    links. – **4.** Gehen Sie geradeaus. An der zweiten Kreuzung gehen Sie rechts und dann einfach
    geradeaus bis ans Ende der Straße. – **5.** Hier vorne biegen Sie links ab. Dann die zweite Straße
    rechts und Sie sind fast da.

5   **1.** Im – **2.** um – **3.** Am – **4.** im – **5.** a) Am b) um – **6.** a) Am b) am

6   **1.** Iwona und Pierre sind gestern einkaufen gegangen. / Gestern sind Iwona und Pierre
    ... – **2.** Du hast die Aufgabe richtig gemacht! – **3.** Wann hat Martina im Hotel eingecheckt?
    – **4.** Was hast du in München gesehen? – **5.** Ich bin gestern nach Hamburg gefahren. /
    Gestern bin ich nach H. gefahren. / Nach H. bin ich gestern gefahren.

7   Listening text
    1. Und wann gehen wir dann ins Theater? – **Am Mittwoch, den 3. Juli**. – **2.** Oh, ich dachte wir
    gehen am 6. Juli. – **Nein, am Samstag wollen wir eine Radtour machen**. – **3.** Ach so, stimmt. Und
    um wie viel Uhr beginnt das Theater? – **Um 19.30 Uhr**. – **4.** Gut. Wie kommen wir zum Theater?
    – **Am besten nehmen wir den Bus**. – **5.** Gibt es dort denn eine Bushaltestelle? – **Nicht direkt.**
    Wir müssen noch 5 Minuten laufen.
    Not used: Im Sommer fahren wir Fahrrad.

8   **1.** uns – **2.** a) sich b) mich – **3.** dich – **4.** sich – **5.** euch

9   **1.** wrong – **2.** right – **3.** wrong – **4.** right – **5.** right
    Listening text
    In Berlin scheint heute die Sonne. Die Temperaturen liegen dabei um 20 Grad. Am Abend
    ziehen Wolken auf und es ist mit Gewittern zu rechnen. – München. Vormittags bewölkt
    und windig, nachmittags starker Regen und kühl. Die Höchsttemperaturen liegen bei 11
    Grad. – Guten Morgen in Köln. Achtung auf den Straßen: Dichter Nebel und Temperaturen
    um -2 Grad. Fahren Sie vorsichtig! – Hallo Hamburg! Heute haben wir wieder richtiges
    Sommerwetter. Der Regen ist vorbei, die Sonne scheint und es wird bis zu 30 Grad heiß! –
    Stuttgart. Heute den ganzen Tag Temperaturen unter null Grad und Schnee.

10 **1.** denn – **2.** aber – **3.** und – **4.** oder – **5.** und – **6.** aber – **7.** denn

11 **1.** 15 Minuten. – **2.** Aus Hamburg. – **3.** Nach Potsdam. – **4.** Der Eurocity (146). – **5.** Auf Gleis
    7. – **6.** Nach München.
    Listening text
    Bitte Vorsicht an Gleis 3. Der Intercity aus Hamburg fährt soeben ein. – Verehrte Fahrgäs-
    te, der ICE 935 nach München, planmäßige Abfahrt 9.15 Uhr, hat voraussichtlich 15 Minuten
    Verspätung. Ich wiederhole: Der ICE 935 nach München hat voraussichtlich 15 Minuten
    Verspätung. – Verehrte Reisende, aufgrund von Gleisarbeiten fährt der Regionalexpress
    nach Potsdam heute von Gleis 7 ab. Ich wiederhole: Der Regionalexpress nach Potsdam fährt
    heute von Gleis 7 ab. – Herzlich Willkommen in Berlin Hauptbahnhof. Sie haben Anschluss an
    den Eurocity 146 nach Hamburg, Abfahrt 14.27 Uhr auf Gleis 2.

12 Im Frühling gibt es selten Schnee. Aber es regnet oft und es ist kühl. Es ist auch häufig windig. – Im Sommer ist es oft heiß. Manchmal gibt es Gewitter und ab und zu regnet es. – Im Herbst ist es oft bewölkt und neblig. Manchmal scheint die Sonne. Es schneit selten, aber es ist oft kalt. – Im Winter ist es oft kalt. Manchmal schneit es und ab und zu regnet es auch. Es gibt auch oft Eis.

13 *Think about a city you'd like to visit and say, what you would do there. Use* **"ich will"** *and* **"ich möchte"** *or* **"ich plane"**. *You'll find additional vocabulary in lesson 9.*

14 **1.** Körperteile – **2.** Fahrgeschäfte – **3.** Züge / Bahn – **4.** Wetter – **5.** Bahnhof – **6.** Krankenhaus – **7.** Krankheiten

15 **1.** Als – **2.** wenn – **3.** a) Als b) wenn – **4.** Wenn – **5.** wenn

16 **Grippe**: Ich habe Fieber und Kopfweh. – **Allergie**: Ich muss oft niesen. – **Erkältung**: Ich muss husten und fühle mich schlecht. – **Halsweh**: Mein Hals tut weh (und ich muss husten). – **Verletzung am Knöchel**: Mein Knöchel ist geschwollen und schmerzt.

17 **1.** Grippe – **2.** niesen – **3.** Halsweh – **4.** Bauch – **5.** Erkältung – **6.** Hand – **7.** Knochen – **8.** Krankheit – **9.** Fieber – **10.** husten – **Solution**: Gesundheit

Intermediate test 3

1 **1.** Jugendherberge – **2.** sind – **3.** haben – **4.** Doppelzimmer – **5.** Betten – **6.** Stockwerk – **7.** Morgens – **8.** für – **9.** Wir – **10.** einen Fahrradverleih – **11.** Wollen – **12.** immer – **13.** Fragen – **14.** Sehenswürdigkeiten – **15.** denn – **16.** Englisch – **17.** sprechen – **18.** uns

2 **1.** wrong – **2.** right – **3.** right – **4.** wrong – **5.** wrong – **6.** wrong – **7.** right – **8.** right

3 **1.** 4) – **2.** 5) – **3.** 2) – **4.** 1) – **5.** 3)

Listening text

1.
▸ Du, wollen wir damit auch fahren?
◂ Na klar, mit der Achterbahn wollte ich immer schon mal fahren!

2.
▸ Guten Tag, was kann ich für Sie tun?
◂ Ich möchte heute abreisen.
▸ Kein Problem. Ich brauche dann den Zimmerschlüssel und mache die Rechnung fertig.

3.
▸ Entschuldigen Sie bitte. Können Sie mir sagen, wie ich zum Bahnhof komme?
◂ Ja, natürlich. Gehen Sie die nächste Straße rechts und an der Baustelle links. Dann einfach geradeaus.
▸ Vielen Dank. Auf Wiedersehen.

4.
▸ Guten Tag, Herr Schirmer. Haben Sie Ihre Versicherungskarte dabei?
◂ Ja ... bitte schön.
▸ Danke. Sie können dann im Wartezimmer Platz nehmen.

5.
▸ Der Zug nach Hamburg fährt von Gleis 12. Das ist dort hinten.
◂ Ja, ich weiß. Ich brauche aber noch eine Fahrkarte ...

4 **1.** aus – **2.** nach – **3.** zur – **4.** a) nach b) mit dem c) mit der – **5.** Seit – **6.** beim

5 **1.** c) – **2.** b) – **3.** c) – **4.** b) – **5.** c)

Listening text

Hallo, ich bin David. Das sind meine Pläne für den Sommer: Am 14. Juli gehe ich
nach England. Dort bleibe ich 8 Tage. Zuerst besichtige ich London. Dort bin ich 4 Tage. Dann
fahre ich nach Oxford und zuletzt nach Brighton. In London will ich den Tower sehen und zu
Madame Tussauds. Ich möchte auch in den Hyde Park, aber nicht ins British Museum. Weil ich
Geschichte* sehr spannend finde und Städte mag, fahre ich danach nach Oxford. Das wollte ich
schon immer sehen. In Brighton möchte ich dann schwimmen und faulenzen, aber nichts mehr
besichtigen und nichts einkaufen.

* die Geschichte = *history*

6 **1.** was du in Prag besichtigt hast. – **2.** wo das Hotel „Seeblick" ist? – **3.** wie Sie sich verletzt
haben. – **4.** wer dir geschrieben hat? – **5.** wann du im Urlaub warst. –
6. warum du das gemacht hast?

Evaluation

maximal:	50 points
sehr gut:	45–50
gut:	35–44
in Ordnung:	25–34

Day 23

Dialogue questions

1. wrong – **2.** wrong – **3.** right – **4.** right

1 Listening text

1.

▸ Wollen Sie eine Nachricht hinterlassen?

◂ Ja. Richten Sie Frau Meier bitte aus, dass sie mich zurückrufen soll.

▸ Wie ist Ihre Telefonnummer?

◂ **0165 238723219**.

2. Sabine Keller. Rufen Sie mich bitte zurück. Meine Nummer ist **0049 89 874650**.

3.

▸ Silke Hinrichs.

◂ Pfeiffer, guten Tag. Kann ich bitte mit Herrn Rösner sprechen?

▸ Tut mir leid, Herr Rösner ist nicht hier. Aber Sie können ihn am Handy erreichen. Seine
Nummer ist **0187 90274823**.

◂ Gut, vielen Dank. Auf Wiederhören!

4. Guten Tag. Sie sprechen mit dem Anschluss der Rufnummer **0221 2347854**.
Bitte hinterlassen Sie eine Nachricht nach dem Piepston.

5.

▸ Gibst du mir deine Telefonnummer?

◂ Ja, gern. **069 134963**.

▸ Klasse! Ich melde mich bei dir!

6.

▸ Hallo?

◂ Becker hier, kann ich bitte Frau Greis sprechen?

▸ Nein, hier gibt es keine Frau Greis.

◂ Ist das nicht der Anschluss **0511 129873**?

▸ Nein, Sie haben sich verwählt.

◂ Entschuldigung, auf Wiederhören.

▸ Wiederhören.

2 **1.** Rufen Sie mich bitte zurück. – **2.** Meine Telefonnummer ist 030 998766. – **3.** Kann ich bitte mit Frau Meisner sprechen? – **4.** Am Apparat. – **5.** Bleiben Sie bitte am Apparat. – **6.** Entschuldigung, ich habe mich verwählt. – **7.** Kann ich etwas ausrichten? – **8.** Sagen Sie ihm bitte, dass ich angerufen habe. – **9.** Auf Wiederhören.

3 **1.** keinen – **2.** a) einen b) keinen – **3.** niemand / keiner – **4.** nichts / niemand / keinen – **5.** a) jemand / einer b) alle – **6.** keiner

Day 24

Dialogue questions

1. Ein paar Tipps für seine Bewerbung. – **2.** Er will in Deutschland arbeiten / weiterarbeiten / bleiben. – **3.** Per E-Mail. – **4.** Er scannt seine Zeugnisse ein. / Er verschickt seine Zeugnisse per E-Mail. / Er macht eine PDF-Datei aus seinen Zeugnissen.

1 **1.** Besprechung – **2.** Sehr geehrte – **3.** telefoniert – **4.** schicken – **5.** zwei – **6.** geplant – **7.** Fragen – **8.** Sie – **9.** mich – **10.** Mit freundlichen Grüßen

2 **1.** Iwona soll (Frau List) Details zur Besprechung schicken. – **2.** Drei Personen. – **3.** Wenn Frau List Fragen hat, soll sie Iwona anrufen oder eine E-Mail schreiben. / Sie soll (Iwona) anrufen oder eine E-Mail schicken.

3 **1.** Ich esse etwas, wenn ich Hunger habe. – **2.** Wenn wir nach München fahren, (dann) gehen wir auf das Oktoberfest. – **3.** Ich rufe dich an, wenn du mir deine Telefonnummer gibst.

Day 25

Dialogue questions

1. ~~Maler~~ | Gleisser – **2.** ~~Kaffee und Kuchen~~ | einem Bewerbungsgespräch – **3.** ~~ein Bewerbungsgespräch~~ | einen Zahnarzttermin – **4.** ~~an der Rezeption warten~~ | direkt ins Büro gehen

1 **1.** Am 4.5. – **2.** a) Im September. b) Um 14 Uhr. – **3.** a) Um 16 Uhr. b) Nein, er hat keine Zeit. – **4.** Der Termin ist am Donnerstag, im Juni 2011, um 9.30 Uhr (halb zehn). – **5.** Um 13.42 Uhr.

Listening text

1. ▸ Wann haben Sie denn Zeit?

   ◂ Ich habe am Dienstag, den 4. Mai, Zeit. Geht das?

   ▸ Ja, das geht! Danke.

2. ▸ Ich kann Ihnen einen Termin am 13.9. um 14 Uhr anbieten.

   ◂ Am 13.9.? Ja, das passt mir.

3. ▸ Können Sie am Freitagnachmittag um 4 Uhr zu mir kommen?

   ◂ Nein, tut mir leid. Am Freitagnachmittag habe ich keine Zeit.

4. ▸ Und wie ist es am Donnerstag, den 29.6.2011, um 9.30 Uhr morgens?

   ◂ Moment bitte ... Ja, der Termin passt – da habe ich Zeit!

5. ▸ Wann fahren Sie wieder nach Hause?

   ◂ Mein Zug fährt ab am Dienstag, um 13.42 Uhr.

2 **1.** Am Montag. / Im Juli. / Am Mittwoch um 16 Uhr. – **2.** An diesem Tag habe ich keine Zeit. / Tut mir leid. Leider nicht. / Ich habe meinen Terminkalender leider nicht hier. – **3.** An diesem Tag habe ich keine Zeit. / Ja, das passt mir gut. / Tut mir leid. Leider nicht. – **4.** An diesem Tag habe ich keine Zeit. / Ja, das passt mir gut. / Tut mir leid. Leider nicht. / Ich habe meinen Terminkalender leider nicht hier. – **5.** Am Montag. / Im Juli. / Am Mittwoch um 16 Uhr. – **6.** Am Mittwoch um 16 Uhr. / Am Montag.

3 **1.** die – **2.** der – **3.** den – **4.** dem – **5.** die

Day 26

Dialogue questions

1. wrong – **2.** right – **3.** wrong

1 **1.** a), b) – **2.** a), b) – **3.** b) – **4.** a), c)

2 **1.** wrong – **2.** wrong – **3.** right – **4.** right – **5.** right – **6.** wrong

Listening text

Pierre	Iwona, bist du Mitglied bei einem Business-Netzwerk im Internet?
Iwona	Ja, ich bin bei einigen Netzwerken Mitglied. Ich habe so schon einige interessante Kontakte geknüpft.
Pierre	Denkst du auch, dass das wichtig ist?
Iwona	Ja, das ist wichtig. Aber es ist auch sehr wichtig, dass man persönlich Kontakte knüpft und vor allem pflegt – nicht nur im Internet.
Pierre	Aha. Und wie?
Iwona	In deinem Beruf ist das vielleicht nicht wichtig, Pierre. Aber wenn man direkt mit Kunden arbeitet, dann ist das wichtig. Du gehst auf Veranstaltungen, redest mit den Leuten, verteilst deine Visitenkarten und so weiter.
Pierre	Ah, ich verstehe. Vielleicht reicht ein Netzwerk im Internet für mich! Jens ist Mitglied bei Xing und ich seit zwei Tagen auch. Bist du dort auch?
Iwona	Ja, aber noch nicht lange. Erst seit ich in Deutschland bin.
Pierre	Cool, dann werde ich dich zu meinen Kontakten hinzufügen!
Iwona	Mach das!

Day 27

Dialogue questions

1. a) – **2.** a) – **3.** b) – **4.** b)

1 Listening text
1. Guten Tag, **meine Damen und** Herren. – **2.** Ich **begrüße Sie sehr herzlich** zur heutigen Besprechung. – **3.** Ich möchte kurz **die Tagesordnungspunkte vorstellen**. – **4.** In der Präsentation **geht es um** neue Strategien. – **5.** Gibt es noch **Fragen?** – **6.** Dann sind alle Fragen **beantwortet**. – **7.** Vielen Dank **für Ihre Aufmerksamkeit**. – **8.** Auf **Wiedersehen**.

2 **1.** Geschäftsbericht 2009 – **2.** 11 Uhr – **3.** Frau Leser – **4.** Frau Leser

3 **1.** Das langweilige Buch. – **2.** Der schicke Anzug. – **3.** Die weißen Hemden. – **4.** Die sportlichen Schuhe.

Day 28

Dialogue questions

1. Sie findet sie wirklich hervorragend. – **2.** Das war das erste größere Projekt auf Deutsch. – **3.** Sie findet die Kollegen nett. – **4.** Auf das nächste Projekt, das Iwona übernimmt.

1 **1.** Achten Sie beim nächsten Mal bitte auf die Zeit. – **2.** Das war hervorragend. – **3.** Ihre Präsentation war etwas kurz. – **4.** Vermeiden Sie bitte die Anrede mit Du. – **5.** Dieses Verhalten ist hier unüblich. – **6.** Das haben Sie gut gemacht. – **7.** Ich habe eine Bitte: Seien Sie bitte etwas pünktlicher.

2 **1.** interessanten – **2.** langweiliges – **3.** guten – **4.** schnelles – **5.** großes – **6.** toller

3 **1.** b) – **2.** b) – **3.** b) – **4.** a) – **5.** a)

Listening text

Herr Kern	Frau Roth, vielen Dank, dass Sie den Vortrag gehalten haben.
Frau Roth	Gern geschehen, Herr Kern.
Herr Kern	Sie haben das gut gemacht. Aber achten Sie bitte etwas mehr auf die Zeit. Es war ein wenig lang.
Frau Roth	Ja, entschuldigen Sie. Ich hatte wenig Zeit für die Vorbereitung.
Herr Kern	Ich weiß. Das ist auch kein großes Problem. Aber Ihr Handout war sehr gut! Beim nächsten Mal bereiten Sie sich länger vor, dann ist die Präsentation sicher einwandfrei!
Frau Roth	In Ordnung. Ich hätte auch eine Bitte: Können Sie mir bitte beim nächsten Mal die Materialien früher schicken?
Herr Kern	Ja, natürlich.
Frau Roth	Vielen Dank.

Day 29

Dialogue questions

1. wrong – **2.** right – **3.** right – **4.** right

1 **1.** werde – **2.** wird – **3.** werden – **4.** werden – **5.** Werdet – **6.** Wirst

2 Ich würde (gern / am liebsten) eine Reise machen / anderen Menschen helfen / ...

3 Listening text

1. Was willst du später von Beruf werden? – **Ich will Lehrerin werden.** – **2.** Wo willst du in der Zukunft arbeiten? – **Ich würde gern in Deutschland arbeiten.** – **3.** Bleibst du nach deinem Praktikum in Deutschland? – **Nein. Ich würde gern in Deutschland arbeiten, aber ich muss zurück nach Japan.** – **4.** Ich würde mich gerne mit dir treffen. – **Ich auch, aber ich habe leider keine Zeit.** – **5.** Welche Sprache möchtest du am liebsten lernen? – **Ich würde am liebsten Russisch lernen!**

Day 30

1 **1.** Dokument – **2.** Schuhe – **3.** verschicken – **4.** Wunsch – **5.** Kantine – **6.** nervös

2 **1.** 3) – **2.** 2) – **3.** 1) – **4.** 4) – **5.** —

Listening text

1.

▶ Herzlich Willkommen. Als erstes spricht heute Herr Hahn von der Situation in der Firma.

◀ Ja, danke Frau Winkler. Kommen wir gleich zum ersten Punkt: dem aktuellen Geschäftsbericht ...

2.

▶ Haben Sie denn am Dienstag Zeit?

◀ Nein, tut mir leid. Da muss ich zum Arzt. Geht es auch am Mittwochnachmittag?

▶ Ja, das geht auch.

3.

▶ Kann ich bitte mit Frau Lorenz sprechen?

◀ Am Apparat!

▶ Ah, guten Tag, Frau Lorenz!

4.

▶ Wo haben Sie denn vorher gearbeitet?

◀ Ich habe nach meinem Studium ein Praktikum in einer deutschen Maschinenbaufirma gemacht.

3 **1.** Welcher – **2.** Was für einen – **3.** Welchen – **4.** a) welcher b) was für eine

4 **1.** schön, Das schöne – **2.** rot, Der rote – **3.** jung, Die jungen – **4.** langweilig, Die langweilige – **5.** spannend, Das spannende – **6.** lang, Die langen – **7.** zufrieden, Der zufriedene – **8.** voll, Die volle

5 Possible solution
(You normally say your name first. It's not necessary but polite to use a hello and a goodbye.)
1. Herr Beck, rufen Sie mich bitte zurück. Meine (Telefon-) Nummer ist 89771. (Auf Wiederhören.) – **2.** Frau Sander, ich brauche einen Beamer für meine Präsentation am Montag, den 22. (Auf Wiederhören.) – **3.** Hallo Brian. Hast du am Freitag Zeit? Wir können ins Kino gehen. (Tschüs!) – **4.** Guten Tag, Herr Schumacher. Ich habe am Dienstag eine E-Mail geschrieben. Haben Sie die Zusammenfassung gelesen, die ich Ihnen geschickt habe? – **5.** Frau Engel, die Präsentation findet um 11 Uhr statt und nicht um 9 Uhr.

6 **1.** d) – **2.** e) – **3.** f) – **4.** b) – **5.** g) – **6.** a) – **7.** c)

7 **1.** a) – **2.** c) – **3.** a) – **4.** b) – **5.** c)

Listening text

Pierre	Iwona, wer ist das dort auf dem Foto?
Iwona	Wen meinst du?
Pierre	Den Mann im langen, schwarzen Mantel.
Iwona	Das ist mein Großvater.
Pierre	Aha ... und der Mann daneben mit dem grünen Jackett – ist das dein Vater?
Iwona	Nein, sein Bruder, also mein Onkel.
Pierre	Dann ist der Mann mit dem braunen Hut dein Vater, ja?
Iwona	Genau! Auf dem Foto hier: Pierre, bist du der kleine Junge mit der roten Mütze?
Pierre	Nein, das ist mein Freund Jean. Ich bin der mit der blauen Mütze.
Iwona	Oh, ihr seid euch aber sehr ähnlich.
Pierre	Stimmt. Und das Mädchen im roten Kleid ist meine Schwester Camille.
Iwona	Und deine andere Schwester?
Pierre	Julie? Sie ist nicht auf dem Bild. Sie ist da erst ein paar Monate alt.

8 **1.** jemand – **2.** a) dieser b) viele – **3.** a) einen b) keiner – **4.** a) jemand b) niemand – **5.** man – **6.** a) etwas b) ein paar – **7.** alles – **8.** a) ein b) jeden c) keiner

9 *Start your sentences with the same temporal adverbs as already there and then use* **"werde ich"** *and whatever your plans are. For example:* **"Heute Abend werde ich in eine Kneipe gehen."**

10 *Build your sentences with* **"Ich ziehe ... an."** *or like the two examples already there. Use the accusative. Possible combinations are:* einen roten Pullover, ein weißes Hemd, eine schwarze Jacke, eine blaue Hose, braune Schuhe, eine gelbe Mütze, einen grünen Schal, rote Socken, eine schwarze Jeans, ein grünes T-Shirt

11 **1.** in – **2.** oft – **3.** dass – **4.** viele – **5.** weil – **6.** die – **7.** Deshalb

12 **1.** Ein Mann | ~~eine Frau~~ – **2.** brauchen Zeit für die Familie | ~~sind keine Manager~~ – **3.** ~~Viele~~ | wenige – **4.** ~~Männer~~ | Frauen – **5.** mehr | ~~weniger~~

13 Listening text
   1.
   ► Können wir uns am **24. März** treffen?
   ◄ Ja, wir können uns am 24. März treffen.
   2.
   ► Hast du am **8. September** Zeit?
   ◄ Nein, ich habe am 8. September keine Zeit.
   3.
   ► Und geht es vielleicht am **13.10.**?
   ◄ Ja, am 13.10. geht es.
   4.
   ► Haben Sie am **6. Juli** Zeit?
   ◄ Nein, am 6. Juli habe ich keine Zeit.

14 **1.** Ich lese das Buch, das ich vor einer Woche gekauft habe. – **2.** Deine Schwester, die jünger ist, geht noch in die Schule. – **3.** Ich bringe den Kindern, die ich besuche, Geschenke mit. – **4.** Meine Freunde, mit denen ich in Urlaub fahre, sind toll. – **5.** Pierres Mutter, an die er / Pierre oft denkt, lebt in Frankreich. – **6.** Ich denke an meinen Bruder, dem ich noch eine E-Mail schreiben muss.

15 **1.** elegant – **2.** schick – **3.** Hut – **4.** Handschuh – **5.** gepflegt – **6.** locker – **7.** auffällig – **8.** Unterwäsche – **9.** Schmuck – **10.** Schal – **11.** Kostüm – **12.** Kleid – **13.** Kleidung – **14.** Krawatte – **15.** Mantel – **16.** anziehen – **17.** Schuh – **18.** bunt
   Solution: Bluse

Final test

1 **1.** fährt – **2.** schläfst – **3.** gehen – **4.** hält – **5.** läufst – **6.** sind

2 **1.** machen – **2.** klettern – **3.** schwimmen – **4.** spielen – **5.** sein – **6.** (Rad) fahren – **7.** haben – **8.** ausleihen – **9.** machen – **10.** wollen – **11.** mitnehmen – **12.** finden

3 **1.** a) schwarze b) elegantes – **2.** a) guter b) beste (bessere) – **3.** schnellste – **4.** netten – **5.** a) kleinen b) roten c) großen – **6.** tollen

4 **1.** Hals – **2.** Film – **3.** Hobby – **4.** Tante – **5.** Müll – **6.** Suppe

5 **1.** 4) – **2.** 1) – **3.** – – **4.** 2) – **5.** 3) – **6.** –
   Listening text
   1.
   ► Möchten Sie mit Kreditkarte zahlen?
   ◄ Ja. Hier, bitte.
   ► Möchten Sie auch eine Tüte?
   ◄ Oh ja, bitte.

2.
- ► Ich hätte gerne das Schnitzel mit Reis und einen Salat.
- ◄ Gut. Wollen Sie auch eine Suppe?
- ► Nein, danke.

3.
- ► Mensch, ist das langweilig.
- ◄ Ja, das nächste Mal sehen wir uns einen Thriller an.

4.
- ► Wo stehen denn die Getränke?
- ◄ Dort, im Wohnzimmer. Da gibt es auch etwas zu essen.
- ► Danke!

6   **1.** du – **2.** euch – **3.** ihr – **4.** ihm – **5.** Sie – **6.** es

7   *m* (der): Vortrag, Punkt, Kontakt, Termin, Terminkalender, Abschluss, Arbeitgeber –
f (die): Bewerbung, Kleidung, Verabredung, Nachricht, Abteilung, Ausbildung, Karriere, Rente
– *n* (das): Thema, Telefon, Gespräch, Büro, Buch, Dokument, Zeugnis, Verhalten, Projekt

8   **1.** In der Küche. / Das dreckige Geschirr ist in der Küche. – **2.** Im Schrank (im Schlafzimmer).
/ Die Kleidung ist im Schrank. – **3.** Auf dem Tisch. / Die sauberen Teller stehen auf dem
Tisch. – **4.** Im Regal. / Die Gläser stehen im Regal. – **5.** Am Tisch. / Johanna sitzt (nach dem
Aufräumen) am Tisch.

Listening text
Hallo, ich bin Johanna. Wenn ich aufräume, dann trage ich zuerst das dreckige Geschirr in
die Küche. Dann lege ich meine Kleidung in den Schrank im Schlafzimmer. Dann staubsauge
ich und spüle ab. Wenn das Geschirr sauber ist, dann stelle ich zwei Teller auf den Tisch. Die
Gläser kommen ins Regal. Wenn ich dann fertig bin, setze ich mich an den Tisch und lese ein
Buch.

9   **1.** Hallo, kommt bitte herein! Toll, dass ihr da seid. – **2.** Entschuldigung, wie komme ich zum
nächsten Supermarkt? – **3.** Lass uns doch ins Kino gehen. –
4. Darf ich dir Philipp vorstellen? Wir arbeiten zusammen. – **5.** Morgen koche ich für meine
Freunde. Deshalb muss ich jetzt noch einkaufen. – **6.** Das haben Sie wirklich sehr gut
gemacht.

10   **1.** dein – **2.** mein – **3.** seine – **4.** ihrem – **5.** deine – **6.** ihre – **7.** deinen – **8.** euren –
9. unseren

11   **1.** ~~immer so viele Kontakte wie möglich~~ | nur wenige gute Kontakte – **2.** mit seinem Kontakt
auch kurz sprechen | ~~von seinem Kontakt nur eine Visitenkarte nehmen~~ – **3.** schon vor |
~~erst auf~~ – **4.** Interessen | ~~Hobbys~~.

12   **1.** Ja, ich sehe ihn. – **2.** Nein, ich will keins. – **3.** Ja, wir geben ihnen Geschenke. – **4.** Ja, ich habe
eine. – **5.** Nein, sie ist nicht da. – **6.** Nein, die E-Mail / sie ist nicht von ihr.

13   **1.** Iwona will viele deutsche Bücher lesen. – **2.** Pierre muss für seinen Abschluss lernen. –
3. Martina fliegt (mit Jens) ein paar Tage nach London.

Listening text

Martina	Und was werdet ihr machen, wenn unser Deutschkurs zu Ende ist?
Iwona	Ich habe wirklich viel gelernt. Ich glaube nicht, dass ich wieder einen Kurs mache. Aber ich will viele deutsche Bücher lesen.
Martina	Das ist eine gute Idee! Und du, Pierre?
Pierre	Zuerst werde ich jetzt für meinen Abschluss lernen. Vielleicht mache ich danach wieder einen Kurs, aber das weiß ich noch nicht. Was wirst du denn machen, Martina?
Martina	Nach dem Kurs habe ich zwei Wochen frei und muss nicht arbeiten. Ich werde ein paar Tage mit Jens nach London fliegen.

| Pierre | Das ist toll. Viel Spaß dabei. |
| Martina | Danke. |

14 **1.** Haus – **2.** Jahreszeiten – **3.** Wetter – **4.** Monate – **5.** Sport – **6.** Obst

15 Listening text
1. Wie wird das Wetter morgen? – **Ich glaube, dass es morgen regnen wird.** – **2.** Was ist passiert? – **Ich bin hingefallen und habe mich an der Hand verletzt.** – **3.** Wann wollen wir uns treffen? – **Am liebsten am Donnerstag.** – **4.** Was hätten Sie denn gerne? – **Eine große Tasse Kaffee, bitte.** – **5.** Wie fahren wir denn nach Köln? – **Am besten mit dem Auto.** – **6.** Was machst du nach deinem Studium? – **Ich will Lehrer werden.**

16 **1.** i) – **2.** e) – **3.** h) – **4.** d) – **5.** f) – **6.** a) – **7.** c) – **8.** g)

17 **1.** ihrem – **2.** einen – **3.** viel – **4.** vielen – **5.** ein paar – **6.** der – **7.** viel – **8.** sein – **9.** seinen – **10.** das – **11.** die – **12.** den

18 **1.** Claudia hat 6 / sechs Stühle. – **2.** Der gelbe Tisch steht in der Küche. – **3.** Ein weißer Schrank steht im Wohnzimmer und im Bad. – **4.** Die Regale sind grün. – **5.** Im Wohnzimmer stehen ein brauner Tisch, (vier) schwarze Stühle, ein weißer Schrank, (zwei) Regale (und der Fernseher).

19 **1.** Wenn ihr wollt, dann **helfen** wir euch. – **2.** Ich **kaufe** gern auf dem Markt **ein.** – **3.** Du **bezahlst** heute die Rechnung im Restaurant. – **4. Können** Sie mir bitte **sagen,** wo der Bahnhof ist? – **5.** Wir fahren am Wochenende nach Hamburg, denn ich **war** noch nicht in Hamburg. – **6.** Ich denke, dass du den Vortrag gestern gut **gemacht hast.**

20 **1.** Ich habe einen wichtigen Termin am Donnerstag um 9 Uhr. / Am Donnerstag um 9 Uhr habe ich einen wichtigen Termin. / Ich habe am Donnerstag um 9 Uhr einen wichtigen Termin. – **2.** Wir werden zusammen einen interessanten Vortrag halten. / Wir werden einen interessanten Vortrag zusammen halten. – **3.** Wann hast du die E-Mail verschickt? – **4.** Werdet ihr jetzt in ein Café gehen? **5.** Er musste erst einen Termin vereinbaren. / Erst musste er einen Termin vereinbaren. – **6.** Wen haben Sie gestern angerufen?

21 **1.** c) – **2.** b) – **3.** c) – **4.** c)
Listening text
▸ Firma Maurer. Gabriele Schneider am Apparat.
◂ Paul Meyer. Guten Tag, Frau Schneider.
▸ Guten Tag, wie kann ich Ihnen helfen?
◂ Ich würde gerne mit Herrn Thomas sprechen. Ist er da?
▸ Nein, tut mir leid. Herr Thomas ist heute nicht im Büro. Kann ich Ihnen helfen?
◂ Ja, vielleicht. Es geht um einen Termin nächste Woche. Ich bin am Donnerstag, den 17.4., um 9.30 Uhr mit Herrn Thomas verabredet.
▸ Einen Moment bitte. Ich sehe eben im Terminkalender nach. Ah ja, hier steht ihr Termin.
◂ Gut. Leider habe ich vor 11 Uhr nun doch keine Zeit. Mein Chef braucht mich zu dieser Zeit. Kann ich um 11 Uhr kommen?
▸ Nein, tut mir leid. Herr Thomas hat schon einen Termin um 11 Uhr. Haben Sie am Nachmittag Zeit? Vielleicht um 14 Uhr?
◂ Ja, 14 Uhr geht bei mir auch.
▸ Gut. Kann ich Ihnen sonst noch helfen?
◂ Ja, können Sie Herrn Thomas bitte ausrichten, dass er mich zurückrufen soll. Ich muss ihm persönlich noch einige Fragen stellen, bevor wir uns treffen.
▸ Ich werde das ausrichten. Hat er Ihre Telefonnummer?
◂ Nein. Meine Nummer ist 0431 92833.

▸ 0431 92833. Gut, er wird sie anrufen.

◂ Vielen Dank. Auf Wiederhören.

▸ Auf Wiederhören.

22 **1.** arbeiten – **2.** E-Mail – **3.** telefonieren (sprechen) – **4.** Nachmittag – **5.** Besprechung –
6. Kneipe / Bar – **7.** fährt – **8.** Bett

Evaluation

maximal:	150 points
sehr gut:	125–150
gut:	100–124
in Ordnung:	75–99

Alphabetical word list

A

abbiegen ['apbiːgn] turn

Abend, -e m [aːbənt] evening

Abendessen, – n ['aːbəntˌɛsn] dinner

abends ['abənts] in the evening

aber ['aːbɐ] but

abfahren ['apfaːrən] depart

Abfahrt, -en f ['apfaːrt] departure

abgeben ['apgeːbn] deliver

ablenken ['aplɛŋkn] distract

Abreise, -n f ['apraɪzə] departure

Abschluss, -schlüsse m ['apʃlʊs] degree

Abschlusstest, -s m ['apʃlʊstɛst] final test

Absender, – m ['apzɛndɐ] sender

abspülen ['apʃpyːlən] wash up

Abteilung, -en f [ap'taɪlʊŋ] department

Ach! [ax] Oh!, Alas!

achten auf ['axtn auf] mind, pay attention

Achterbahn, -en f ['axtɐbaːn] roller coaster

Actionfilm, -e m ['ɛkʃnfɪlm] action movie

ägyptisch [ɛ'gʏptɪʃ] Egyptian

Aha! [a'ha(ː)] I see!

ähnlich ['ɛːnlɪç] similar, alike

Aikido (only Sg) n [ai'kiːdo] aikido

aktuell [aktu'ɛl] current

alle ['alə] all

Allergie, -n f [alɛr'giː] allergy

alles ['aləs] all, everything

Alles Gute! ['aləs 'guːtə] All the best!

als [als] than

also ['alzo] thus

alt [alt] old

am [am] on

am Apparat [am apa'raːt] speaking

Amerika (only Sg) n [a'meːrika] America

Ampel, -n f ['ampəl] traffic light

an [an] to, at, by

anbieten ['anbiːtn] offer

anderer, andere, anderes ['andərɐ, 'andərə, 'andərəs] other

anders ['andɐs] different

Angebot, -e n ['angəboːt] offer

angenehm ['angəneːm] kind, pleasant

Anhang, -hänge m ['anhaŋ] attachment

ankommen ['ankomən] arrive

Ankunft, -künfte f ['ankunft] arrival

anmelden ['anmɛldn] register

anmerken ['anmɛrkn] notice

Anrede, -n f ['anreːdə] title

Anreise, -n f ['anraɪzə] arrival

anreisen ['anraɪzn] arrive

Anruf, -e m ['anruːf] call

Anrufbeantworter, – m ['anruːfbə-antvɔrtɐ] answering machine

anrufen ['anruːfn] call, phone

Anschluss, -schlüsse m ['anʃlʊs] line, telephone connection

ansehen ['anzeːən] see, view

ansprechen ['anʃprɛçn] address

anstoßen ['anʃtoːsn] chink glasses

Antwort, -en f ['antvɔrt] reply, answer

antworten ['antvɔrtn] reply, answer

anziehen ['antsiːən] dress

Anzug, Anzüge m ['antsuːk] suit

Apfel, Äpfel m ['apfəl] apple

Apotheke, -n f [apo'teːkə] pharmacy

April (only Sg) m [a'pril] April

Arbeit (only Sg) f ['arbaɪt] job, work

arbeiten ['arbaɪtn] work

Arbeitgeber, – m [ˌarbaɪt'geːbɐ] employer

Arbeitnehmer, – m [ˌarbaɪtˈneːmɐ] employee

arbeitslos [ˈarbaɪtsloːs] unemployed

Arbeitsplatz, -plätze m [ˈarbaɪtsplats] job, position

Architekt, -en m [arçiˈtɛkt] architect (male)

Architektin, -nen f [arçiˈtɛktɪn] architect (female)

Arm, Arme m [arm] arm

Art, -en f [aːrt] kind, type

Arzt, Ärzte m [artst] doctor (male)

Ärztin, -nen f [ˈɛrtstɪn] doctor (female)

Asien (only Sg) n [ˈaːzjən] Asia

auch [aux] too

auf [auf] on, to

Auf Wiederhören! [auf ˈviːdɐˌhøːrən] Good-bye! (on the phone)

Auf Wiedersehen! [auf ˈviːdɐˌzeːən] Good-bye!

Aufenthalt, -e m [ˈaufɛnthalt] stay

auffällig [ˈauffɛlɪç] flashy

Aufgabe, -n f [ˈaufgaːbə] exercise

aufgehen [ˈaufgeːən] rise

aufhängen [ˈaufhɛŋən] put, hang up

Aufmerksamkeit (only Sg) f [ˈaufmɛrksamkaɪt] attention

aufräumen [ˈaufrɔʏmən] clean up

aufrufen [ˈaufruːfn] call

aufstehen [ˈaufʃteːən] get up

auftreten [ˈauftreːtən] tread; appear

Aufzug, -züge m [ˈauftsuːk] elevator

August (only Sg) m [auˈgʊst] August

aus [aus] from

Ausbildung, -en f [ˈausbɪldʊŋ] education

auschecken [ˈaustʃɛkn] check out

ausdrucken [ˈausdrʊkn] print

Ausflug, -flüge m [ˈausfluːk] trip, tour

ausfüllen [ˈausfʏlən] fill

Ausgang, -gänge m [ˈausgaŋ] exit

ausgerechnet [ˈausgərɛçnət] just

ausleihen [ˈauslaɪən] borrow

ausrichten [ˈausrɪçtn] leave/deliver a message

ausrutschen [ˈausrʊtʃn] slip

außerhalb [ˈausɐhalp] out of

aussteigen [ˈausʃtaɪgn] alight, get off

Ausstellung, -en f [ˈausʃtɛlʊŋ] exhibition

aussuchen [ˈaussuːxən] choose

Australien (only Sg) n [ausˈtraːljən] Australia

ausweichen [ˈausvaɪçn] dodge

ausziehen [ˈaustsiːən] undress

authentisch [auˈtɛntɪʃ] authentic

Auto, -s n [ˈauto] car

Autobahn, -en f [ˈautobaːn] motorway

B

Bäckerei, -en f [ˈbɛkəraɪ] baker's shop

Bad, Bäder n [baːt] bathroom

Badezimmer, – n [ˈbaːdəˌtsɪmɐ] bathroom

Bahn, -en f [baːn] train, railway

Bahnhof, -höfe m [ˈbaːnhoːf] station

Bahnsteig, -e m [ˈbaːnʃtaɪk] platform

bald [balt] soon

Banane, -n f [baˈnaːnə] banana

Bar, -s f [baːɐ] bar

Bauch, Bäuche m [baux] stomach, belly

Bauchweh (only Sg) n [ˈbauxveː] stomachache

bauen [ˈbauən] build

Baustelle, -n f [ˈbauʃtɛlə] construction site

beachten [bəˈaxtn] mind

Beamer, – m [ˈbiːmɐ] video projector

beantworten [bəˈantvɔrtn] answer

Becher, – m [ˈbɛçɐ] pot, cup

bedeuten [bə'dɔʏtn] mean

bedienen (sich) [zɪç bə'diːnən] help oneself

beeilen (sich) [zɪç bə'aɪlən] hurry

Beförderung, -en f [bə'fœrdərʊŋ] promotion

befreundet sein mit [bə'frɔʏndət] be friends with

beginnen [bə'ɡɪnən] start

begrüßen [bə'ɡryːsən] greet

Begrüßung, -en f [bə'ɡryːsʊŋ] welcome, reception

behandeln [bə'handəln] treat

Behandlung, -en f [bə'handlʊŋ] treatment

Behandlungsraum, -räume m [bə'handlʊŋsˌraum] surgery

bei [baɪ] at, by, next to

beide ['baɪdə] both, the two

beides ['baɪdəs] both, either

Beilage, -n f ['baɪlaːɡə] side dish

Bein, -e n [baɪn] leg

Beispiel, -e n ['baɪʃpiːl] example

bekommen [bə'kɔmən] get

benutzen [bə'nʊtsən] use

Beruf, -e m [bə'ruːf] profession

beruflich [bə'ruːflɪç] job-related

besichtigen [bə'zɪçtɪɡən] visit

besprechen [bə'ʃprɛçn] talk, discuss

Besprechung, -en f [bə'ʃprɛçʊŋ] meeting

Besprechungszimmer, – n [bə'ʃprɛçʊŋsˌtsɪmɐ] meeting room

besser ['bɛsɐ] better

Bestätigung, -en f [bə'ʃtɛːtɪɡʊŋ] confirmation

bestellen [bə'ʃtɛlən] order

Besuch, -e m [bə'zuːx] visit

besuchen [bə'zuːxn] visit

Betreff, -e m [bə'trɛf] subject

Bett, -en n [bɛt] bed

bewegen [bə'veːɡn] move

bewerben (für) [bə'vɛrbn] apply

Bewerbung, -en f [bə'vɛrbʊŋ] job application

Bewerbungsgespräch, -e n [bə'vɛrbʊŋsɡəʃprɛːç] job interview

bewölkt [bə'vœlkt] cloudy, overcast

bezahlen [bə'tsaːlən] pay

Bier, -e n [biːɐ] beer

Biergarten, -gärten m ['biːɐɡartn] beer garden

bieten ['biːtn] offer

Bild, -er n [bɪlt] picture, image

billig ['bɪlɪç] cheap, inexpensive

Birne, -n f ['bɪrnə] pear

bis [bɪs] until, to

Bis bald! [bɪs balt] See you!

Bis später! [bɪs 'ʃpɛːtɐ] See you (later)!

bitte ['bɪtə] please

Bitte schön! ['bɪtə ʃøːn] Here you are!

bitten (um) ['bɪtn] ask

blau [blau] blue

bleiben ['blaɪbn] stay

Bluse, -n f ['bluːzə] blouse

Bodybag, -s n ['bɔdiːbɛk] shoulder/cross-body bag

Bonbon, -s m+n [bɔŋ'bɔŋ, bõ'bõː] sweet, candy

Bratwurst, -würste f ['braːtvʊrst] bratwurst

brauchen ['brauxn] need

braun [braun] brown

brechen ['brɛçn] break

Bretagne (only Sg) f [bre'tanjə] Brittany

Brezel, -n f (Brezn, –f) ['breːtsl ('breːtsn)] pretzel

bringen ['brɪŋən] get, bring

britisch ['brɪtɪʃ, 'briːtɪʃ] British

Brosche, -n f ['brɔʃə] brooch

Brot, -e *n* [bro:t] bread
Brötchen, – *n* ['brø:tçən] bun
Bruder, Brüder *m* ['bru:dɐ] brother
Buch, Bücher *n* [bu:x] book
buchen ['bu:xn] book
Buchung, -en *f* ['bu:xʊŋ] booking
Buchungsbestätigung, -en *f* ['bu:xʊŋs-
   bɛˌʃtɛ:tɪgʊŋ] booking confirmation
bügeln ['by:gəln] iron
Büro, -s *n* [bʏ'ro:] office
Bundesland, -länder *n* ['bʊndəsˌlant]
   German state
bunt [bʊnt] colourful
Burg, -en *f* [bʊrk] castle
Bus, -se *m* [bʊs] bus
Bushaltestelle, -n *f* ['bʊshaltəˌʃtɛlə]
   bus stop
Business-Netzwerk, -e *n* ['bɪznɛs-
   nɛtsvɛrk] business network
Butter *(only Sg) f* ['bʊtɐ] butter

C

Café, -s *n* [ka'fe:] café
Cent, (-s) *m* [(t)sɛnt] cent
Chef, -s *m* [ʃɛf] boss, manager (male)
Chefin, -nen *f* ['ʃɛfɪn] boss, manager
   (female)
chinesisch [çi'ne:sɪʃ] Chinese
Chip, -s *m* [tʃɪp] crisp
Cola, –/-s *n/f* ['ko:la:] coke
Computer, – *m* [kɔm'pju:tɐ] computer
Consultingfirma, -firmen *f* [kɔn'saltɪŋ-
   fɪrma] consulting ompany
cool ['ku:l] cool, awesome

D

da [da:] here, there
dabeihaben [da'baɪha:bn] have

Dame, -n *f* ['da:mə] madam, lady
danach [da'na:x] afterwards
danke ['daŋkə] thanks, thank you
danken (für) ['daŋkn] thank
dann [dan] then
Darf ich ... vorstellen? [darf ɪç 'fo:ɐ̯ʃtɛlən]
   May I introduce ...?
darauf [da'rauf, 'da:rauf] afterwards;
   on it
darin [da'rɪn, 'da:rɪn] in that
darum [da'rʊm] therefore, that's why
dass [das] that
Datei, -en *f* [da'taɪ] file
Daten *(only Pl)* ['da:tn] data
dauern ['dauɐn] take
Daumen drücken ['daumən ˌdrʏkn] keep
   one's fingers crossed
Daumen, – *m* ['daumən] thumb
davon [da'fɔn, 'da:fɔn] thereof, of it
dazu [da'tsu:] thereto, to it
dazukommen [da'tsu:kɔmən] join
denken (an) ['dɛŋkn] think
denn [dɛn] for, because
der, die, das [de:ɐ̯, di:, das] the
deshalb ['dɛshalp] therefore, thus,
   hence
Detail, -s *n* [de'taj] detail
deutsch [dɔʏtʃ] German
Deutsche, -n *m* ['dɔʏtʃə] German
Deutschkurs, -e *m* ['dɔʏtʃkʊrs] German
   class
Deutschland *(only Sg) n* ['dɔʏtʃlant]
   Germany
Deutschlehrer, – *m* ['dɔʏtʃle:rɐ] German
   teacher (male)
Deutschlehrerin, -nen *f* ['dɔʏtʃle:rərɪn]
   German teacher (female)
Deutschunterricht *(only Sg) m*
   ['dɔʏtʃʊnterɪçt] German class/lesson

Dezember *(only Sg)* m [de'tsɛmbɐ]
December

Dialog, -e m [dia'loːk] dialogue

Dienstag, -e m ['diːnstaːk] Tuesday

dieser, diese, dieses ['diːzɐ, diːzə, diːzəs]
this, that

diese *Pl* ['diːzə] these

Ding, -e n [dɪŋ] thing

direkt [di'rɛkt] direct(ly)

Diskussion, -en f [dɪskʊ'sjoːn]
discussion

doch [dɔx] however, yet

Dokument, -e n [dɔkʊ'mɛnt] document

Dom, -e m [doːm] cathedral

Donnerstag, -e m ['dɔnɐstaːk] Thursday

Doppelbett, -en n ['dɔpəlˌbɛt] double
bed

Doppelzimmer, – n ['dɔpəlˌtsɪmɐ]
double room

dort [dɔrt] there

Dose, -n f ['doːzə] can

downloaden ['daunloːdn] download

Drama, Dramen n ['draːma] drama

draußen ['drausn] out here, outside

dreckig ['drɛkɪç] dirty

dringend ['drɪŋənt] badly

drucken ['drʊkn] print

drücken ['drʏkn] press

du [duː] you

dürfen ['dʏrfn] may

durch [dʊrç] through, by

Durchschnitt, -e m ['dʊrçʃnɪt] average

Dusche, -n f ['duːʃə, 'dʊʃə] shower

duschen ['duːʃn, 'dʊʃn] take a shower

DVD, -s f [deːvauˈdeː] DVD

E

eben ['eːbn] a moment ago

ebenso ['eːbnzoː] the same,
likewise

echt [ɛçt] real, really

Ehefrau, -en f ['eːəfrau] wife

ehemalig ['eːəmaːlɪç] former

Ehemann, -männer m ['eːəman]
husband

Ei, -er n [ai] egg

eigener, eigene, eigenes ['aigən] own

eigentlich ['aigntlɪç] actually

ein bisschen [ain 'bɪsçən] a bit

ein paar [ain 'paːɐ] (a) few

ein wenig [ain 'veːnɪç] a little bit of

ein, eine, ein [ain, ainə, ain] a/an

Einbahnstraße, -n f ['ainbaːnˌʃtraːsə]
one-way street

einchecken in ['aintʃɛkn in] check in

einfach ['ainfax] just, simply

einige [ainɪgə] some

Einkauf, -käufe m ['ainkauf] shopping

einkaufen ['ainkaufn] go shopping,
shop

Einkaufsliste, -n f ['ainkaufsˌlɪstə]
shopping list

einladen ['ainlaːdn] invite

Einladung, -en f ['ainlaːdʊŋ] invitation

Einleitung, -en f ['ainlaitʊŋ]
introduction

einmal ['ainmaːl] once

einsammeln ['ainzaməln] collect

einscannen ['ainskɛnən] scan

einschlafen ['ainʃlaːfn] fall asleep

einsteigen in ['ainʃtaign in] board,
get on

einstellen ['ainʃtɛlən] hire, employ

eintönig ['aintøːnɪç] monotonous

Eintrittskarte, -n f ['aintrɪtsˌkartə] ticket

einwandfrei ['ainvantˌfrai] flawless

einzeln ['aɪntsəln] single

Einzelzimmer, – n ['aɪntsəlˌtsɪmɐ] single room

Eis (only Sg) n [aɪs] ice

eisig ['aɪzɪç] icy

elegant [ele'gant] elegant

Eltern (only Pl) ['ɛltɐn] parents

E-Mail, -s f ['iːmeːl] e-mail

E-Mail-Adresse, -n f ['iːmeːlatrɛsə] e-mail address

empfangen [ɛm'pfaŋən] welcome, receive

Empfänger, – m [ɛm'pfɛŋɐ] recipient, receiver

Ende, -n (mostly Sg) n ['ɛndə] end

endlich ['ɛndtlɪç] finally

England (only Sg) n ['ɛŋlant] England

englisch ['ɛŋlɪʃ] English

Enkel, – m ['ɛŋkəl] grandchild (male)

Enkelin, -nen f ['ɛŋkəlɪn] grandchild (female)

entscheiden [ɛnt'ʃaɪdn] decide

entschuldigen [ɛnt'ʃʊldigən] excuse

Entschuldigung! [ɛnt'ʃʊldigʊŋ] Sorry!

Entschuldigung, -en f [ɛnt'ʃʊldigʊŋ] apology

er [eːɐ] he

erfolgreich [ɛɐ'fɔlkraɪç] successful

ergeben, sich [zɪç ɛɐ'geːbn] come along, arise

Erkältung, -en f [ɛɐ'kɛltʊŋ] cold

erklären [ɛɐ'klɛːrən] explain

erleben [ɛɐ'leːbn] experience

erleichtern [ɛɐ'laɪçtɐn] make ... easy

Ermäßigung, -en f [ɛɐ'mɛːsigʊŋ] discount

ermitteln [ɛɐ'mitəln] investigate

erreichen [ɛɐ'raɪçn] reach

erst [eːɐst] first; only

erster, erste, erstes ['ɛɐstɐ, 'ɛɐstə, 'ɛɐstəs] first

Erwachsene, -n m/f [ɛɐ'vaksənə] adult, grown-up

erzählen [ɛɐ'tsɛːlən] tell

es [ɛs] it

essen ['ɛsn] eat

Essen, – n ['ɛsn] meal

Etage, -n f [e'taːʒə] floor, level

etwa ['ɛtva] about

etwas ['ɛtvas] somewhat, a little; something

Euro, (-s) m ['ɔyro] Euro

Europa (only Sg) n [ɔy'roːpa] Europe

F

fahren ['faːrən] go, ride, drive

Fahrgeschäft, -e n ['faːɐgəʃeft] ride

Fahrkarte, -n f ['faːɐkartə] ticket

Fahrplan, -pläne m ['faːɐplaːn] timetable

Fahrrad, -räder n ['faːɐraːt] bicycle, bike

Fahrradverleih, -e m ['faːɐraːtfɛɐlaɪ] bike rental

Fahrt, -en f [faːrt] journey, trip; drive

Fall, Fälle m [fal] case

falsch [falʃ] wrong, false

Familie, -n f [fa'miːljə] family

fantastisch [fan'tastɪʃ] great, fantastic

Farbe, -n f ['farbə] colour

fast [fast] almost, nearly

faulenzen ['faulɛntsn] do nothing

Februar (only Sg) m ['feːbruaːɐ] February

fegen ['feːgn] sweep

fehlen ['feːlən] miss, be missing

Feiertag, -e m ['faɪɐtaːk] holiday

Ferien (only Pl) ['feːrjən] holiday

fernsehen ['fɛrnzeːən] watch TV

Fernsehen *(only Sg)* n ['fɛrnzeːən] television, TV

Fernseher, – m ['fɛrnzeːɐ] television

Fernsehturm, -türme m ['fɛrnzeːtʊrm] television tower

Fernsehzeitschrift, -en f ['fɛrnzeːtsaɪtʃrɪft] TV guide

fertig ['fɛrtɪç] ready, done

Festnetzanschluss, -schlüsse m ['fɛstnɛtsanʃlʊs] landline

Festzelt, -e f ['fɛsttsɛlt] festival tent

Fieber *(only Sg)* n ['fiːbɐ] fever

Film, -e m [fɪlm] film, movie

Filmverleih, -e m ['fɪlmfɐlaɪ] film rental

finden ['fɪndn] find, think

Firma, Firmen f ['fɪrma] company

Fisch, -e m [fɪʃ] fish

Flasche, -n f ['flaʃə] bottle

Fleisch *(only Sg)* n [flaɪʃ] meat

fliegen ['fliːgən] fly

Flipchart, -s n ['flɪptʃaːɐt] flip chart

Flug, Flüge m [fluːk] flight

Flugzeug, -e n ['fluːktsɔʏk] plane

Flur, -e m [fluːɐ] corridor

folgen [fɔlgn] follow

Formular, -e n [fɔrmʊ'laːr] form

fortfahren ['fɔrtfaːrən] continue

Frage, -n f ['fraːgə] question

Fragebogen, -bögen m ['fraːgəboːgn] questionnaire

fragen (nach) ['fraːgn] ask

Frankreich ['fraŋkraɪç] France

französisch [fran'tsøːsɪʃ] French

Frau *(abbr. Fr.)* [frau] woman, wife, Ms

frei [fraɪ] free

Freitag, -e m ['fraɪtaːk] Friday

Freizeit *(only Sg)* f ['fraɪtsaɪt] leisure time

freuen, sich [zɪç 'frɔʏən] be pleased/ glad/happy

Freund, -e m [frɔʏnt] friend (male), boyfriend

Freundin, -nen f ['frɔʏndɪn] friend (female), girlfriend

frisch [frɪʃ] fresh

frisch machen (sich) ['frɪʃ maxn] freshen up

froh [froː] glad

früh [fryː] early

früher ['fryːɐ] earlier

Frühling, -e *(mostly Sg)* m ['fryːlɪŋ] spring

Frühstück, -e *(mostly Sg)* n ['fryːʃtʏk] breakfast

frühstücken ['fryːʃʏkn] eat breakfast

fühlen ['fyːlən] feel

Führungsposition, -en f ['fyːrʊŋspozɪtsjoːn] leadership position

für [fyːɐ] for

Fuß, Füße m [fuːs] foot

Fußball, -bälle m ['fuːsbal] football, soccer

Fußballplatz, -plätze m ['fuːsbalplats] football ground

G

Gabel, -n f ['gaːbəl] fork

ganz [gants] complete, completely

gar nicht [gaːɐ nɪçt] not at all

Garten, Gärten m ['gartn] garden

Gast, Gäste m [gast] guest

Gästezimmer, – n ['gɛstətsɪmɐ] guest room

geben ['geːbn] give

Geburtsdatum, -daten n [gə'buːɐtsdaːtʊm] date of birth

Geburtstag, -e m [gə'buːɐtstaːk] birthday

Geburtstagsgeschenk, -e n [gə'buːɐtstaːksgəʃɛŋk] birthday present

Gedanke, -n m [gə'daŋkə] thought

geeignet [gə'aignət] suitable

gefallen [gə'falən] appeal, please; like

gehen ['geːən] go

gelb [gɛlp] yellow

Geld (only Sg) n [gɛlt] money

Gelenk, -e n [gə'lɛŋk] joint

gelten (für) ['gɛltn] apply

gelungen [gə'luŋən] successful

gemeinsam [gə'mainzaːm] common; together

Gemüse (only Sg) n [gə'myːzə] vegetable

genau [gə'nau] exactly

genießen [gə'niːsən] enjoy

Genre, -s n ['ʒãːrə] genre

genug [gə'nuːk] enough

gepflegt [gə'pfleːkt] neat, groomed

gerade [gə'raːdə] right now

geradeaus [gə'raːdəaus] straight on

Gern geschehen! [gɛrn gə'ʃeːən] You're welcome!

gern, gerne ['gɛrn(ə)] gladly

geschäftlich [gə'ʃɛftlɪç] on business, commercial

Geschäftsfrau, -en f [gə'ʃɛftsfrau] businesswoman

Geschäftsmann, -männer m [gə'ʃɛftsman] businessman

Geschenk, -e n [gə'ʃɛŋk] gift, present

Geschirr (only Sg) n [gə'ʃɪr] dishes

Geschirrspüler, – m [gə'ʃɪrʃpyːlɐ] dishwasher

geschlossen [gə'ʃlɔsn] closed

Geschwister (only Pl) [gə'ʃvistɐ] brothers and sisters

Gesetz, -e n [gə'zɛts] law

Gespräch, -e n [gə'ʃprɛːç] conversation, talk

gestern ['gɛstɐn] yesterday

gesund [gə'zunt] healthy

Gesundheit (only Sg) f [gə'zunthait] health

Getränk, -e n [gə'trɛŋk] beverage, drink

Gewitter, – n [gə'vɪtɐ] thunderstorm

Gift, -e n [gɪft] poison

Glas, Gläser n [glaːs] glass

glauben (an) ['glaubn] think, believe

gleich [glaiç] immediately, soon, same

gleichberechtigt ['glaiçbə,rɛçtɪkt] equal

Gleis, -e n [glais] rails

Glück (only Sg) n [glʏk] luck

Glück haben [glʏk haːbn] be lucky

glücklich ['glʏklɪç] happy

Gott, Götter m [gɔt] god

Gramm (only Sg) n [gram] gramme, gram

gratulieren zu [gratu'liːrən] congratulate

Grippe, -n f ['grɪpə] flu

groß [groːs] big

großartig ['groːsartɪç] awesome

Großeltern (only Pl) ['groːsɛltɐn] grandparents

Großmutter, -mütter f ['groːs,mʊtɐ] grandmother

Großvater, -väter m ['groːs,faːtɐ] grandfather

grün [gryːn] green

grüßen ['gryːsən] greet

Gruppe, -n f ['grʊpə] group

Gruß, Grüße m [gruːs] greeting, salutation

günstig ['gʏnstɪç] low priced

Gurke, -n f ['gʊrkə] cucumber

gut [guːt] good
Gute Nacht! [ˌguːtə ˈnaxt] Goodnight!
Guten Abend! [ˌguːtn ˈaːbnt] Good evening!
Guten Morgen! [ˌguːtn ˈmɔrgn] Good morning!
Guten Tag! [ˌguːtn ˈtaːk] Good day/afternoon!

H

haben [ˈhaːbn] have
Hähnchen, – n [ˈhɛːnçn] chicken
halb [halp] half
Hallo! [ˈhaloː] Hello!
Hals, Hälse m [hals] neck, throat
Halsschmerzen (only Pl) [ˈhalsʃmɛrtsn] sore throat
Halsweh (only Sg) n [ˈhalsveː] sore throat
halten [ˈhaltən] hold
halten von [ˈhaltən fɔn] think
Haltestelle, -n f [ˈhaltəʃtɛlə] stop
Hand, Hände f [hant] hand
Handout, -s n [ˈhɛndaut] handout
Handschuh, -e m [ˈhantʃuː] glove
Handy, -s n [ˈhɛndi] mobile phone
Handzettel, – m [ˈhantˌtsɛtəl] handout
häufig [ˈhɔʏfɪç] often
Hauptbahnhof, -höfe m [ˈhauptbaːnˌhoːf] main station
Hauptgericht, -e n [ˈhauptɡəˌrɪçt] main dish
Hauptteil, -e m [ˈhaupttaɪl] main part/section
Haus, Häuser n [haus] house
Hausarbeit, -en f [ˈhausarbaɪt] chore
Hausnummer, -n f [ˈhausˌnʊmɐ] house number

heiß [haɪs] hot
heißen [ˈhaɪsn] be called
helfen [ˈhɛlfən] help
Hemd, -en n [hɛmt] shirt
Herbst, -e (mostly Sg) m [hɛrpst] autumn
hereinkommen [hɛˈraɪnˌkɔmən] come in
Herr, -en m (abbr. Hr.) [hɛr] sir, mister
herrichten [ˈheːərɪçtn] prepare
hervorragend [hɛɛˈfoːəraːɡənt] excellent
herzlich [ˈhɛrtslɪç] dearly
Herzlich willkommen! [ˈhɛrtslɪç vɪlˈkɔmən] Welcome!
Herzlichen Glückwunsch! [ˈhɛrtslɪçən ˈɡlʏkvʊnʃ] Congratulations!
heute [ˈhɔʏtə] today
heutig [ˈhɔʏtɪç] today's
hier [hiːɐ] here
hineingehen [hɪˈnaɪnɡeːən] go inside
hinfahren [ˈhɪnfaːrən] get/drive there
Hinfahrt, -en f [ˈhɪnfaːrt] journey there
hinfallen [ˈhɪnfalən] fall over
hinten [ˈhɪntn] (at the) back
hinter [ˈhɪntɐ] behind
hinterlassen [ˈhɪntɐlasn] leave
Hobby, -s n [ˈhɔbiː] hobby
hoch [hoːx] high
Hochhaus, -häuser n [hoːxhaus] high-rise building
hoffen [ˈhɔfn] hope
hoffentlich [ˈhɔfntlɪç] hopefully
holen [ˈhoːlən] get, fetch
Honig (only Sg) m [ˈhoːnɪç] honey
hören [ˈhøːrən] listen; hear
Hose, -n f [ˈhoːzə] trousers
Hosenanzug, -züge m [ˈhoːzənˌantsuːk] pantsuit
Hotel, -s n [hoˈtɛl] hotel

Hotelangestellte, -n *m* [ho'tɛl,angəʃtɛltə] hotel clerk

Hunger *(only Sg) m* ['hʊŋɐ] hunger

hungrig ['hʊŋriç] hungry

Hurra! [hʊ'ra:] Hooray!

husten ['hu:stn] cough

Hut, Hüte *m* [hu:t] hat

I

ich [ɪç] I

Idee, -n *f* [i'de:] idea

ihr [i:ɐ] you

im Folgenden [ɪm 'fɔlgndən] in the follwing, hereafter

Im Notfall [ɪm 'no:tfal] if need be

immer ['ɪmɐ] always

in [ɪn] in

in der Nähe von [ɪn de:ɐ nɛ:ə] near, not far from

in Ordnung [ɪn 'ɔɐtnʊŋ] all right, be OK/fine

Informatiker, – *m* [ɪnfɔr'ma:tɪkɐ] computer scientist

Information, -en *f* [ɪnfɔrma'tsjo:n] information

informativ [ɪnfɔrma'ti:f] informative

informieren [ɪnfɔr'mi:rən] inform

inklusive [ɪnklʊ'zi:və] inclusive

Innenstadt, -städte *f* ['ɪnɛnʃtat] city centre

interessant [ɪnt(ə)rɛ'sant] interesting

Interesse, -n *n* [ɪnt(ə)'rɛsə] interest, hobby

international [ɪntɛnatsjo'na:l] international

Internet *(only Sg) n* ['ɪntɛnɛt] internet

irgendwelche [ɪrgnt'vɛlçə] any

Italien [i'ta:ljən] Italy

italienisch [ital'je:nɪʃ] Italian

J

ja [ja:] yes

Jacke, -n *f* ['jakə] jacket

Jackett, -s *n* [ʒa'kɛt] jacket, suit jacket

Jahr, -e *n* [ja:ɐ] year

Jahreszeit, -en *f* [ja:rəstsaɪt] season

Januar *(only Sg) m* ['janua:ɐ] January

Japan ['ja:pan] Japan

japanisch [ja'pa:nɪʃ] Japanese

Jeans, – *f/*Jeans *(only Pl)* [dʒi:ns] jeans

jedenfalls ['je:dn'fals] anyway

jeder, jede, jedes ['je:dɐ, 'je:də, 'je:dəs] each

jemand ['je:mant] someone, somebody

jetzt [jɛtst] now

Job, -s *m* [dʒɔp] job

joggen ['dʒɔgən] run, jog

Joghurt, -s/– *m* ['jo:gʊrt] yogurt

Judo *(only Sg) n* ['ju:do] judo

Jugendherberge, -n *f* ['ju:gənt,hɛrbɛrgə] youth hostel

Juli *(only Sg) m* ['ju:li:] July

jung [jʊŋ] young

Juni *(only Sg) m* ['ju:ni] June

K

Kaffee *(only Sg) m* ['kafe:, ka'fe:] coffee

kalt [kalt] cold

Kantine, -n *f* [kan'ti:nə] canteen

kaputt [ka'pʊt] broken, in pieces

kaputtmachen [ka'pʊtmaxn] break

Karate *(only Sg) n* [ka'ra:tə] karate

Karotte, -n *f* [ka'rɔtə] carrot

Karriere *(only Sg) f* [kar'je:rə] career

Karte, -n *f* ['kartə] ticket; map

Kartoffel, -n *f* [kar'tɔfl] potatoe

Karton, -s *m* [kar'tɔŋ] carton

Karussell, -s *n* [karʊ'sɛl] roundabout

Käse *(only Sg) m* ['kɛːzə] cheese
kaufen ['kaufn] buy
Kaufhaus, -häuser *n* ['kaufhaus]
  department store
kaum [kaum] hardly
kehren ['keːrən] sweep
kein [kaɪn] no
keinmal [kaɪnmaːl] not once, never
Kellner, – *m* ['kɛlnɐ] waiter
Kellnerin, -nen *f* ['kɛlnərɪn] waitress
kennen ['kɛnən] know
kennen (sich) [zɪç 'kɛnən] know each
  other
kennenlernen ['kɛnənlɛrnən] meet, get
  to know
Kilo, (-s) *n* ['kiːlo] kilo
Kind, -er *n* [kɪnt] child
Kindergarten, -gärten *m* ['kɪndɐˌgartn]
  nursery
Kindergärtner, – *m* ['kɪndɐˌgɛrtnɐ]
  nursery teacher (male)
Kindergärtnerin, -nen *f* ['kɪndɐˌgɛrtnərɪn]
  nursery teacher (female)
Kinderzimmer, – *n* ['kɪndɐtsɪmɐ]
  nursery, children's room
Kino, -s *n* ['kiːno] cinema
Kirche, -n *f* ['kɪrçə] church
klappen ['klapn] go off all right
klar [klaːr] clear
Klasse, -n *f* ['klasə] class
Kleid, -er *n* [klaɪt] dress
Kleidung *(only Sg) f* ['klaɪdʊn] clothes
Kleidungsstück, -e *n* ['klaɪdʊnsʃtʏk]
  piece of clothing
klein [klaɪn] small, little
klettern ['klɛtɐn] climb
Klima *(only Sg) n* ['kliːma] climate
klingeln ['klɪŋəln] ring
Kneipe, -n *f* ['knaɪpə] pub, bar
Knöchel, – *m* ['knœçl] ankle

Knochen, – *m* ['knɔxn] bone
Koch, Köche *m* [kɔx] chef, cook (male)
kochen ['kɔxn] cook
Köchin, -nen *f* ['kœçɪn] chef,
  cook (female)
Kollege, -n *m* [kɔˈleːgə] colleague (male)
Kollegin, -nen *f* [kɔˈleːgɪn] colleague
  (female)
komfortabel [kɔmfɔɐ̯ˈtaːbəl]
  comfortable
kommen ['kɔmən] come; get to;
  be on TV
Kommissar, -e *m* [kɔmɪˈsaːɐ̯] detective,
  commissar
Kommode, -n *f* [kɔˈmoːdə] chest of
  drawers
Komödie, -n *f* [kɔˈmøːdiə] comedy
können ['kœnən] can
Könnte ich ...? ['kœntə ɪç] Could I ...?
Kontakt, -e *m* [kɔnˈtakt] contact
Kontakte knüpfen [kɔnˈtaktə ˌknʏpfn]
  make new contacts, socialise,
  network
Kontinent, -e *m* ['kɔntinɛnt] continent
Kontrolle, -n *f* [kɔnˈtrɔlə] control
Konzert, -e *n* [kɔnˈtsɛrt] concert
Kopf, Köpfe *m* [kɔpf] head
Kopfschmerzen *(only Pl)* ['kɔpfʃmɛrtsn]
  headache
Kopfweh *(only Sg) n* ['kɔpfveː] headache
kosten ['kɔstn] cost
kostenlos ['kɔstnloːs] (for) free
Kostüm, -e *n* [kɔsˈtyːm] female suite
krank [kraŋk] ill
Krankenhaus, -häuser *n* ['kraŋknˌhaus]
  hospital
Krankenkasse, -n *f* ['kraŋknkasə]
  health insurance company
Krankenschwester, -n *f*
  ['kraŋknˌʃvɛstɐ] nurse

Krankheit, -en f ['kraŋkhaɪt] illness
Krawatte, -n f [kra'vatə] tie
Kreditkarte, -n f [kre'diːt,kartə] credit card
Kreuzung, -en f ['krɔytsʊŋ] crossroads
Krimi, -s m ['krɪmi] crime series, detective story
Kritik, -en f [kri'tiːk] criticism
kritisieren [kriti'ziːrən] criticise
Kuchen, – m ['kuːxn] cake, pie
Küche, -n f ['kʏçə] kitchen
kühl [kyːl] chilly, cool
Kunde, -n m ['kʊndə] client
Kurs, -e m [kʊrs] class, course
Kurve, -n f ['kʊrvə] turn
kurz [kʊrts] short(ly), brief(ly)

L

Laden, Läden m ['laːdn] shop
Lampe, -n f ['lampə] lamp
Land, Länder n [lant] country
lang(e) [laŋ] long
langsam ['laŋzaːm] slow(ly)
langweilig ['laŋvaɪlɪç] boring
Laptop, -s m/f ['lɛptɔp] laptop
lassen ['lasn] let
laufen ['laufn] run, jog
Laufstrecke, -n f ['lauf,ʃtrɛkə] running route
leben ['leːbn] live
Leben, – (mostly Sg) n ['leːbn] life
Lebensmittel, – (mostly Pl) n ['leːbnsmɪtl] food
lecker ['lɛkɐ] delicious, tasty
legen ['leːgən] lay
Lehrer, – m ['leːrɐ] teacher (male)
Lehrerin, -nen f ['leːrərɪn] teacher (female)
leicht [laɪçt] easy

leider ['laɪdɐ] unfortunately
leidtun ['laɪdtuːn] be sorry
leihen ['laɪən] borrow, lend
Leistung, -en f ['laɪstʊŋ] performance
Lektion, -en f [lɛktsi'oːn] lesson
lernen ['lɛrnən] learn
Lerner, – m ['lɛrnɐ] student
lesen ['leːzn] read
letzter, letzte, letztes ['lɛtstɐ, 'lɛtstə, lɛtstəs] last
Leute (only Pl) ['lɔytə] people
lieb [liːp] nice, dear, beloved, good
lieb haben ['liːp ,haːbn] like/love you, be fond of
Liebe (only Sg) f ['liːbə] love
Liebe/Lieber ... ['liːbə, 'liːbɐ] Dear ...
lieber ['liːbɐ] rather, preferably
liegen ['liːgn] lie
links [lɪŋks] left
Liter, – m ['liːtɐ, 'lɪtɐ] litre
Lob (only Sg) n [loːp] praise
loben ['loːbn] praise
locker ['lɔkɐ] casual
Löffel, – m ['lœfl] spoon
Lust haben auf ['lʊst haːbn auf] be up for sth

M

machen ['maxn] make
Macht nichts! ['maxt nɪçts] Never mind!
Mai (only Sg) m [maɪ] May
mal, einmal [maːl] once
man [man] one, you
Manager, – m ['mɛnɛdʒɐ] manager
manche ['mançə] some
manchmal ['mançmaːl] sometimes
Mann, Männer m [man] man

Mantel, Mäntel *m* ['mantəl] coat
Markt, Märkte *m* [markt] market
Marktplatz, -plätze *m* [marktplats]
    market place
Marmelade, -n *f* [marmə'la:də] jam
März *(only Sg)* *m* [mɛrts] March
Maschinenbau *(only Sg)* *m* [ma'ʃi:nə
    nbau] mechanical engineering
Material, -ien *n* [mater'ja:l] material
Mauer, -n *f* ['mauɐ] wall
Medium, Medien *n* ['me:diʊm]
    medium
mehr [me:r] more
mehrere ['me:rərə] several
Meine Güte! ['maɪnə 'gy:tə] Blimey!
meinen ['maɪnən] think, mean
Mensch! [mɛnʃ] Gosh!, Blimey!
Mensch, -en *m* [mɛnʃ] human (being),
    man
merken ['mɛrkn] notice
Messer, – *n* ['mɛsɐ] knife
Milch *(only Sg)* *f* [mɪlç] milk
Milchkaffee, -s *m* ['mɪlçkafe:] café au lait
Milchprodukt, -e *n* ['mɪlçpro,dʊkt]
    dairy product
Minute, -n *f* [mi'nu:tə] minute
mit [mɪt] with
Mitarbeiter, – *m* ['mɪtar,baɪtɐ]
    personnel
mitbringen ['mɪtbrɪŋən] bring along
Mitglied, -er *n* ['mɪtgli:t] member
mitkommen ['mɪtkɔmən] come along
mitnehmen ['mɪtne:mən] take along
Mittag, -e *m* ['mɪta:k] noon
Mittagessen, – *n* ['mɪta:k,ɛsn] lunch
mittags ['mɪta:ks] at noon
Mittwoch, -e *m* ['mɪtvɔx] Wednesday
Möbel, – *(mostly Pl)* *n* ['mø:bl] furniture
Mobiltelefon, -e *n* [mo'bi:ltele,fo:n]
    mobile phone

möcht- ['mœçt-] would like to
Moderation, -en *f* [modera'tsio:n]
    moderation
moderieren [mode'ri:rən] moderate
mögen ['mø:gn] like
möglich ['mø:klɪç] possible
Möglichkeit, -en *f* ['mø:klɪçkaɪt]
    possibility
Möhre, -n *f* ['mø:rə] carrot
Moment! [mɔ'mɛnt] Just a moment!
Moment, -e *m* [mɔ'mɛnt] moment
Monat, -e *m* ['mo:nat] month
Montag, -e *m* ['mo:nta:k] Monday
Mord, -e *m* [mɔrt] murder
Mörder, – *m* ['mœrdɐ] murderer
morgen ['mɔrgn] tomorrow
Morgen, – *m* ['mɔrgn] morning
morgens ['mɔrgns] in the morning
motivieren [mɔti'vi:rən] motivate
Müll *(only Sg)* *m* [mʏl] rubbish, trash
Müsli, -s *n* ['my:sli] muesli
müssen ['mʏsn] have to, must
Mütze, -n *f* ['mʏtsə] cap
Museum, Museen *n* [mʊ'ze:ʊm]
    museum
Mutter, Mütter *f* ['mʊtɐ] mother
Muttersprache, -n *f* ['mʊtɐ,ʃpra:xə]
    native language

N

na (ja) [na] well
Na klar! [na 'kla:r] Of course!
nach [na:x] to, toward, past, after
nach Hause [na:x 'hauzə] home
Nachbar, -n *m* ['naxba:r] neighbour
Nachmittag, -e *m* ['na:xmita:k] after-
    noon
nachmittags ['na:xmita:ks] in the
    afternoon

Nachname, -n *m* ['naːxnaːmə]
  last name
Nachricht, -en *f* ['naːxrɪçt] message
Nachrichten *(only Pl)* ['naːxrɪçtn] news
nachschauen, nachschlagen ['naːxʃauən]
  look up
nächster, nächste, nächstes ['nɛːkstɐ,
  'nɛːkstə, 'nɛːkstəs] next
Nacht, Nächte *f* [naxt] night
Nachtisch *(only Sg) m* ['naːxtɪʃ] dessert
nah [naː] close, nearby
Name, -n *m* ['naːmə] name
Nase, -n *f* ['naːzə] nose
natürlich [naˈtyːɐlɪç] naturally, of
  course, sure, certainly
Nebel *(only Sg) m* ['neːbl] fog
neben ['neːbən] at, by, next to
neblig ['neːblɪç] foggy
nehmen ['neːmən] take
nein [naɪn] no
nennen ['nɛnən] mention
nervös [nɛrˈvøːs] nervous
nett [nɛt] nice
Netzwerk, -e *n* ['nɛtsvɛrk] network
neu [nɔɣ] new
nicht [nɪçt] not
nicht mehr [nɪçt meːɐ] not anymore,
  no longer
nichts [nɪçts] nothing
nicken ['nɪkn] nod
nie [niː] never
niemand ['niːmant] nobody, no one
niesen ['niːzən] sneeze
noch [nɔx] still
noch einmal [nɔx 'aɪnmaːl] once again
normal [nɔrˈmaːl] normal
normalerweise [nɔrˈmaːlɐvaɪzə]
  usually
Notfall, -fälle *m* ['noːtfal] emergency
Notiz, -en *f* [noˈtiːts] note

November *(only Sg) m* [noˈvɛmbɐ]
  November
Nudel, -n *f* ['nuːdəl] noodles
Nummer, -n *f* ['nʊmɐ] number
nun [nuːn] now
nur [nuːɐ] only, just
Nutzen *(only Sg) m* ['nʊtsən] use

O

ob [ɔp] if, whether
oben ['oːbən] above
Obst *(only Sg) n* [oːpst] fruit
oder ['oːdɐ] or
offen ['ɔfən] open
Öffnungszeit, -en *(mostly Pl) f*
  ['œfnʊŋstsaɪt] opening hours
oft [ɔft] often, a lot
Ohr, -en [oːɐ] ear
Ohrenschmerzen *(only Pl)*
  ['oːrənʃmɛrtsn] earache
Oje! [oːˈjeː] Oh dear!
Oktober *(only Sg) m* [ɔkˈtoːbɐ]
  October
Onkel, – *m* ['ɔŋkl] uncle
online ['ɔnlaɪn] online
Online-Bewerbung, -en *f* ['ɔnlaɪn-
  bəvɛrbʊŋ] online application
Orange, -n *f* [oˈrãːʒə, oˈranʒə] orange
Ordnung, -en *f* ['ɔrtnʊŋ] order
organisieren [ɔrganiˈziːrən] organise
Overheadprojektor, -en *m* ['oːvɐhɛt-
  proːjɛktɐ] overhead projector

P

Packung, -en *f* ['pakʊŋ] package, pack
Papier *(only Sg) n* [paˈpiːr] paper
Paprika, -s *m/f* ['paprika] peppers
Park, -s *m* [park] park

Parkplatz, -plätze *m* ['parkplats]
  parking (space)
Party, -s *f* ['paːrti] party
Passant, -en *m* [pa'sant] passerby
  (male)
Passantin, -nen *f* [pa'santɪn] passerby
  (female)
passen (zu) ['pasn] fit, suit
passend ['pasnt] suitable, appropriate
passieren [pa'siːrən] happen
Pause, -n *f* ['pauzə] break
per [pɛr] by
Person, -en *f* [pɛr'zoːn] person
Personalausweis, -e *m*
  [pɛrzo'naːlausvaɪs] ID card
Personalchef, -s *m* [pɛrzo'naːlʃɛf]
  personnel manager
persönlich [pɛr'zøːnlɪç] personally
Pfirsich, -e *m* ['pfɪrzɪç] peach
pflegen ['pfleːgn] maintain; nurse
Pfleger, – *m* ['pfleːgɐ] male nurse
Piepston, -töne *m* ['piːpstoːn] beep, pip
Plan, Pläne *m* [plaːn] plan
planen ['plaːnən] plan, arrange, design
Planung, -en *f* ['plaːnʊŋ] planning
Platz nehmen ['plats ˌneːmən] take/
  have a seat
Platz, Plätze *m* [plats] place; seat
plötzlich ['plœtslɪç] suddenly
Polen *(only Sg) n* ['poːlən] Poland
polnisch ['pɔlnɪʃ] Polish
Pommes (frites) *(only Pl)* ['pɔməs,
  pɔmfrɪt] chips, fries
populär [pɔpʊ'lɛːɐ] popular
Position, -en *f* [pozi'tsjoːn] position
Post *(only Sg) f* [pɔst] mail; post (office)
Posteingang, -gänge *m* ['pɔstaɪŋaŋ]
  in-box
Postleitzahl, -en *f* ['pɔstlaɪttsaːl] postal
  code

Praktikum, Praktika *n* ['praktikʊm]
  placement
Präsentation, -en *f* [prɛzɛnta'tsjoːn]
  presentation
präsentieren [prɛzɛn'tiːrən] present
Preis, -e *m* [praɪs] price
prima ['priːma] great
privat [pri'vaːt] private
Privatsender, – *m* [pri'vaːtˌsɛndɐ]
  private (TV) station
pro [proː] per
probieren [pro'biːrən] taste, try
Problem, -e *n* [pro'bleːm] problem
Professor, -en *m* [pro'fɛsoːɐ] professor
Programm, -e *n* [pro'gram] programme;
  channel
Projekt, -e *n* [pro'jɛkt] project
prüfen ['pryːfn] check
pünktlich ['pʏnktlɪç] punctual
Pullover, – *m* [pu'loːvɐ] jumper,
  sweater
Punkt, -e *m* [pʊŋkt] topic; point
putzen ['putsn] clean

Q

Quartal, -e *n* [kvar'taːl] quarter
Quizsendung, -en *f* [kvizsɛndʊŋ] quiz
  show

R

Rad fahren ['raːt faːrən] cycle
Rad, Räder *n* [raːt] bike; wheel
Radio, -s *n* ['raːdjo] radio
Radtour, -en *f* ['raːttuːɐ] bicycle tour
Radverleih, -e *m* ['raːtfɛɐlaɪ]
  bike rental
Ratgeber, – *m* ['raːtgeːbɐ] guide
Raum, Räume *m* [raum] room

Rechnung, -en *f* ['reçnʊŋ] bill

recht haben ['rɛçt haːbn] be right

rechts [rɛçts] right

Rechtsanwalt, -anwälte *m* ['rɛçtsanvalt] lawyer (male)

Rechtsanwältin, -nen *f* ['rɛçtsanvɛltɪn] lawyer (female)

reden ['reːdn] talk

Regal, -e *n* [re'ɡaːl] shelf

Regen *(only Sg) m* ['reːɡn] rain

Regenschirm, -e *m* ['reːɡnʃɪrm] umbrella

regnen ['reːɡnən] rain

regnerisch ['reːɡnərɪʃ] rainy

reichen ['raɪçn] be enough

Reis *(only Sg) m* [raɪz] rice

Reise, -n *f* ['raɪzə] journey, trip, tour

reisen ['raɪzn] travel

Reisepass, -pässe *m* ['raɪzəpɛsə] passport

Reiseziel, -e *n* ['raɪzətsiːl] destination

Rente, -n *f* ['rɛntə] pension

reservieren [rezɛr'viːrən] book, retain

Restaurant, -s *n* [rɛsto'rãː] restaurant

restlich ['rɛstlɪç] remaining

Rezeption, -en *f* [retsɛp'tsioːn] reception, front desk

richtig ['rɪçtɪç] right, correct; really, quite

Richtung, -en *f* ['rɪçtʊŋ] direction

Riesenrad, räder *n* ['riːznraːt] big wheel

Rock, Röcke *m* [rɔk] skirt

röntgen ['rœntɡn] x-ray

Röntgen *(only Sg) n* ['rœntɡn] X-ray

rot [roːt] red

Rotwein, -e *m* ['roːtvaɪn] red wine

Rücken, – *m* ['rʏkn] back

Rückenschmerzen *(only Pl)* ['rʏknʃmɛrtsn] backache

Rückfahrt, -en *f* ['rʏkfaːrt] return journey

rufen ['ruːfn] call, shout

Rufnummer, -n *f* ['ruːfnumɐ] phone number

Ruhe *(only Sg) f* ['ruːə] peace, quiet

Ruhestand *(only Sg) m* ['ruːəʃtant] retirement

rund [rʊnt] round

rund um [rʊnt ʊm] about

russisch ['rʊsɪʃ] Russian

Russland *(only Sg) n* ['rʊslant] Russia

S

Sache, -n *f* ['zaxə] thing

Saft, Säfte *m* [zaft] juice

sagen ['zaːɡn] say

Sahne *(only Sg) f* ['zaːnə] cream

Salat, -e *m* [za'laːt] salad

Samstag, -e *m* ['zamstaːk] Saturday

Satz, Sätze *m* [zats] sentence, phrase, clause

sauber ['zaubɐ] clean

Sauerkraut *(only Sg) n* ['zauɐkraut] sauerkraut

Sauna, -s/Saunen *f* ['zauna] sauna

scannen ['skɛnən] scan

Schal, -s *m* [ʃaːl] scarf

Schalter, – *m* ['ʃaltɐ] ticket office

schauen ['ʃauən] look

scheinen ['ʃaɪnən] shine

Scherbe, -n *f* ['ʃɛrbə] shard

schick [ʃik] chic, fashionable

schicken ['ʃɪkn] send

Schinken, – *m* ['ʃɪŋkn] ham

schlafen ['ʃlaːfn] sleep

Schlafzimmer, – *n* ['ʃlaːftsɪmɐ] bedroom

Schlagsahne *(only Sg) f* ['ʃlaːɡzaːnə] whipped cream

schlecht [ʃlɛçt] bad

schließlich ['ʃliːslɪç] after all

schlimm [ʃlɪm] bad

Schlüssel, – m ['ʃlʏsl] key

Schluss, Schlüsse (mostly Sg) m [ʃlʊs] conclusion, end

schmecken ['ʃmɛkn] taste

Schmerz, -en m [ʃmɛrts] pain

schmerzen ['ʃmɛrtsn] hurt

Schmuck (only Sg) m [ʃmʊk] jewellery

Schnee (only Sg) m [ʃneː] snow

schneien ['ʃnaɪən] snow

schnell [ʃnɛl] fast

Schnitzel, – n ['ʃnɪtsl] schnitzel

Schokolade, -n f [ʃokoˈlaːdə] chocolate

Schokoladentorte, -n f [ʃokoˈlaːdntɔrtə] chocolate gateau

schon [ʃoːn] already, yet

schön ['ʃøːn] nice, beautiful

Schorle, -n f ['ʃɔrlə] juice or wine mixed with sparkling water

Schottland (only Sg) n ['ʃɔtlant] Scotland

Schrank, Schränke m [ʃraŋk] cupboard

schreiben ['ʃraɪbn] write

Schuh, -e m [ʃuː] shoe

Schule, -n f ['ʃuːlə] school

Schulung, -en f ['ʃuːlʊŋ] training

schwarz [ʃvarts] black

Schwellung, -en f ['ʃvɛlʊŋ] swelling

schwer [ʃveːɐ] difficult, hard; heavy

Schwester, -n f ['ʃvɛstɐ] sister

Schwimmbad, -bäder n ['ʃvimbaːt] swimming pool

schwimmen ['ʃvimən] swim

sehen ['zeːən] see

Sehenswürdigkeit, -en f ['zeːənsvʏrdɪçkaɪt] sight

sehr [zeːɐ] very

sein [zain] be

seit [zaɪt] for, since

Seite, -n f ['zaɪtə] side; page

selbst [zɛlpst] oneself

selten ['zɛltn] rare(ly)

seltsam ['zɛltzaːm] strange

senden (an) ['zɛndn] send

Sender, – m ['zɛndɐ] channel, station; sender

Sendung, -en f ['zɛndʊŋ] broadcast, show, programme

September (only Sg) m [zɛpˈtɛmbɐ] September

Serie, -n f ['zeːrjə] serial, series

Service, -s m ['zœrvɪs] service

Serviette, -n f [zɛrviˈɛtə] napkin

setzen ['zɛtsn] put, place

setzen, sich [zɪç 'zɛtsn] sit down

shoppen ['ʃɔpn] go shopping, shop

sich [zɪç] oneself

sicher ['zɪçɐ] sure(ly), for sure; safe

sicherstellen ['zɪçɐʃtɛlən] ensure

sie [ziː] she, they

Sie [ziː] you (formal)

simsen ['zɪmzn] text

singen ['zɪŋən] sing

Single, -s ['sɪŋl] single

Situation, -en f [zituaˈtsjoːn] situation

sitzen ['zitsn] sit

Sitzplatz, -plätze m ['zitsplats] seat

Small Talk (only Sg) m ['smɔːltɔːk] small talk

SMS, – f [ɛsɛmˈɛs] SMS, text (message)

so [zoː] so, as, such

Socke, -n f ['zɔkə] sock

Sofa, -s n ['zoːfa] couch

Software (only Sg) f ['sɔftvɛːr] software

sogar [zoˈgaːɐ] even

Sohn, Söhne m [zoːn] son

sollen ['zɔlən] shall, are to

sollt- ['zɔlt-] should

Sommer, – (mostly Sg) m ['zɔmɐ] summer

Sonderangebot, -e n ['zɔndɐangəboːt]
  special offer
Sonne, -n f ['zɔnə] sun
sonnig ['zɔnɪç] sunny
Sonntag, -e m ['zɔntaːk] Sunday
sonst [zɔnst] else
Spanien (only Sg) n ['ʃpaːniən] Spain
spanisch ['ʃpaːnɪʃ] Spanish
spannend ['ʃpanənt] fascinating
Spaß, Späße m [ʃpaːs] fun
spät [ʃpɛt] late
später [ʃpɛːtɐ] later
spazieren [ʃpaˈtsiːrən] stroll, walk
Spaziergang, -gänge m
  [ʃpaˈtsiːrgaŋ] walk
Speisekarte, -n f ['ʃpaɪzekartə] menu
Speiseraum, -räume m ['ʃpaɪzeraum]
  dining room
Spezialität, -en f [ʃpetsialiˈtɛːt]
  specialty
spielen ['ʃpiːlən] play
Sport (only Sg) m [ʃpɔrt] sport
Sportart, -en f ['ʃpɔrtart] sport
sportlich ['ʃpɔrtlɪç] casual; athletic
Sportplatz, -plätze m ['ʃpɔrtplats]
  sports ground
Sportverein, -e m ['ʃpɔrtfɛɐˈaɪn]
  sports club
Sprachkurs, -e m ['ʃpraːxkurs] language
  course/class
sprachlich ['ʃpraːxlɪç] linguistic
Sprachschule, -n f ['ʃpraːxʃuːlə] language
  school
sprechen ['ʃprɛçn] speak, talk
Sprudel, – m ['ʃpruːdl] sparkling water
Staatsangehörigkeit, -en f ['ʃtaːtsangə
  høːrɪçkaɪt] nationality
Stadt, Städte f [ʃtat] town, city
Stadtrundfahrt, -en f ['ʃtatrʊntfaːrt]
  sightseeing tour

Stadtzentrum, -zentren (mostly Sg) n
  ['ʃtattsɛntrʊm] city center
Stand, Stände m [ʃtant] (market) stand
ständig [ʃtɛndɪç] all the time, constantly
stark [ʃtark] heavy; strong
starten [ʃtartn] start, set off
Statistik, -en f [ʃtaˈtɪstɪk] statistics
stattfinden ['ʃtatfɪndn] take place
Stau, -s m [ʃtau] traffic jam
staubsaugen ['ʃtaupzaugn] hoover
stehen ['ʃteːən] stand, be
Stelle, -n f ['ʃtɛlə] job; position; place
stellen ['ʃtɛlən] put, place
Stellenanzeige, -n f ['ʃtɛlənˈantsaɪgə] job
  advertisement
stimmen ['ʃtɪmən] be right
Stimmt! ['ʃtɪmt] True!, Right!
Stock, – m [ʃtɔk] floor, level
Stockwerk, -e n ['ʃtɔkvɛrk] floor, level
Straße, -n f ['ʃtraːsə] street, road
Straßenbahn, -en f ['ʃtraːsənbaːn]
  tram(way)
Straßenbahnhaltestelle, -n f
  ['ʃtraːsənbaːnhaltəʃtɛlə] tram stop
Strategie, -n f [ʃtrateˈgiː] strategy
Student, -en m [ʃtuˈdɛnt] student
Studentenausweis, -e m
  [ʃtuˈdɛntn-ausvaɪs] student ID
studieren [ʃtuˈdiːrən] study
Studium, Studien (mostly Sg) n
  ['ʃtuːdiʊm] studies
Stück, -e n [ʃtʏk] piece
stürmen ['ʃtʏrmən] storm
stürmisch ['ʃtʏrmɪʃ] stormy
Stufe, -n f ['ʃtuːfə] stair
Stuhl, Stühle m [ʃtuːl] chair
Stunde, -n f ['ʃtʊndə] hour; lesson
Sturm, Stürme m [ʃtʊrm] storm
suchen [zuːxn] search, look for
süß [zyːs] sweet, cute

super ['zuːpɐ] great
Supermarkt, -märkte *m* ['zuːpɐmarkt] supermarket
Suppe, -n *f* ['zupə] soup

T

Tag, -e *m* [taːk] day
Tageslichtprojektor, -en *m* ['taːgəs lɪçtproːjɛktoːɐ] overhead projector
Tagesordnungspunkt, -e *m* ['taːgə sortnʊŋspʊnkt] topic
Tante, -n *f* ['tantə] aunt
Tasse, -n *f* ['tasə] cup
Tatort, -e *m* ['taːtɔrt] crime scene
Team, -s *n* [tiːm] team
Tee, -s *m* [teː] tea
Teilnehmer, – *m* ['taɪlneːmɐ] member, participant
Telefon, -e *n (abbr. Tel.)* [teleˈfoːn] (tele)phone
telefonieren [telefoˈniːrən] call, phone, talk over the phone
Telefonnummer, -n *f* [teleˈfoːnnʊmɐ] phone number
Teller, – *m* ['tɛlɐ] plate, dish
Tennis *(only Sg) n* ['tɛnis] tennis
Termin, -e *m* [tɛrˈmiːn] appointment
Terminkalender, – *m* [tɛrˈmiːnkalɛndɐ] diary
Test, -s *m* [tɛst] test
teuer ['tɔyɐ] expensive
Theater, – *n* [teˈaːtɐ] theatre
Thema, Themen *n* ['teːma] topic
Thriller, – *m* ['θrɪlɐ] thriller
Tipp, -s *m* [tɪp] tip
Tisch, -e *m* [tɪʃ] table
Tischtennisplatte, -n *f* ['tɪʃtɛnɪsplatə] table tennis table
Titel, – *m* ['tiːtl, tɪtl] (academic) title

Tochter, Töchter *f* ['tɔxtɐ] daughter
Toilette, -n *f* [toaˈlɛtə] bathroom, lavatory
toll [tɔl] cool, awesome, great
Tomate, -n *f* [toˈmaːtə] tomato
Torte, -n *f* ['tɔrtə] gateau
total [toˈtaːl] totally
tragen ['traːgn] carry; wear
Transport, -e *(mostly Sg) m* [transˈpɔrt] transport
treffen (sich) ['trɛfn] meet
Treppe, -n *f* ['trɛpə] stairs
trinken ['trɪŋkn] drink
Trinkgeld *(only Sg) n* ['trɪŋkgɛlt] tip
trotzdem ['trɔtsdeːm] anyway
Tschüs! [tʃyːs] Bye!
T-Shirt, -s *n* ['tiːʃœrt, 'tiːʃøːɐt] T-shirt
Tür, -en *f* [tyːɐ] door
Tüte, -n *f* ['tyːtə] bag
tun [tuːn] do
TV, -s *n* [teːˈfau] TV

U

über ['yːbɐ] over
überhaupt [yːbɐˈhaupt] at all
übermorgen ['yːbɐmɔrgn] day after tomorrow
übernachten [yːbɐˈnaxtn] stay/spend the night
Übernachtung, -en *f* [yːbɐˈnaxtʊŋ] overnight stay
übernehmen [yːbɐˈneːmən] take over
übersehen [yːbɐˈzeːən] overlook
übersetzen [yːbɐˈzɛtsn] translate
üblich ['yːblɪç] common, normal
übrig ['yːbrɪç] left (over)
übrigens ['yːbrɪgns] by the way
Uhr, -en *f* [uːɐ] clock, watch

Uhrzeit, -en f ['uːrtsaɪt] time (of day)

um [ʊm] at; about

umdrehen ['ʊmdreːən] turn around

umknicken ['ʊmknɪkn] twist

umsteigen ['ʊmʃtaɪgn] change

und [ʊnt] and

und so weiter (usw.) [ʊnt zoː waɪtɐ] and so on

Unfall, -fälle ['ʊnfal] accident

ungefähr [ʊngəfɛːɐ] about, around

Universität, -en f (abbr. Uni, -s f) [univɛrziˈtɛːt (ˈʊni)] university

unnötig ['ʊnnøːtɪç] unnecessary

unten ['ʊntn] below

unter ['ʊntɐ] beneath

Unterlagen (only Pl) ['ʊntɐlaːgn] documents

unternehmen [ʊntɐˈneːmən] do, undertake

Unterricht (only Sg) m ['ʊntərɪçt] class

Unterrichtsstunde, -n f ['ʊntərɪçtsʃtʊndə] lesson

Unterwäsche (only Sg) f ['ʊntɐvɛʃə] underwear

unüblich ['ʊnyːblɪç] uncommon

Urlaub, -e m ['uːɐlaup] holiday

USA (only Pl) [uː ɛs ˈaː] USA

US-amerikanisch [uː ˈɛs amerikaːnɪʃ] American

V

Vater, Väter ['faːtɐ] father

Verabredung, -en f [fɛɐˈapreːdʊŋ] appointment, date, rendezvous

verabschieden [fɛɐˈapʃiːdn] say good-bye

Veranstaltung, -en f [fɛɐˈanʃtaltʊŋ] event

verbinden [fɛɐˈbɪndn] put through; connect

Verbindung, -en f [fɛɐˈbɪndʊŋ] connection

verbringen [fɛɐˈbraxt] spend

verdienen [fɛɐˈdiːnən] earn

vereinbaren [fɛɐˈaɪnbaːrən] agree, arrange

Verhalten (only Sg) n [fɛɐˈhaltn] behaviour

verheiratet [fɛɐˈhaɪraːtət] married

Verkäufer, – m [fɛɐˈkɔyfɐ] salesman

Verkäuferin, -nen f [fɛɐˈkɔyfərɪn] saleslady

Verkehrsmittel, – n [fɛɐˈkeːɐsmɪtl] means of transport

verlassen [fɛɐˈlasn] leave

verleihen [fɛɐˈlaɪən] lend

verletzen (sich) [zɪç fɛɐˈlɛtsn] hurt (oneself), injure

Verletzung, -en f [fɛɐˈlɛtsʊŋ] injury

vermeiden [fɛɐˈmaɪdn] avoid

Verpackung, -en f [fɛɐˈpakʊŋ] packaging

verschicken an [fɛɐˈʃɪkn] send

verschieden [fɛɐˈʃiːdn] different

verschneit [fɛɐˈʃnait] snowy

Verspätung, -en f [fɛɐˈʃpɛːtʊŋ] delay

verstehen [fɛɐˈʃteːən] understand

verteilen [fɛɐˈtaɪlən] distribute, hand out

verwählen [fɛɐˈvɛːlən] dial the wrong number

Verwandte, -n m+f [fɛɐˈvantə] relative (male and female)

viel [fiːl] much

Viel Spaß! [fiːl ˈʃpaːs] Have fun!

Viele Grüße [ˌfiːlə ˈgryːsə] (kind/best) regards

Vielen Dank! [ˌfiːlən ˈdaŋk] Thank you very much!

vielleicht [fi'laɪçt] maybe
Viertel, – n ['fɪrtl] quarter
Visitenkarte, -n f [vi'siːtnkartə] business card
Volksfest, -e n ['fɔlksfɛst] fair
voll [fɔl] crowded, full
Volleyball, -bälle m ['vɔlibal] volleyball
von [fɔn] from, of
vor [foːɐ̯] before, to, in front of
Voraussetzung, -en f [for'auszɛtsʊn] requirement
vorbei [foɐ̯'baɪ] over; past
vorbeigehen [foːɐ̯'baɪgeːən] pass
vorbereiten ['foːɐ̯bəraɪtn] prepare
Vorbereitung, -en f ['foːɐ̯bəraɪtʊn] preparation
Vorgehen, – n ['foːɐ̯geːən] actions
vorgestern ['foːɐ̯gɛstɐn] day before yesterday
vorkommen ['foːɐ̯kɔmən] occur, happen
Vormittag, -e m ['foːɐ̯mɪtaːk] morning
Vorname, -n m ['foːɐ̯naːmə] first name
vorn(e) ['fɔrn(ə)] in front
Vorschlag, -schläge m ['foːɐ̯ʃlaːk] proposition, suggestion
vorschlagen ['foːɐ̯ʃlaːgn] suggest
vorstellen (sich) ['foːɐ̯ʃtɛlən] introduce, present
Vortrag, -träge m ['foːɐ̯traːk] speech

W
wählen ['vɛːlən] dial
während ['vɛːrənt] during; while
Wand, Wände f [vant] wall
wann [van] when
warm [varm] warm
Wartebereich, -e m ['vartəbəraɪç] waiting area

warten ['vartn] wait
Wartezimmer, – n ['vartətsɪmə] waiting room
warum [va'rʊm] why
was [vas] what
was für ein [vas fyːr aɪn] what (kind of)
Wäsche (only Sg) f [vɛʃə] laundry
waschen (sich) ['vaʃn] wash
Wasser (only Sg) n ['vasɐ] water
WC, -s n [veː'tseː] toilet
Webseite, -n f ['vɛpzaɪtə] web page, website
Wechselgeld (only Sg) n ['vɛksəlgɛlt] change
weg [vɛk] away
Weg, -e m [veːk] way
wegen ['veːgn] because of
wegfahren ['vɛkfaːrən] go away (on a trip)
wehtun ['veːtuːn] hurt
weil [vaɪl] because
Weile (only Sg) f ['vaɪlə] while
Wein, -e m [vaɪn] wine
Weinglas, -gläser n ['vaɪnglaːs] wine glass
Weintraube, -n f ['vaɪntraubə] grape
weiß [vaɪs] white
weit [vaɪt] far, long
weit weg [vaɪt 'vɛk] far away
weiter ['vaɪtɐ] continuing, further, next
weiterarbeiten ['vaɪtɐarbaɪtn] continue working
Weiterbildung, -en f ['vaɪtɐbɪldʊn] further education
weiterhelfen ['vaɪtɐhɛlfn] help
weiterhin ['vaɪtɐhɪn] furthermore
weiterleiten ['vaɪtɐlaɪtn] forward
weitermachen ['vaɪtɐmaxn] continue
welcher, welche, welches ['vɛlçɐ, 'vɛlçə, 'vɛlçəs] which, what

Welt, -en f [vɛlt] world

weltweit ['vɛltvaɪt] worldwide

wenig ['ve:nɪç] little

wenn [vɛn] when; if

wer [ve:ɐ] who

werden ['ve:ɐdən] become

Westen (only Sg) m ['vɛstn] west

Wetter (only Sg) n ['vɛtɐ] weather

Whiteboard, -s n ['vaɪtbɔːɐt] whiteboard

wichtig ['vɪçtɪç] important

wie [vi:] how

Wie geht's? [vi: 'ge:ts] How are you?,
What's up?

wie lange [vi: 'laŋə] how long

wie oft [vi: 'ɔft] how often

wie viel [vi: 'fi:l] how much

wie viele [vi: 'fi:lə] how many

wieder ['vi:dɐ] again

wiederholen [vi:dɐ'ho:lən] repeat

wieso [vi'zo:] why

willkommen [vɪlkɔmən] welcome

Wind, -e m [vɪnt] wind

winden ['vɪndn] blow

windig ['vɪndɪç] windy

Winter, – (mostly Sg) m ['vɪntɐ] winter

wir [vi:ɐ] we

wirklich ['vɪrklɪç] really

Wirklichkeit (only Sg) f ['vɪrklɪçkaɪt]
reality

wissen ['vɪsn] know

wo [vo:] where

Woche, -n f ['vɔxə] week

Wochenende, -n n ['vɔxnɛndə]
weekend

Wochenmarkt, -märkte m ['vɔxnmarkt]
weekly farmer's market

woher [vo:'he:r] where from

wohin [vo:'hɪn] where to

wohl [vo:l] probably

wohlfühlen ['vo:lfy:lən] be comfortable,
feel good

wohnen ['vo:nən] live

Wohngemeinschaft, -en f (abbr. WG, -s f)
['vo:ngəmaɪnʃaft (ve:'ge:)] flat share

Wohnort, -e m ['vo:nɔrt] residence

Wohnung, -en f ['vo:nʊŋ] flat

Wohnungsanzeige, -n f ['vo:nʊŋs-
antsaɪgə] flat advertisement

Wohnzimmer, – n ['vo:ntsɪmɐ] living
room

Wolke, -n f ['vɔlkə] cloud

wollen ['vɔlən] want

worauf [vo:'rauf] what

Wort, Wörter n [vɔrt] word

worüber [vo:'ry:bɐ] what about

wünschen ['vʏnʃən] wish

würd- [vʏrd-] would

wunderbar ['vʊndɐbaɐ] marvelous

Wunsch, Wünsche m [vʊnʃ] wish

Wurst, Würste f [vʊrst] sausage

Wurzel, -n f ['vʊrtsəl] root

Z

zahlen ['tsa:lən] pay

Zahn, Zähne m [tsa:n] tooth

Zahnarzt, -ärzte m ['tsa:nartst] dentist

Zähne putzen ['tsɛ:nə 'pʊtsn] brush
one's teeth

Zahnschmerzen (only Pl) ['tsa:nʃmɛrtsn]
toothache

Zebrastreifen, – m ['tse:braʃtraɪfn]
zebra crossing

Zeit, -en (mostly Sg) f [tsaɪt] time

Zeitschrift, -en f ['tsaɪtʃrɪft] magazine,
journal

Zeitung, -en f ['tsaɪtʊŋ] newspaper

Zelt, -e n [tsɛlt] tent

Zeugnis, -se n ['tsɔʏknɪs] certificate

ziemlich ['tsiːmlɪç] pretty, quite

Zimmer, – n ['tsɪmɐ] room

Zimmerservice (only Sg) m
['tsɪmɐzœrvɪs] room service

zu [tsuː] to, toward

Zucchini, -s f [tsʊ'kiːni] courgette

zuerst [tsu'eːɐst] (at) first

Zufall, -fälle m ['tsuːfal] coincidence,
chance

zufrieden [tsu'friːdən] satisfied

Zug, Züge m [tsuːk] train

Zugfahrt, -en f ['tsuːkfaːrt] train ride

zuhören ['tsuhørən] listen

zukünftig ['tsukʏnftɪç] future

Zukunft (only Sg) f ['tsukʊnft] future

zuletzt [tsu'lɛtst] lastly

zum Beispiel (abbr. z. B.) [tsʊm 'baɪʃpiːl]
for example, for instance

zum einen [tsʊm 'aɪnən] on the one
hand

zumachen ['tsuːmaxn] close

zurück [tsu'rʏk] back

zurückhaltend [tsu'rʏkhaltnt]
conservative, modest

zurückrufen [tsu'rʏkruːfn] call back

zusammen [tsu'zamən] together

Zusammenarbeit (only Sg) f
[tsu'zamənarbaɪt] cooperation

zusammenarbeiten [tsu'zamənarbaɪtn]
cooperate

Zusammenfassung, -en f
[tsu'zamənfasʊn] summary

zusammensitzen [tsu'zamənzɪtsn] sit
together

zusätzlich ['tsuzɛtslɪç] additionally

zustimmen ['tsuʃtɪmən] agree

Zutat, -en f ['tsutaːt] ingredient

Zwiebel, -n f ['tsviːbl] onion

zwischen ['tsvɪʃn] between

Trackangaben

CD 1

Track no.	Day (Lesson)	Track no.	Day (Lesson)
1	Introduction	22	L 7/3
2	L 2/dialogue	23	L 8/dialogue
3	L 2/d. slow	24	L 8/d. slow
4	L 2/2	25	L 8/2
5	L 2/4	26	L 9/dialogue
6	L 3/dialogue	27	L 9/d. slow
7	L 3/d. slow	28	L 9/3
8	L 3/3	29	L 10/dialogue
9	L 4/dialogue	30	L 10/d. slow
10	L 4/d. slow	31	L 10/2
11	L 4/2	32	L 11/dialogue
12	L 5/dialogue	33	L 11/d. slow
13	L 5/d. slow	34	L 11/1
14	L 5/2	35	L 12/dialogue
15	L 6/5	36	L 12/d. slow
16	L 6/17	37	L 12/1
17	L 6/19	38	L 13/dialogue
18	IT 1/3	39	L 13/d. slow
19	IT 1/8	40	L 13/1
20	L 7/dialogue	41	L 13/3
21	L 7/d. slow		

CD 2

Track no.	Day (Lesson)	Track no.	Day (Lesson)
1	L 14/3	24	IT 3/5
2	L 14/9	25	L 23/dialogue
3	L 14/15	26	L 23/1
4	L 14/18	27	L 24/dialogue
5	IT 2/3	28	L 25/dialogue
6	L 15/dialogue	29	L 25/1
7	L 15/1	30	L 26/dialogue
8	L 15/4	31	L 26/2
9	L 16/dialogue	32	L 27/dialogue
10	L 17/dialogue	33	L 27/1
11	L 18/dialogue	34	L 28/dialogue
12	L 18/3	35	L 28/3
13	L 19/dialogue	36	L 29/dialogue
14	L 19/1	37	L 29/3
15	L 20/dialogue	38	L 30/2
16	L 20/2	39	L 30/7
17	L 21/dialogue	40	L 30/13
18	L 21/2	41	FT 5
19	L 22/4	42	FT 8
20	L 22/7	43	FT 13
21	L 22/9	44	FT 15
22	L 22/11	45	FT 21
23	IT 3/3		

CD 3

Track no.	Day (Lesson)	Track no.	Day (Lesson)
1	Introduction	14	Vocabulary L16
2	Vocabulary L2	15	Vocabulary L17
3	Vocabulary L3	16	Vocabulary L18
4	Vocabulary L4	17	Vocabulary L19
5	Vocabulary L5	18	Vocabulary L20
6	Vocabulary L7	19	Vocabulary L21
7	Vocabulary L8	20	Vocabulary L23
8	Vocabulary L9	21	Vocabulary L24
9	Vocabulary L10	22	Vocabulary L25
10	Vocabulary L11	23	Vocabulary L26
11	Vocabulary L12	24	Vocabulary L27
12	Vocabulary L13	25	Vocabulary L28
13	Vocabulary L15	26	Vocabulary L29

Picture credits

Getty Images: George Doyle – 159; Niko Guido – 19 (unten); Jasmina007 – 17; Martin Leigh – 143; Photo Alto/Odilon Dimier – 183; Stockbyte – 201; Stephan Zabel – 45

iStock: no_limit_pictures – 144; Sean Warren – 34

Thinkstock: akarelias – 19 (oben); Helder Almeida – 166; Eileen Bach – 189; Marcin Balcerzak – 184; Robert Brown – 138; cmfotoworks – 120; Steve Cole – 61; Comstock – 119; dekadi – 149; Digital Vision – 97; Barbara Dudzinska – 137; elxeneize – 68; Petro Feketa – 172; fotobauer – 6; Fuse – 85; gielmichal – 92; Good Mood Photo – 86; Peter Gudella – 114; Ingram Publishing – 165, 171; insagostudio – 178; Brian Jackson – 18, 39, 40; Jupiterimages – 33, 108, 196; Maksym Khytra – 67; Levent Konuk – 126; kosmos111 – 91; lentolo – 22; LuminaStock – 28; Robyn Mackenzie – 62; Maridav – 80; matthewennisphotography – 56; Ryan McVay – 21; mila1974 – 177; Dean Mitchel – 195; moodboard – 74; ronaldino3001 – 132; shironosov – 160; Alison Stieglitz – 131; Maria Teijeiro – 55; wavebreakmedia – 190; Mikkel William Nielsen – 79; xyno – 113; xyno6 – 125: Catherine Yeulet – 27; Hongqi Zhang – 107; Zheka-Boss – 73; Katarzyna Zwolska – 20

Langenscheidt

„Einfach besser nachschlagen!"

Rund 50.000 Stichwörter, Wendungen und Beispiele. Mit **neuen farbigen Illustrationen** zu wichtigen Wortfeldern und Alltagsthemen. Komplett überarbeitet, mit leicht verständlichen Definitionen und hilfreichen Lerntipps.

Das einsprachige Wörterbuch für alle jüngeren Deutschlerner!

Langenscheidt
Power Wörterbuch

Deutsch
als Fremdsprache

www.langenscheidt.de/daf